Greenberg's® Guide

to

Marx Trains

Volume II

By Eric J. Matzke, BSCE

Edited by Georges Denzene

With the Assistance of Donna J. L. Dove and Linda F. Greenberg

Copyright © 1990

Greenberg Publishing Company, Inc.
7566 Main Street
Sykesville, MD 21784
(301) 795-7447

Third Edition

Manufactured in the United States of America

Greenberg Publishing Company, Inc. offers the world's largest selection of Lionel, American Flyer, LGB, Ives, and other toy train publications as well as a selection of books on model and prototype railroading, dollhouse miniatures, and toys. For a copy of our current catalogue, send a stamped, self-addressed envelope to Greenberg Publishing Company, Inc. at the above address.

Greenberg Shows, Inc. sponsors the world's largest public model railroad, dollhouse, and toy shows. The shows feature extravagant operating model railroads for N, HO, O, Standard, and 1 Gauges as well as a huge marketplace for buying and selling nearly all model railroad equipment. The shows also feature a large selection of dollhouses and dollhouse furnishings. Shows are currently offered in metropolitan Baltimore, Boston, Ft. Lauderdale, Cherry Hill and Teaneck in New Jersey, Long Island in New York, Philadelphia, Pittsburgh, Richmond, and Tampa. To receive our current show listing, please send a self-addressed stamped envelope marked *Train Show Schedule* to the address above.

ISBN   0-89778-132-5

Library of Congress Cataloging-in-Publication Data

Matzke, Eric.

Greenberg's Guide to Marx Trains.

1. Louis Marx & Co. 2. Railroads — Models.

I. Denzene, Georges. II. Greenberg, Linda F. III. Dove, Donna J. L. IV. Title: Guide to Marx Trains.

TF197.M296 1989   625.1'9   89-16979

ISBN 0-89778-131-7 (V. 1)

ISBN 0-89778-132-5 (V. 2)

Front cover (left to right): Blue Missouri Pacific GE-70-ton diesel switcher pulling plastic four-wheel cars: a maroon Erie flatcar with two farm tractors and a blue Erie flatcar with two cars. On the second track is the red 112 Lehigh Valley GE 70-ton diesel switcher pulling plastic four-wheel cars: a green 715100 NYC gondola, a yellow 3280 SFRD boxcar, and an orange Gulf Oil tank car. On the third track is the green and gold 702 Western Pacific GE 70-ton diesel switcher pulling a red 347100 Pennsylvania gondola, a maroon Cities Service tank car with green twin tanks, a yellow 54099 Missouri Pacific stock car with a brown door, and a tuscan brown 259199 Canadian Pacific Railway boxcar. On the last track is the black and red 799 Rock Island GE 70-ton diesel switcher pulling a blue 467100 Baltimore & Ohio boxcar, a black 24 Illinois Central searchlight car, and a green 176393 New York Central boxcar. R. Burgio Collection, B. Greenberg photograph.

Back cover: 2940 Grand Central Station. J. Armacost Collection, M. Feinstein photograph.

Table Of Contents

Acknowledgments

As in-house editor of Volume II, as well as Volume I, I have spent the past year and a half immersed in Marx Trains. I have acquired a great appreciation for these trains and the Marx enthusiasts who collect them. I am grateful to the collectors who have spent many hours "explaining" Marx trains to me.

My sincere thanks to the following Marx collectors:

Georges Denzene, Minnesota, provided the inspiration for "tackling Marx" and brought new information to bear on each listing and the general introductions. His perseverance and careful review provided the key to lengthy research for both volumes. It was a pleasure to work with him.

Larry Jensen, Virginia, revised the chapters on scale cars and seven-inch cars. He added significant new information to both chapters and was one of the principal readers for the entire book. Larry's cheerful assistance — particularly the many days he spent in our office — is particularly appreciated.

Hansford Diehl, Florida, allowed us to photograph his large and beautiful collection. Always a gracious host, Hansford spent three long weekends assisting with selecting and photographing equipment for the diesel and plastic chapters.

Keith Wills, Quebec, contributed his article from *Railroad Model Craftsman* on Marx HO which substantially expanded our knowledge of this specialty. Keith also urged the rewriting of the diesel chapter. A special thanks to **Harold Carstens,** publisher of *Model Craftsman,* for permitting the use of Keith Wills' article.

Paul Gailey, Florida, reorganized the motor listings to correspond with the gear drawings, extensively reviewed the chapters and photographs on plastic cars, and provided many insights into Marx production methods and dates.

Al Osterud, Minnesota, reviewed the plastic chapters and photographs, spending many hours on the phone explaining "plastic" to me. His counsel was particularly appreciated in identifying the factory production plastic cars and organizing them into their proper categories.

Gary Anderson, Minnesota, reviewed each chapter extensively and worked with Al Osterud in reviewing the plastic chapter and photographs. He also provided important data on train toys and motor gears through letters and personal conversations with Georges at train meets.

Dick MacNary, Georgia, answered many inquiries about diesel engines and sent slides of the Sears sets. A long time collector and authority on Marx trains, Dick has shared his knowledge with many novices. Larry Jensen attributes his interest in Marx trains to the encouragement he received from Dick.

Robert Burgio, Maryland, graciously lent his trains to be photographed for the cover and HO chapter.

John Malcovsky, Vermont, provided moral support through his comprehensive correspondence with Georges over the last three years and sent photographs and information about HO sets.

Robert Whitacre, Ohio, supplied the chapter on Marx Sets. He also answered many technical questions for Georges.

James Flynn, Illinois, contributed to the chapters on plastic cars, train toys, and scale cars.

Thomas Croyts, Ohio, helped with accessory and train toy descriptions.

Roy Jackson, Illinois, generously allowed us to use his TCA article, with modifications, on girder bridges; he also added information on HO sets.

William Dyson, Maryland, added material on signals.

Stephen Anderson, New York, sent photographs and new information.

Bill Nelsen, Virginia, graciously invited my family to enjoy his operating Marx layout.

Ray Price, Ohio, provided photographs, blueprints, and information which enhanced this new edition.

Allan Miller, West Virginia, scrutinized each chapter and painstakingly documented corrections and additions.

Other readers included **Dave Ashworth, Tasker Brush, Michael Denuty, Marc DeRaleigh, John Fox, David Hoover, Marty Johnson, Eric Matzke, Marvin Meyer, Fred Pauling, Larry Reed, Trip Riley,** and **Jim Salko.**

At Greenberg's, **Dallas Mallerich, III,** fellow editor and model railroader, assisted in rewriting the diesel chapter and back cover. **Bruce Greenberg** directed photography and Bruce and **Linda Greenberg** edited the introductions to each chapter. **Mable Sager** researched the accessories and wrote their captions. **Donna Price** and **Cyndie Bare** carefully proofread each chapter. In addition, Donna sized the photographs and prepared the book for the printer. **Maureen Crum** designed the cover. **Bill Wantz** printed the many black and white photographs. **Bill Dove** prepared the stats for the last chapter.

Donna Dove
March 1990

Introduction

The colorful and imaginative world of Marx trains holds a fascination for many toy train enthusiasts. Mass-distributed through large retailers, these low-cost trains were designed as durable toys for children to enjoy. In fact, "durable" may not be a strong enough word when one considers the almost brute energy that a child can expend when playing with his or her toys. Louis Marx, more than any other toy maker, recognized the necessity of producing trains that would withstand this hard use *and* still provide hours of enjoyment. Quite simply, Marx trains stayed on the track well, their motors did not burn out, and the sets included cars that appealed to children, such as gondolas and flatcars, with their attractive and variable loads. Being able to run their own trains with very limited difficulty helped many children to develop a love for model railroading (and, eventually, train collecting!).

Volume II of *Greenberg's Guide to Marx Trains* provides continued coverage of this exciting and growing area in train collecting. As in Volume I, we have revised and updated all of the listings, added numerous color photographs, and greatly expanded the narrative text.

Generally, toy train manufacturers designed their diesel locomotives after real trains, called prototypes. Marx was no exception, although his diesels may not have been advertised as such. Because Marx diesels were made for play, liberties were taken in their design and, therefore, some of the diesels may be similar to more than one prototype. Nevertheless, after much consultation with collectors, each diesel has been assigned its prototype name.

Those readers interested in the design models that began the Marx scale and seven-inch lines will enjoy reading the new information presented by Larry Jensen in chapters two and three. Larry discusses design models, in particular, and includes photographs.

Although the four-wheel plastic cars are easily identified, some confusion occurs in distinguishing between a deluxe plastic car and a plain eight-wheel plastic car. For this reason, we have divided the plastic chapter into three separate sections: four-wheel, eight-wheel, and deluxe. When purchased directly from Marx, the eight-wheel cars came wrapped in brown paper, whereas the deluxe cars came in a box marked "deluxe." Since secondhand items often come without boxes or wrappings, the differences between the cars have been defined to help collectors identify both the pieces in their collections and the pieces they may find at train shows.

As with the tin-plated cars of Volume I, color shading differences can be perceived when looking at plastic cars. Color variations within the same basic hue often arise unintentionally. A supplier may provide a different shade of plastic or paint even though the color ordered had the same catalogue number as a previous order. Denoting these variations is often difficult; for example, several shades of what might be called yellow may be perceived as orange, yellow-orange, deep yellow, bright yellow, light yellow, or even beige. Discoloration occurs in toy trains due to age, sun-fading, and chemicals in the air. The color blue is especially susceptible to change. For these reasons, we have not noted variations based on subtle shadings in color.

Pricing

The train values in this book are based on READY SALES obtained at train meets during the summer of 1989, and from private transactions reported by our panel of reviewers. A ready sale is one that occurs within an hour after the train is put on display. If a train is still unsold at the end of the day, it would most likely have had a higher price tag than shown in this Guide.

Supply and demand are the ultimate arbiters of value. There can be substantial short term fluctuations in price due to available supply at a given marketplace.

If you plan to sell your trains to someone who will then resell them at another train marketplace, you will NOT obtain the prices reported in this book. Rather, you may expect to achieve about 50 percent of these prices. Basically, for your items to be of interest to a dealer, he must buy them for considerably less than the prices listed here.

For each item we provide prices for two conditions: Good and Excellent. These conditions are defined as:

GOOD (Gd) — Scratches, small dents, dirty.

EXCELLENT (Exc) — Minute scratches or nicks, no dents or rust.

In some cases, **NRS** has been inserted rather than a price. NRS is the abbreviation for **No Reported Sales**.

In the toy train field there is greater concern with exterior appearance and lesser concern with operation. If operation is important to you, ask the seller whether the train runs. If the seller does not know, test it before making your purchase. Most train meets provide test tracks for that purpose.

We have had a number of inquiries as to whether or not a particular piece is "a good value." This Guide will help you to answer that question and will sensitize you to the factors affecting train values. There is, nevertheless, NO substitute for experience in the marketplace.

Our work is never finished; there is always more to learn and document. If you discover an error or an item that has been omitted, please tell us about them on the Correction/Addition form provided so that is may be used in the Guide's next edition.

Photo of the FT103 demonstrator in the Electro-Motive paint scheme. Marx's 21 Santa Fe diesel was modeled after this prototype. Note the four closely spaced portholes. Courtesy Electro-Motive Division, General Motors Corporation.

Chapter I

Diesel Locomotives

*All of the diesels were patterned after locomotive prototypes and for this reason, we have elected to use these prototype names in describing the variety of diesel locomotives manufactured by Louis Marx & Company. Our reference was the **Diesel Spotter's Guide** by Jerry A. Pinkepank.*

As the large, efficient diesel locomotives began to replace the chugging steam locomotives on the prototype railroads, a similar transition occurred in the product lines of America's toy makers. Soon after Lionel introduced its famous Santa Fe F-3 in 1948, Marx offered its large FT unit, number 21 locomotive (introduced in 1950), which just happened to have a die-cast knuckle adapter that coupled to Lionel cars. Marx's locomotive also reproduced Santa Fe's red and silver "war bonnet" paint scheme — one of the most popular in real and model railroading history. This locomotive sold well through Sears and Allied Toy Distributors.

In the following years, the diesel became a staple item in the Marx locomotive line-up and a modern companion to the steam locomotives so loved by Louis Marx himself. In 1950 Marx introduced the 6000 Southern Pacific F-7 diesel. The plastic GE 70-ton switcher was conceived late in 1957 as R & D model 2282. This model was constructed by using cut-up pieces from the shell of a 1998 plastic Alco S-3 switcher. If one compares these two switchers, their identical details immediately become apparent. The first GE 70-ton switcher produced for the market was the black NYC 588. Interestingly, one of the last R & D models was a GE 70-ton diesel fitted with a windup motor. It was numbered 3780 and dated February 1974.

Cataloging Marx diesels is difficult because of the discrepancy between what was actually produced and what was advertised. The 1950 Montgomery Ward Catalog illustrated a colorful Rock Island version of the large number 21 locomotive. Although a company called Unique Art did offer such a locomotive, Marx did not. The illustration in Ward's catalogue

remains an interesting conversation piece for those who like to consider "what if?"

Another example of a locomotive that was advertised but not produced is the C & O Alco S-3 switcher pictured in some 1955 Sears catalogues. Yet another is the lithographed Missouri-Kansas-Texas (MKT) A unit, similar to the 6000 Southern Pacific, which appeared in Allied Toy Distributors 1950 and 1951 catalogues. It existed only as an R & D model in the (former) Erie Archives. A later "missing" item was the Penn Central industrial switcher (GE 70-ton diesel), similar to the 799 Rock Island.

It is often thought that Marx chose the railroad paint schemes based on their colors (and thus their appeal to youngsters), rather than other factors, such as road name recognition or locality. In some cases, Marx used railroad calendars and promotional materials as inspiration for models.

Traction tires were added to the later versions of the Marx diesels to increase pulling power. They are usually found on the geared wheels of E-7 and 70-ton diesels, but can be found on other Marx motive power as well. The metal wheels were cast with a recessed channel to accommodate the rubber tire which was designed and made to fit snugly on the wheel. After considerable running time, these tires would become enlarged, oil soaked, and loose, and would no longer be effective. With the demise of the Marx Company replacement tires are virtually impossible to find, but some operators have had success finding suitable replacements at IBM typewriter repair shops, hardware stores, and O ring distributors.

As time wore on Marx began, in the 1960s, to use more steam locomotives than diesels. By 1970, very few new diesels were manufactured. In the early 1970s, under the management of the Quaker Oats Company, the GE 70-ton switcher was revived introducing the faithful Santa Fe as well as the new plastic F-7 turquoise Penn Central A unit.

Metal EMD F-3 diesels. *Top shelf:* 62 "BALTIMORE & OHIO" AA units with tab and slot couplers. *Second shelf:* 62 "BALTIMORE & OHIO" AA units with tilt automatic couplers. *Third shelf:* Red and white 6000 "SOUTHERN PACIFIC". *Bottom shelf:* Red and silver 6000 "SOUTHERN PACIFIC". H. Diehl Collection, M. Feinstein photograph.

Over the years, the roster of Marx diesels included an E-unit locomotive in metal, plastic E-7s, the EMD F-7 in metal, the Alco S-3 and GE 70-ton switchers in plastic, the Marxtronic switcher, and the plastic Budd Rail Diesel Car.

METAL EMD FT DIESEL

Note: We have labeled this unit as an EMD FT because of the four closely spaced portholes which are unique to the FT. The other body characteristics are similar, yet Marx chose to give it passenger trucks instead of freight trucks.

The EMD FT locomotive was once commonly used on real railroads for heavy, long-distance road freight service in all kinds of terrain. In modeling these units, Marx opted to use simulated trucks. They have a total of only eight actual wheels. This design was produced in only one stock number in the metal category — the 21 Santa Fe. It is the largest of the passenger-type diesel locomotives modeled by Marx.

METAL EMD F-3 DIESEL

Note: We have labeled these diesels as EMD F-3 diesels because the F-3 is the only prototype with two round portholes separated by rectangular louvered grilles.

The EMD F-3 diesels modeled by Marx are eight-wheel diesels used for both freight and passenger service by real railroads. The model is identified by its smoothly-rounded nose, and mixture of round and square *portholes* on the side. Marx manufactured only two of these diesels, the 62 Baltimore and Ohio and the 6000 Southern Pacific. Double reduction motors are found occasionally in these disc-wheeled diesels. They were an effort by Marx to expand the motive power options available to include diesels that were more speed manageable. This made a smoother running engine which enabled it to pull the 3/16" scale cars, bought singly or in sets, as well as other heavier loads.

Metal FM diesels. *Top shelf:* 54 "KANSAS CITY SOUTHERN" AA units. *Second shelf:* Two B units. (55) "KANSAS CITY SOUTHERN"; 82 "MONON". Note that the units are joined together by tilt automatic couplers. *Third shelf:* 4000 "SEABOARD" ABA set. 4000 dummy A; (4001) dummy B; 4000 powered A. *Bottom shelf:* 81 "MONON" ABA set. 81 dummy A; 82 dummy B; 81 powered A. H. Diehl Collection, M. Feinstein photograph.

METAL FM DIESEL

Note: With the Marx factory being based in Erie, it is logical to think that Marx may have patterned its small metal diesel line after the FM prototypes. We have taken the liberty of labeling these diesels as such.

The Erie-built Fairbanks Morse A units of 1945 to 1949 were used by many well-known railroads such as the New York Central, Milwaukee Road, Pennsylvania, Union Pacific, Santa Fe, Chicago North Western, and Kansas City Southern. Marx's smallest main line locomotive was offered in three paint schemes; the 54 Kansas City Southern, the 81 Monon, and the 4000 Seaboard. Their stamping approximates the FM design with the long nose and heavy pilot. The side fuel tank, other access panels in the skirt, and the lithographed simulated four-wheel trucks closely resemble the FM prototypes. The round portholes are not found on the prototypes but apparently the Marx designers thought they made the model look more like a real diesel. However, the metal stamping allowed for an inaccurate reproduction of the nose. Marx used either a large four-wheel motor or a small two-wheel non-reversing motor depending on the selling price of the particular example. The larger motor powered all four wheels and was positioned in the locomotive housing so that the front wheel axle was located near the middle of the locomotive. The smaller motor powered only two wheels and was positioned toward the rear with a separate two-wheel axle placed at the front of the locomotive.

PLASTIC EMD E-7 DIESEL

Note: In 3/16" scale this diesel is six feet short of prototype length. However, the top and sides of the plastic molding accurately duplicate the E-7 prototype.

Like the large 21 diesel (made of metal), the plastic EMD locomotives represent the E-7 units used to haul passenger trains on real railroads. On the models, the plastic truck side frames are detailed as though they were six-wheel trucks, when in fact they have only four wheels. The trucks are too large and the shell too wide to simulate the E-7 prototype, but this was a necessary modification to enable it to run on O Gauge track. Because the models have a total of only eight actual wheels, they give the impression of the shorter F-7 diesels and are often identified as such by collectors. However, we have chosen to label them E-7s based on the side frame design, and the accurate panel and side grille molding of the car body.

Most of these diesels were sold as AA or AB units. However, there were four diesel units that were sold in the ABA combination. These were the Rock Island, Santa Fe, Allstate, and the gray Western Pacific. The B unit is fitted with a tab and slot coupler at each end which allows it to couple to the A units. Because very few of these ABA sets were sold, it has become difficult to find a B unit fitted with two tab and slot couplers.

Plastic EMD E-7 diesels; AA sets. *Top shelf:* (52) "UNION PACIFIC". *Second shelf:* 99 "ROCK ISLAND". *Third shelf:* (51) "ALLSTATE". *Bottom shelf:* 901 "WESTERN PACIFIC", gray version. H. Diehl Collection, M. Feinstein photograph.

ALCO S-3 SWITCHER

Note: This switcher bears many similarities to both the Alco S-3 and the LIMA 800 hp switchers. It does not match either exactly. However, we have chosen to call this an Alco S-3.

The Alco S-3 switcher is an eight-wheel locomotive used on prototype railroads for yard switching and for light main line service. The model is identified by its arched roof and small rounded fuel tank between the trucks. The model has swiveling plastic side frames imitating four-wheel trucks. Unlike the 4-4 wheel arrangement of the prototype, the model has a 2-4-2 wheel arrangement with only four middle wheels being powered. The S-3 has a vertical front end, as opposed to the sloped front found on the GE 70-ton switcher. The ornamental horn is mounted on the front of the cab, just below the eave of the roof. Because these locomotives were suitable for both main line and switching operations, they are often referred to as *road switchers*. Marx manufactured these in both powered and dummy versions.

GE 70-TON SWITCHER

Note: Even though the prototype does not have the side and top radiators like the Marx model, this is the only prototype switcher with a sloped front. Therefore, we have labeled these as such.

The GE 70-ton switcher is an eight-wheel locomotive used on prototype railroads for a variety of light functions, including switching and servicing of industrial spurs. The model was designed to 3/16" scale and is identified by its sloping front end and slightly rounded roof. The 70-ton switcher also has a "rolled-up" awning above the cab window on either side. Like the prototype, the model has four-wheel truck side frames. However, there are two single axles, thus only four actual wheels. The ornamental horn is mounted on the hood of the locomotive, just ahead of the cab. Since these locomotives are frequently used by small industrial railroads, mining companies, etc., they are often referred to as *industrial switchers*. Prototype branch line switchers ran on lighter rails that could not take heavy locomotives. The branch line had a twisting roadbed with tight curves which a light, short locomotive could better maneuver.

Top shelf: 4000 "PENN CENTRAL" A unit; (51) "ALLSTATE" A unit. *Second shelf:* 4000 "NEW YORK CENTRAL" A unit with short flags; 2124 "BOSTON & MAINE" Budd RDC. *Third shelf:* 4000 "NEW YORK CENTRAL" AA set with long flags. *Bottom shelf:* Metal EMD FT diesel, the 21 "SANTA FE". H. Diehl Collection, M. Feinstein photograph.

BUDD RDC

One of the most characteristic sights on the heavily-traveled commuter lines of America's eastern corridor is that of the fluted-side Budd Rail Diesel Cars (RDCs) whisking passengers to their destinations. Marx chose the RDC prototype which is essentially a self-propelled passenger car powered by a diesel engine. Because the unit provides both the motive power and the passenger capacity, it was an ideal prototype for Marx to model.

MARXTRONIC

The Marxtronic Electric Train System was a battery-operated plastic switcher modeled after the Plymouth industrial switcher. The prototype Plymouth industrial switcher was a small engine usually owned privately by industries which had use of a locomotive on their own property. The Marxtronic came in a set with two gondolas and plastic two-rail track. It was advertised on television as the "Train

with the Brain" which automatically switches, loads, reverses, couples, and uncouples.

Note: *The following listings are in numerical order within each class.*

Metal EMD FT Diesel

                                                                    Gd Exc

21 "SANTA FE": 1950-54, lithographed A unit; "MADE BY MARX" on rear; silver body with red front; silver and red roof and sides; black plastic roof horns; yellow and black trim with red along bottom; black lettering, white numbers; silver and black detail; die-cast long truck sides; tab and slot coupler.
(A) Powered A unit; catalogue number (1595); clear light lens.
                                                                    15   20
(B) Dummy A unit; catalogue number (1595D); red light lens.
                                                                    12   18
(C) Dummy A unit; catalogue number (1596); clear light lens.
                                                                    12   18
(D) Dummy A unit; catalogue number (1596D); red light lens; metal non-tilt automatic coupler on front pilot.   12   18

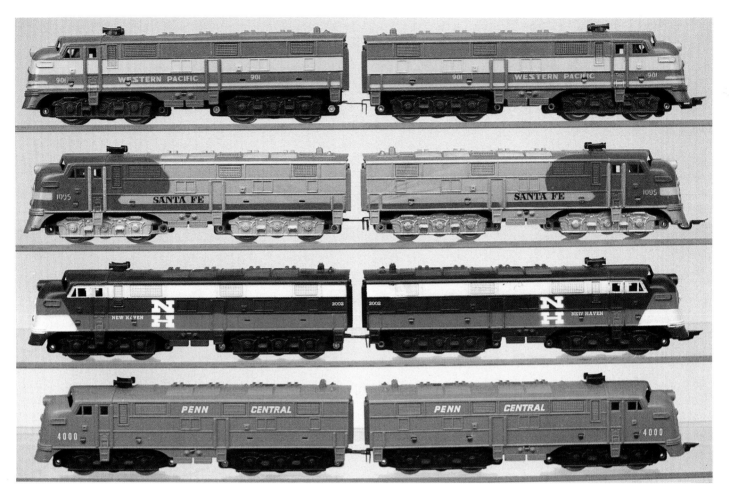

Plastic EMD E-7 diesels, AA sets. *Top shelf:* 901 "WESTERN PACIFIC", the green version. *Second shelf:* 1095 "SANTA FE". *Third shelf:* 2002 "NEW HAVEN". *Bottom shelf:* 4000 "PENN CENTRAL". H. Diehl Collection, M. Feinstein photograph.

Metal EMD F-3 Diesel

Gd Exc

62 "BALTIMORE & OHIO": 1953-54, 1958, 1967, lithographed A unit; B & O capitol dome logo on front; "MADE BY MARX" and Marx winged logo on rear; silver roof with blue front and sides; black details on roof and with black plastic roof horns; white and black detail; black stripe with yellow accent trim; white lettering and numbers; long sheet metal side frames; eight wheels; tab and slot coupler.
(A) Powered A unit; catalogue number (294); clear light lens.
15   20
(B) Powered A unit; clear light lens; double reduction motor.
30   40
(C) 1953-54, 1967, dummy A unit; catalogue number (294D); red light lens; not illuminated.
10   15
(D) 1958, dummy A unit; catalogue number (294/D), red light lens; not illuminated; plastic tilt automatic coupler. (Note: Tilt coupler was added to accommodate 3/16" scale cars.)
10   15

6000 "SOUTHERN PACIFIC": 1950-54, lithographed A unit; red setting sun logo on front with "SOUTHERN PACIFIC LINES"; "MADE BY MARX" and Marx winged logo on rear; black plastic roof horns; red-orange roof and body; silver or white band at bottom on front and sides; black and white detail; black stripe across pilot; black and white lettering and numbers; long sheet metal side frames; eight wheels; tab and slot coupler.
(A) Powered A unit; catalogue number (295); silver band; clear light lens.
5   10

Gd Exc

(B) Powered A unit; same as (A), but double reduction motor.
10   20
(C) 1950-54, dummy A unit; catalogue number (295D); silver band; red light lens.
10   15
(D) Powered A unit; white band; clear light lens.
25   35
(E) Dummy A unit; white band.
25   35
(F) Powered A unit; double reduction motor.
35   45

Metal FM Diesel

54 "KANSAS CITY SOUTHERN": 1956-60, lithographed A unit; front logo "KANSAS CITY SOUTHERN LINES"; red, black, and yellow body; black roof; black stripes with yellow trim; yellow lettering and white numbers; white and black details; lithographed truck detail and horns; clear light lens.
(A) 1956-60, powered A unit; large four-wheel reversing motor; tab and slot coupler.
18   25
(B) 1956-60, powered A unit; small two-wheel non-reversing motor; tab and slot coupler.
18   25
(C) 1956-58, dummy A unit; plastic knuckle coupler.
20   35

(55) "KANSAS CITY SOUTHERN": 1957-60, lithographed B unit; similar to 54(A), but with "KANSAS CITY SOUTHERN"; Marx trademark on rounded corner; lithographed truck detail.
(A) 1957-60, four-wheel; tab and slot coupler at one end and plastic tilt automatic coupler at other.
20   35

Plastic EMD E-7 diesels; B units. *Top shelf:* (99X) "ROCK ISLAND"; (52) "UNION PACIFIC". *Second shelf:* Two (902) "WESTERN PACIFIC". *Third shelf:* Two (1096) "SANTA FE". Notice the variation in the winged logo. *Bottom shelf:* (2003) "NEW HAVEN", (51) "ALLSTATE". H. Diehl Collection, M. Feinstein photograph.

	Gd	Exc

(B) 1959-60, four-wheel; tab and slot coupler at one end and plastic knuckle coupler at other. **20 35**

(C) Eight-wheel; tab and slot coupler at one end and tilt automatic coupler at other. **25 40**

81 "MONON": 1955-56, 1958-59, lithographed A unit; "MONON" on front; "MONON" and "M" on sides; Marx logo on rear; "81F" on sides; gray roof and body with wide red stripe and red front; lithographed horns on roof; yellow and white trim; with black and white details; yellow and white lettering; four-wheel motor version made both with light and without light; lithographed truck detail; tab and slot coupler.
(A) Powered A unit; large four-wheel reversing motor; clear light lens. **15 20**
(B) Powered A unit; small two-wheel non-reversing motor; clear light lens. **15 20**
(C) 1955-56, dummy A unit; catalogue number (1092/1), red light lens; not illuminated. **15 20**
(D) Powered A unit; windup motor; yellow and gray; slot in roof for lever; porthole cut out for key hole. **NRS**

(82) "MONON": 1958-59, lithographed B unit; non-powered; catalogue number (1095/ID); "MONON" Marx logo on end at bottom; gray roof; gray body with wide red stripe; yellow and white trim; yellow and white lettering; black, white, and red details; lithographed truck detail.

	Gd	Exc

(A) Four-wheel; plastic tilt automatic coupler. **18 25**
(B) Four-wheel; tab and slot coupler at one end and plastic knuckle coupler at other. **18 25**
(C) Eight-wheel; tab and slot coupler at one end, and tilt automatic coupler at other. **23 30**

4000 "SEABOARD": 1955-62, lithographed A unit; "SEABOARD" and "MADE BY MARX" on sides; "4000" at front; red heart Seaboard RR logo on front; green body with yellow and red trim; horns lithographed on green roof; Marx logo on rear door; low yellow bridle on green nose; yellow and red trim on sides; black pin stripes along bottom; yellow lettering and white numbers; black, white, and yellow detail; hole to simulate headlight; lithographed truck detail; tab and slot coupler.
(A) Powered A unit; catalogue number (892); small two-wheel non-reversing motor, no reverse. **25 35**
(B) Dummy A unit; catalogue number (895-D). **25 35**
(C) Powered A unit; catalogue number (895-D); four-wheel motor, reverse. **25 35**
(D) Powered A unit; catalogue number (895M); windup motor with die-cast thin-spoked wheels; porthole cut out for keyhole; ringing bell. **20 30**

(4001) "SEABOARD": 1962, lithographed B unit; non-powered; matches 4000; four-wheel; tab and slot couplers. **125 150**

Alco S-3 switchers. *Top shelf:* Maroon 1998 "A.T. & S.F." *Second shelf:* Red 1998 "ROCK ISLAND" with white lettering and silver trucks. *Third shelf:* Blue 1998 "ALLSTATE". *Bottom shelf:* Black 1998 "A.T. & S. F." H. Diehl Collection, M. Feinstein photograph.

Plastic EMD E-7 Diesel

Gd Exc

(51) "ALLSTATE": 1957-59, A or B unit; orange body with black band from nose along middle of sides; black plastic horns and Marx logo on roof; black nose bridle stripe; with or without "U.S. PAT. OFF." underside logo; small black stripe along bottom of pilot; black lettering and numbers; clear light lens; black plastic truck frames.
(A) Powered A unit; tab and slot coupler.   65   85
(B) 1957-59, dummy A unit; plastic tilt automatic coupler.   65   85
(C) Dummy B unit; non-powered; tab and slot coupler at one end and plastic tilt automatic coupler at other.   75   95
(D) Dummy B unit; non-powered; tab and slot couplers at both ends (from ABA sets).   85   105

(52) "UNION PACIFIC": 1960, A or B unit; no number on units; orange body with black trim; black lettering and numbers; clear light lens; black plastic truck frames.
(A) Powered A unit; tab and slot coupler.   50   75
(B) Powered A unit; plastic tilt automatic coupler.   50   75
(C) Dummy A unit; non-powered; tab and slot coupler at one end, and plastic tilt automatic coupler at other.   60   80
(D) 1960, dummy B unit; non-powered; tab and slot coupler at one end and plastic tilt automatic coupler at other.   65   85

99 "ROCK ISLAND": 1958-74, A unit; Rock Island logo on front with "99"; black body with lower red front; black plastic horns and

Gd Exc

Marx logo on black roof; large and small red bands on side with white trim; white lettering and herald; clear light lens; plastic truck frames.
(A) Powered A unit; catalogue number (10993D) after 1972; tab and slot coupler.   15   20
(B) Powered A unit; plastic tilt automatic coupler.   15   20
(C) Dummy A unit; plastic tilt automatic coupler.   15   20

(99X) "ROCK ISLAND": 1958-68, catalogue number (1093B); B unit; non-powered; matches 99.
(A) Tab and slot couplers (from ABA set).   22   30
(B) Tab and slot coupler and plastic tilt automatic coupler.   18   25

901 "WESTERN PACIFIC": 1956-60, A unit; "901" on sides; black plastic horns; Marx logo on roof; yellow nose bridle stripe; clear light lens; plastic truck frames.

Green body: Red and yellow accent trim; yellow lettering and numbers; black trucks.
(A) Powered A unit; catalogue number (1096); tab and slot coupler.
                                                                 20   30
(B) Powered A unit; diesel roar; tab and slot coupler.   35   45
(C) Dummy A unit; catalogue number (1096D); tab and slot coupler at one end and plastic tilt automatic coupler at other.   20   30

Gray body: Black and yellow accent trim; black lettering and numbers; silver trucks.
(A) 1957-58, powered A unit; catalogue number (1096); tab and slot coupler.   50   75

Alco S-3 switchers. *Top shelf:* **Red 1998 "ROCK ISLAND" with black lettering and silver trucks.** *Second shelf:* **Red 1998 "ROCK ISLAND" with black lettering and black trucks.** *Third shelf:* **1998 "UNION PACIFIC".** *Bottom shelf:* **1998 "UNION PACIFIC" with traction tires.** H. Diehl Collection, M. Feinstein photograph.

	Gd	Exc

(B) 1957-58, powered A unit; catalogue number (1096D); plastic tilt automatic coupler. **50 75**
(C) Dummy A unit; catalogue number (1097 DCN); tab and slot coupler at one end, and tilt automatic coupler at the other; clear plastic lens. **50 75**

(902) "WESTERN PACIFIC": 1957-58, B unit; catalogue number (1096B); Marx logo on roof; matches 901.
(A) Green body with red and yellow accent trim; yellow numbers and lettering; black trucks; tab and slot coupler at one end and tilt automatic coupler at the other. **20 30**
(B) Gray body with black and yellow accent trim, numbers, and lettering; silver trucks, tab and slot coupler at one end and tilt automatic coupler at the other. **75 90**
(C) Same as (B), but with tab and slot couplers at both ends (from ABA set). **80 95**

1095 "SANTA FE": 1952, A unit; gray body with red front and cab; black plastic horns and Marx logo on roof; red side stripes; black lettering; clear light lens; silver plastic imitation six-wheel side frames with four wheels.
  Long notched pilot: Yellow vertical nose stripes.
(A) 1952 only; powered A unit; catalogue number (1095); tab and slot coupler. **10 15**

	Gd	Exc

(B) Dummy A unit; catalogue number (1095D); tab and slot coupler at one end and plastic tilt automatic coupler at other. **10 15**
  Short pilot: Yellow vertical and horizontal nose stripes.
(A) 1953-74, powered A unit; catalogue numbers (1095) and (10995D) after 1972; later models rubber-stamped instead of heat-stamped; tab and slot coupler. **10 15**
(B) 1953-74, dummy A unit; tab and slot coupler at one end, and plastic tilt automatic coupler at other. **10 15**

(1096) "SANTA FE": 1955-71, B unit; catalogue number (1095B); red Santa Fe winged Indian head logo on front; Marx logo on roof; rubber-stamped black lettering; matches 1095.
(A) Tab and slot coupler at one end and plastic tilt automatic coupler at the other. **12 20**
(B) Tab and slot couplers at both ends (from ABA set). **15 25**

2002 "NEW HAVEN": 1960-74, A unit; catalogue numbers (1091), (10991D) after 1972; large "N" above large "H" (New Haven) on sides; "2002" on sides; black body with red and white bands; white nose bridle below with red top panels; white lettering and numbers; black plastic horns; Marx logo on roof; black plastic imitation six-wheel side frames with four wheels; clear light lens.
(A) 1960-74, powered A unit; tab and slot coupler; traction tires. **18 25**
(B) 1962-74, dummy A unit; plastic tilt automatic coupler. **18 25**

The top three shelves show GE-70 ton switchers; the bottom shelf shows the Alco S-3 switcher. Notice the difference in size of these models. *Top shelf:* 588 "NEW YORK CENTRAL"; 702 "WESTERN PACIFIC". *Second shelf:* 702 "WESTERN PACIFIC" with cream sides, front, and lettering; 799 "WESTERN PACIFIC". *Third shelf:* 799 "ROCK ISLAND"; 1798 "CAPE CANAVERAL EXPRESS". *Bottom shelf:* 1998 "A.T. & S.F." H. Diehl Collection, M. Feinstein photograph.

Gd Exc

(2003) "NEW HAVEN": 1960-74, B unit; non-powered; catalogue number (1091B), tab and slot coupler at one end, and tilt automatic coupler at other; matches 2002.   20   30

4000 "NEW YORK CENTRAL": 1953-55, 1959-69, 1971- 74, A unit; black body with light gray vent grilles; three white wing-shaped stripes (flag) near front on each side (two different versions of these flags made — short and long); white lettering and numbers; clear light lens; silver plastic horns; Marx logo on roof; silver plastic truck frames.
   Short flags.
(A) 1953-55, 1967-69, powered A unit; catalogue number (1094); tab and slot coupler.   25   35
(B) 1953-55, 1967-69, dummy A unit; catalogue number (1094D); plastic tilt automatic coupler.   25   35
   Long flags.
(A) 1953-55, 1967-69, powered A unit; catalogue number (1094); tab and slot coupler.   25   35
(B) 1953-55, 1967-69; dummy A unit; catalogue number (1094D); plastic tilt automatic coupler.   25   35

4000 "PENN CENTRAL": 1971-73, A unit; powered; catalogue number (10994D); "PENN CENTRAL" and "4000" on sides; turquoise body; no stripes or trim; white lettering and numbers; clear light lens; black plastic horns; Marx logo on roof; black plastic imitation six-wheel side frames with four wheels.

Gd Exc

(A) Powered A unit; tab and slot coupler.   125   150
(B) Dummy A unit; tab and slot coupler at one end and plastic tilt automatic coupler at other.   125   150
(C) 1974, powered A unit; one white stripe at bottom along body sides; pointed at front; white lettering and numbers; white roof vents; plastic tilt automatic coupler.   150   175
(D) Dummy A unit; same as (C).   150   175

Alco S-3 Switcher

1998 "A.T. & S.F.": 1955-62; catalogue number (1998); "A.T. & S.F." on hood sides; "SANTA FE" on cab; same color "1998" cast on cab; black die-cast metal base; clear lens; black plastic side frames; horn on cab front wall; Marx logo on front; front and rear cast handrails, plus handrails on sides near front; plastic tilt automatic couplers.
(A) 1955, maroon body with yellow lettering and numbers; black horn; cab variations for sound unit hole in cab rear door; no traction tires.   20   30
(B) 1962, black body with white lettering and numbers; black horn; traction tires.   35   45

(1998) "ALLSTATE": 1959, no catalogue number; blue body with white lettering; U.S. map outline on cab; white stripes on side of hood at front; plastic tilt automatic couplers.   100   125

GE 70-ton switchers. *Top shelf:* (800) "MISSOURI PACIFIC SYSTEM"; (801) "ILLINOIS CENTRAL GULF". *Second shelf:* 588 "NEW YORK CENTRAL" with tab and slot coupler; 112 "LEHIGH VALLEY". *Third shelf:* 588 "NEW YORK CENTRAL" with plastic knuckle coupler; 588 "NEW YORK CENTRAL" with tab and slot coupler. *Bottom shelf:* 588 "NEW YORK CENTRAL", showing the two shades of gray. H. Diehl Collection, M. Feinstein photograph.

	Gd	Exc

1998 "UNION PACIFIC": 1955-62, same color "1998" cast on cab; red lettering; dark gray roof; black die-cast metal base; black plastic horn on cab front; gray stack on hood; plastic tilt automatic couplers.

Yellowish-tan body.

(A) Powered unit; catalogue number (1998S); no tires; diesel roar sound unit. — 15 20
(B) 1956-60, powered unit; catalogue number (1998); traction tires; no diesel roar sound. — 15 25
(C) 1956, dummy unit; catalogue number (1998D), no diesel roar; no tires; for use with (A). — 25 35

Canary yellow body.

(A) Powered unit; catalogue number (1998S); no tires; diesel roar sound unit. — 15 20
(B) 1956-60, powered unit; catalogue number (1998); traction tires; no diesel roar sound. — 15 25
(C) 1956, dummy unit; catalogue number (1998D), no diesel roar; no tires; for use with (A). — 25 35

1998 "ROCK ISLAND": 1962, catalogue number (1998D); same color "1998" cast on cab; red body with gray roof; black die-cast metal base; black stripes and trim on lower body; plastic tilt automatic couplers.

Black trucks: Black lettering and numbers.

	Gd	Exc
(A) Powered.	35	50
(B) Dummy unit.	35	50

    Silver trucks: White lettering and numbers.

| (A) Powered. | 35 | 50 |
| (B) Dummy unit. | 35 | 50 |

    Silver trucks: Black lettering and numbers.

| (A) Powered. | 35 | 50 |
| (B) Dummy unit. | 35 | 50 |

GE 70-Ton Switcher

112 "LEHIGH VALLEY": 1974-76, DC; white Lehigh Valley flag on cab; "112" on front hood; "BUILT BY MARX" on front; red body with white lettering and numbers; white stripe along running board; red plastic horn on hood; red plastic stack; clear light lens; wire handrails; powered with DC can motor; black plastic truck frames; third rail pickup shoe; plastic knuckle coupler. — 15 20

588 "NEW YORK CENTRAL": 1958-62, "588" on cab; wire handrails; black plastic truck frames; horn on hood by cab; "BUILT BY MARX" on front.

    Black body: White lettering and numbers.

(A) No reverse; lighted; plastic knuckle coupler. — 10 15

	Gd	Exc
(B) 1959, reverse; lighted; tab and slot coupler.	10	15
(C) 1962, no reverse; lighted; plastic tilt automatic coupler.	10	15
(D) 1960-62, no reverse; no lights; plastic knuckle coupler.	10	15

Maroon body: Yellow lettering and numbers.

	Gd	Exc
(A) 1958, catalogue number (588R); reverse; no light; plastic knuckle coupler.	25	35
(B) No reverse; lighted; plastic knuckle coupler.	25	35
(C) Reverse; no light; tab and slot coupler.	25	35

Gray body: Two shades exist; black lettering and numbers.

	Gd	Exc
(A) 1962, no light; tab and slot coupler.	35	45
(B) 1964, light; plastic knuckle coupler.	35	45
(C) Tilt automatic coupler.	35	45

702 "WESTERN PACIFIC": 1972-74, "702" on cab; green body; gold on sides of hood and front; gold lettering and numbers; wire handrails; plastic knuckle coupler.

	Gd	Exc
(A) Catalogue number (798/4); reverse; lighted.	15	25
(B) 1972-74, catalogue number (783/4); no reverse or light.	15	25
(C) Yellow on sides and front; yellow lettering and numbers.	30	45
(D) Cream on sides and front; cream lettering and numbers.	30	45

799 "WESTERN PACIFIC": Square yellow hood and front; yellow lettering and numbers; wire handrails; horn and stack detail; no reverse; plastic knuckle coupler; very limited distribution.   **35 50**

799 "ROCK ISLAND": 1959-65, similar to 702(A), but with "ROCK ISLAND" on hood; "799" on cab; black body; red on side of hood and front; white lettering and numbers; wire handrails; plastic knuckle coupler.   **10 15**

(800) "MISSOURI PACIFIC": 1975-76, no number on engine; "MISSOURI PACIFIC SYSTEM", "Mopac" bird logo on cab; blue body with wire handrails; white stripe along running board; white front, lettering, and logo; light lens; plastic knuckle coupler.

	Gd	Exc
(A) With reverse	25	35
(B) No reverse.	25	35

(801) "ILLINOIS CENTRAL GULF": 1974-75, no number on engine; black Illinois Central Gulf logo on cab; orange cab and lower portion of body; white hood; wire handrails; black lettering; "BUILT BY MARX" on front; black plastic horn on hood; orange stack; clear plastic light lens.

	Gd	Exc
(A) With reverse; lighted; plastic tilt automatic coupler.	15	20
(B) No reverse; no light; plastic knuckle coupler. Reader confirmation requested.	15	20

1798 "CAPE CANAVERAL EXPRESS": 1959-64, powered; Marx logo on cab; "BUILT BY MARX" on front; red cab and lower body with white band and blue top hood; white lettering, numbers, and logo; white nose and hood; blue horn and stack on hood; clear light lens.

	Gd	Exc
(A) 1959-60, with reverse; plastic tilt automatic coupler.	50	75
(B) 1959-60, no reverse; plastic knuckle coupler.	50	75
(C) 1964, red horn; plastic tilt automatic coupler.	50	75
(D) 1959-60, without horn and stack; plastic knuckle coupler.	50	75

Budd RDC

2124 "BOSTON & MAINE": 1956-59, powered; "BOSTON AND MAINE" and "2124" on sides; red B & M Minute Man logos on front and rear ends; gray body; black silhouetted passengers on frosted plastic strip in windows; interior light; black lettering and numbers; black plastic roof horn each end; illuminated red and green plastic marker lights at each end; tab and slot coupler.   **150 175**

Marxtronic

"MARXTRONIC": 1959, catalogue number unknown; automatic switching set locomotive for use on plastic two-rail track; black body; cast-on details; stack on hood. (Two different methods of battery access used: remove motor screws to change battery or slide hood to change battery.) Special die-cast metal coupler for set.   **50 75**

Chapter II

Scale Cars

("Three-sixteenth")

by Larry Jensen

The 1942 Spiegel's Catalog proclaims "FREIGHT CARS MADE FROM ACTUAL RAILROAD BLUE PRINTS TO SCALE OF 3/16 INCH. Perfect in every detail...", in describing one of Marx's first scale train sets. When sold separately, "Scale railroad cars" was printed on the boxes containing each car. Scale cars differed from their predecessors in that each car was designed to be a scale model of the prototype car rather than a freely-designed toy. Accurate in scale, some modelers converted Marx scale cars into two-rail S Gauge operation by changing their couplers and trucks. These cars are generally called 3/16th cars by collectors referring to the ratio between the model and the prototype. Marx labeled these trains *scale*. Therefore, we have chosen to use the term scale to refer to the trains in this series.

MODEL RAILROADING

A. C. Kalmbach first published the magazine *Model Railroader* with the January 1934 edition. The growing interest by adults in the hobby of scale model railroading created a demand for this publication. While children were satisfied with the simplistic designs of the toy trains, adults needed to have greater realism in their train models. With the debut of *Model Railroader*, interest in scale model railroading began to grow in the United States.

The goals of scale model railroading are to build a realistic model of the full-sized prototype and operate it in a suitable setting (layout). To keep things in proper proportion, all dimensions are scaled down or reduced by the same ratio.

In the mid-1800s the British and German toy train manufacturers established the gauge standards known as Number 0, 1, 2, and 3. This allowed trains from various manufacturers to run on the same track. HO, literally *half Number 0*, was developed in the 1920s, when smaller electric motors were available to allow smaller engines to be built. In the late 1930s A. C. Gilbert started using 3/16" per foot which became S scale/gauge. Marx probably chose S scale because it was closest in size to his six-inch trains.

When you measure a Marx scale boxcar using the 3/16 scale on an architect's rule, the side measures 42' long by 10' wide, very close to the 40' size used for prewar prototype boxcars. Both the UP and NYNH & H boxcars had their dimensions lithographed on their sides: IL (interior length) 40-6 (or 40' 6") and IW (interior width) 9-2 (or 9' 2"). Considering the fact that our measurement was taken on the outside and the prototype walls had some thickness, these measurements were quite accurate. The scale height measurement from the floor to the catwalk top was 10'. The UP is marked IH (interior height) 10-9 and the NYNH & H was marked 10-0, which were not as accurate. The PRR cattle car was marked IL 40-5, IW 8-10, and IH 8-11. Some scale cars omitted sizes or the sizes were inaccurate, i.e. IL 50-6 for the GAEX boxcar. One should note that scale model railroaders do not always scale exactly, but sometimes *foreshorten* cars to track better or fit in with the overall layout they are building.

Toy Train Gauges and Scales

Name	Gauge	Scale	Ratio	Comments
3	2-1/2"	1/2"	1:24	Original European Toy Train Gauge (established in the mid-1800s).
Standard	2-1/8"	7/16"	1:27 ~	Established by Lionel circa 1909.
2	2"	7/16"	1:27 ~	Original European Toy Train Gauge.
G	1-3/4"	1/2"	1:24	Follows Narrow Gauge prototype.
1	1-3/4"	3/8"	1:32	Original European Toy Train Gauge.
O	1-1/4"	1/4"	1:48	Original European Toy Train Gauge (called # 0).
S	7/8"	3/16"	1:64	Established by A. C. Gilbert in the late 1930s.
HO	.650"	3.5 mm	1:87 ~	Started in the 1920s.
N	9 mm	.075"	1:160	Established by Arnold Rapido in 1964.
Z	6.5 mm	0.54" ~	1:220	Established by Märklin in 1972.

Gauge is the distance between the rails, scaled approximately to equal the American Railroad's standard of 4' 8-1/2".
Scale is the distance equal to one full foot on the prototype.
Ratio is the model size versus prototype size (e.g. for S scale 1 inch on the model is the same as 64 inches on the prototype).
When ~ is used, the scale or ratio are not exact. The number with the ~ is not the governing one but an approximation. The original number gauges were for toys without regard to scale. The scales shown here came into use later. There are over thirty gauges and almost as many scales used throughout the world. Often the terms scale and gauge are used interchangeably though this is not technically correct.

PREWAR DESIGN AND DEVELOPMENT

Three design models from the Marx Archives suggest that Marx started the design of the scale train line in 1940. Two of the models were tank cars: the one dated 7-26-40, is the same length as a production boxcar and was hand-lettered Texaco; the other dated November 20, 1940 and was hand-lettered the familiar NIAX. The lettering was not the same as that on the production NIAX, but it was the same length. The third model, a tender, was the earliest, with a March 12, 1940 date. The most interesting feature of the tender was its trucks. They were handmade versions of the passenger and 333 tender Type C trucks. Was Marx already thinking of a scale passenger set? If so, why was it not developed in the early 1940s to compliment the freight cars?

Marx planned to have his scale train line ready for the 1942 Christmas season. Tooling was to be finished and production begun early in 1942 to meet contract commitments. Scale trains first appeared in the Montgomery Ward and Spiegel Catalogs of 1942.

Only two design models that date back to the beginning of the scale line are known to the author. These were the NIAX tank car and the C & O flatcar. Only the NIAX was a hand-painted design model. There must be more design models in other collections. We would appreciate knowing of any scale design models that readers have so we can learn more about these cars.

POSTWAR DESIGN AND DEVELOPMENT

After the war there was a flurry of new designs. The earliest known postwar R & D scale design models were passenger cars. In mid-summer 1946, a Delaware and Hudson (D & H) coach and Southern Pacific (SP) observation were made. These had cast side frames on the trucks, but the molds were clearly handmade. The 1948 design model had trucks with production cast side frames that were hand-peened to the sheet metal part of the truck. The last model dated December 6, 1948, had the cast side frames attached by the production method using two vertical crimps across the boss that protruded through the sheet metal. A model of the NYC Vista Dome dated 9-30-48 had the boss hand-peened. Thus, it can be concluded that the NYC passenger cars could have been sold no earlier than 1949.

From the design models sold at the auctions, 1948 seems the pinnacle of scale development. Several new ideas were considered but not produced. A red Erie double-door, automobile-furniture boxcar, as well as several electrically-operated boxcar models, were made from scale production bodies.

One group of design models was plastic and was dated mid-1948. There was a medium height gondola, a regular gondola, a tank, a box, a three-bay hopper, and a caboose. These models were consecutively numbered starting with the regular height gondola and ending with the caboose. They were made by gluing several pieces together. It appears that these pieces were made by pouring liquid plastic into a simple flat mold, (except the tank car which required a round mold), rather than the usual injection-molding technique. These

An assortment of scale boxcars. *Top shelf:* 1950 "GAEX" with Type D trucks and tab and slot couplers; 9100 "U.P." with Type B trucks and metal tilt automatic couplers. *Second shelf:* 1950 "GAEX". Note the yellow stripe contains "GAEX-DF". On the right is the "N.Y.C." Note the rivets and grab-irons on left side at end. *Third shelf:* 1950 "GAEX". Note the yellow stripe contains only "DF". On the right is the 174580 "N.Y.C." with no rivets. *Bottom shelf:* Brown 70311 "P.R.R." Note black wheels indicative of a prewar car. On the right is the brown 3200 "New York, New Haven And Hartford". L. Jensen Collection, B. Greenberg photograph.

plastic models were closer to scale than the production plastic cars; however, there were enough similarities to conclude that they were indirectly related. Production plastic scale car bodies were the same as the eight-wheel plastic cars but they had Type B trucks. Also, the lettering was heat-stamped rather than rubber-stamped, with the exception of the tank car and flatcar.

TRUCKS AND COUPLERS

Type B trucks developed for the scale freight cars had a tin-plated sheet metal piece attached to the outside of the truck, simulating the prototype Bettendorf style frame. This gave the car a realistic appearance. In later years, the plastic tender came with the same trucks, but with a black metal frame. Other types of trucks were used with the scale cars, usually Type D, but occasionally Types F and G. Scale pas-

Left column: Three automatic couplers used on scale cars (shown upside down). The bottom metal coupler is prewar with a slot in the vertical piece that holds the trip shoe. Middle metal coupler is postwar. Top coupler is plastic. *Middle column:* Three side frame pieces that simulate Bettendorf trucks. Bottom is pre- and postwar with slanted fine spring detail. Middle is postwar with slanted coarse spring detail. Top is later postwar with level coarse spring detail. *Right column:* Bottom wheel is black and was used on prewar freight cars and postwar passenger cars. Top wheel is silver and used on postwar freight cars.

An assortment of plastic scale cars. *Top shelf*: Gray 347100 "PENNSYLVANIA" gondola with red lettering; red (035565) "SOUTHERN PACIFIC" caboose. *Middle shelf*: Yellow 13975 "A.T. & S.F." stock car; orange 467110 "BALTIMORE & OHIO" boxcar. *Bottom shelf*: Production samples showing the tags put on the cars by the design department for use as reference in their work. Maroon (03563) "ERIE" flatcar, the near side railing has been removed to allow the reader to see the production sample tag put on trains kept as samples in the Marx Design Department; green 2532 "CITIES SERVICE" white lettering, the tag is on the top right-hand side. L. Jensen Collection, B. Greenberg photograph.

senger cars had Type C trucks originally, but later used Types E and F.

The embossing on die-cast frames of Type C trucks for the earliest passenger cars represented springs and slope from high on the left side to low on the right side. Later passenger cars with plastic couplers have the opposite slope. Marx also used Type B trucks on one six-inch car, some six-inch bodies fitted to scale caboose bases and some plastic cars.

Marx purchased a patent for the automatic tilt coupler in 1942. It was often referred to as the dagger, tilt, or forked coupler. Unlike the one-way couplers, it allowed cars to be placed in either direction. The couplers were first produced in metal for the scale cars when they were introduced in 1942. The coupler was redesigned to be manufactured in plastic. The design model was mounted on a production C & O high-sided gondola dated 4-14-52. The plastic version may have been used in late 1952 for trains shipped to small distributors, if at all. In 1953 is was being used on all Marx train sets.

PASSENGER CARS

The lithographed scale passenger cars were produced with interior lights and attractive window strips featuring Marx V.I.P.s, such as sales manager George Dessler, West

Coast jobber Colonel Jim Stock (the gentleman wearing the hat), other Marx employees as well as the radio and TV stars Rochester and Jack Benny. These window strip notables appeared in striking contrast to the impersonal black silhouettes in Lionel passenger cars. Marx also produced a very plain scale passenger car which omitted the cut-out window panes.

SETS of SCALE TRAINS

The engines usually associated with this group are the 999 with a wedge tender and the 333 with the die-cast metal tender, although other engines were also used as the sheet metal 397 plain black engine. The 397 engine with scale cars was shown in the 1942 Montgomery Ward Catalog for $12.95. That was a dollar less than the 1942 Spiegel Catalog which showed the 999 with open spokes. Was the 397 used because the war limited production of the die casting for the 999 or was it just to provide a lower cost set?

The 1942 Wards Catalog shows the 397 locomotive pulling the NYC wedge tender, PFE reefer, B & M flat with timber load, LNE hopper, and Reading caboose. The 1942 Spiegel Catalog advertised the 999 die-cast locomotive pulling the NYC wedge tender, B & O tile car with load, T & P gondola, AT & SF cattle car, and Reading caboose.

An assortment of scale cars. *Top shelf:* 254000 "B & O" gondola with Type G trucks; 33773 "B & M" flatcar with lumber load and Type F trucks. *Second shelf:* 33773 "B & M" flatcar with pipe load and Type F trucks; 80410 "C & O" flatcar with lumber load and Type B trucks. *Third shelf:* Two flatcars with Type B trucks. On left is 33773 "B & M" with pipe load; on right is 2700 "NYC & St L" with lumber load. *Bottom shelf:* Box used for Marx flatcars, the end labeling identified with the car inside; 2700 "NYC & St L" flatcar without a load. There are no holes for mounting the U-shaped stakes. Notice that the box shows this plain flatcar. L. Jensen Collection, B. Greenberg photograph.

The 397 engine shown in the Wards Catalog validates its inclusion in a scale train set. However, other engines such as the 898 and even the Commodore Vanderbilt have appeared with scale sets. Unfortunately, we cannot validate these sets through catalogues.

The Santa Fe AA diesel, both metal and plastic, came in scale sets with both passenger and freight cars, some sets including both. The B & O diesel came in sets with freight cars, the Western Pacific came in sets with passenger cars, and the 1998 switcher came in scale sets with Santa Fe cattle cars. We presume the 4000 New York Central came in a set with passenger cars, but would appreciate reader confirmation.

DATING

Prewar cars have a slot in the coupler piece that holds the trip. The trip is the part that hits the uncoupler. They also have blackened wheels. Postwar models did not have the slot in their couplers and had tin-plated wheels. Cars made before early 1948 had five fine coils embossed on the truck but were hard to distinguish on later cars because of worn dies. In the summer of 1948 the spring had four heavy and coarse coils.

PAINT AND COLOR

Differences in color shade, shine, and car finish are not considered variations but differences that occurred in the car's production, as when colors were casually mixed during their manufacture. Time and the elements also effect color. If you were to arrange many of the same color car from dark to light, it would be difficult to discern a color change between two adjacent cars. Yet the first car is obviously many shades lighter in color than the last. A crackle finish was caused by exposing the original smooth dry finish to a solvent. Cars with a crackle finish seem to be the earliest. The lubricant first used on the bending dies to prevent the finish from scratching

An assortment of scale cars. *Top shelf:* 567 side dump car called a crossbreed because the body is made from a six-inch car but the base and trucks are from a scale caboose. *Middle shelf:* (3591A) searchlight car with red plastic searchlight; (3561G) searchlight crossbreed car. *Bottom shelf:* Two cabooses. 92812 "READING"; 20102 "NYC". Note the holes at the left end of the Reading. B. Allan Collection, B. Greenberg photograph.

most likely caused the crackling. It was then changed when the crackling was discovered and subsequent cars retained their original lithography finish. A glossy surface occurred when the flattening agent settled to the bottom of the container.

CROSSBREEDS

Crossbreeds are cars made from bodies of six-inch cars mounted on scale caboose frames and trucks. These were used in an early work train. The base for the Reading caboose that had a hole in the side usually has the six slots to attach the six-inch body to the base. A specially modified caboose base was used for the ramp car. The ramp car with two "DELUXE Delivery" trailers as the load was shown in the 1942 Wards Catalog. This set included an 897 engine with six-inch four-wheel cars plus accessories. The ramp car was also sold with a tank as the load.

JAPANESE COPY

The Japanese-made Hudson and Pacific set looked much like the Marx scale set, but had Japanese-designed couplers.

It is interesting to view the two side by side for comparison. The copy is remarkably similar to the Marx product, yet the differences are almost comical. The Hudson and Pacific was made by Sakai and imported by the Center Import Company of Baltimore.

MINOR VARIATIONS

Each of the gondolas has minor variations. The earliest cars had a slot in the side into which was inserted a tab from the floor to give added support. The later cars did not have the slot and tab. This change was made about the same time as the change to plastic couplers. Either a round embossing or four small dimples 90 degrees apart were found around the hole for the truck rivet. "MADE IN USA" or the Marx emblem was stamped into the underside of the base. The B & O gondola sometimes had a load of tile consisting of seven tan paper tubes 1 inch in diameter by 1-1/2 inches long with a collar of 1-3/32 inches (outside diameter) by 3/8 inches long.

Flatcar stakes, like those on the six-inch cars, were smooth. The car side had a small hole in the center where a spring was inserted. The spring held the clamp down against the load to keep the load in place. Later cars had dimples on

Top shelf: Two hand-painted design model passenger cars, "MARLINES" operating REA car; "NEW YORK CENTRAL" mail/baggage car. *Second shelf:* Two "NEW YORK CENTRAL" passenger cars with cut-out windows and passenger strip. Silver 3557; gray 234. *Third shelf:* Two passenger cars with lithographed windows. Silver 3557 "NEW YORK CENTRAL"; silver 3152 "SANTA FE" on Type F trucks. *Bottom shelf:* Two silver passenger cars with cut-out windows, passenger strip, and Type F trucks. 3152 "SANTA FE"; 1217 "WESTERN PACIFIC". L. Jensen Collection, B. Greenberg photograph.

the stakes to hold the clamp on the car. These variations are found on all B & M, C & O, and NKP flatcars.

There are two common loads for flatcars. The first was a set of eight black pasteboard pipes, 5/16 inch in diameter by 7- 3/8 inches long with a connecting collar having a 3/8 of an inch outside diameter, 5/16 of an inch inside diameter, by 1/2 inch long on one end. The second was a set of six timbers, 1/2 inch x 1/2 inch x 7-1/4 inches long. Another load, a set of logs (real sticks with the bark still on), surfaced in the Marx auctions. This would account for the four catalogue numbers found on a production sample flatcar. We presume the numbers are for the three known cars: the *pipe load*, the *timber load*, and the *no stake car*. The final number would have to be the *log load*. It would be interesting to know how many collectors acquired a flat with logs on it and thinking the load was assembled by kids, threw the logs away.

The NYC and GAEX boxcars had a minor variation not found on other boxcars. The number 3555 was lithographed on a smooth rectangular area in the door ribbing on all other boxcars. The NYC and GAEX boxcars sometimes did not have this smooth area. The GAEX had black or green door runners and the NYC had black or red and gray runners.

Reportedly, the PFE reefer can have the ends and base painted red. The PFE reefer lithography sometimes fades to almost white and may lose some or all of the *red sun* in the Southern Pacific (SP) herald.

The Reading caboose sometimes had holes in the sides at one end for marker lights. These holes were present on prewar cars and some postwar cars. The Reading and NYC cabooses have previously been incorrectly described as illuminated. The seven-inch B & O caboose was also made with scale trucks, as well as Type D trucks.

Scale cars are listed numerically within each of the following categories.

Metal passenger cars
Metal freight cars
Metal crossbreed cars
Plastic freight cars

An assortment of scale observation cars showing the variety of the drumheads. *Top shelf:* Two "NEW YORK CENTRAL", "METEOR" with Marx logo drumhead and Type C trucks. Gray; 3558 silver. *Second shelf:* Two silver observation cars. 1007 "WESTERN PACIFIC" with Type F and Western Pacific drumhead; 3558 "NEW YORK CENTRAL" with Type C trucks and the New York Central drumhead. *Bottom shelf:* Two 3197 "SANTA FE" with Type E trucks and El Capitan drumhead. The car on the left has an illuminated drumhead, the car on the right is non-illuminated. L. Jensen Collection, B. Greenberg photograph.

Gd Exc

Metal Passenger Cars

Note: *Except when noted, all passenger cars are illuminated and have cut-out windows, strip with people in full color, and metal or plastic tilt automatic couplers.*

Coaches

234 "NEW YORK CENTRAL": Two-tone gray body; white lettering; Type C trucks.   15   20

1217 "WESTERN PACIFIC: Silver body; white lettering; Type F trucks; plastic tilt automatic couplers.   25   50

3152 "SANTA FE": Silver body; red lettering.
(A) Type E trucks.   8   12
(B) Type F trucks.   8   12
(C) Solid lithographed window panes; not illuminated; Type E trucks.   8   12
(D) Same as (C), but with Type F trucks.   8   12

3557 "NEW YORK CENTRAL": Silver body; blue lettering; plastic tilt automatic couplers; Type C trucks.
(A) Illuminated.   30   45
(B) Solid lithographed window panes; not illuminated.   30   45

Vista Domes

234 "NEW YORK CENTRAL": Short translucent plastic dome; two-tone gray body; white lettering; Type C trucks.   15   20

Gd Exc

1217 "WESTERN PACIFIC": Full length dome; red body; silver lettering; cut-out windows in car body; people strip in dome; illuminated; Type F trucks; plastic tilt automatic couplers.   16   22

3152 "SANTA FE": Short translucent plastic dome; silver body; red lettering; Type F trucks.
(A) Illuminated.   8   12
(B) Solid lithographed windows; not illuminated.   8   12
(C) Full length dome; silver body; red lettering; lithographed windows in car body; people strip in dome; Type F trucks; plastic tilt automatic couplers.   15   20

3557 "NEW YORK CENTRAL": Short translucent plastic dome; silver body; blue lettering; plastic tilt automatic couplers; Type C trucks.
(A) Illuminated.   30   45
(B) Solid lithographed window panes; not illuminated.   30   45

Observations

(236) "NEW YORK CENTRAL": Two-tone gray body; white lettering; "METEOR"; white and gray Marx winged logo drumhead; Type C trucks.   15   20

1007 "WESTERN PACIFIC": Silver body; red lettering; red Western Pacific winged herald drumhead; plastic tilt automatic couplers; Type F trucks.   18   25

3197 "SANTA FE": Silver body; red lettering; red El Capitan winged herald with Marx logo drumhead.
(A) Type E trucks.   8   12
(B) Type F trucks.   8   12

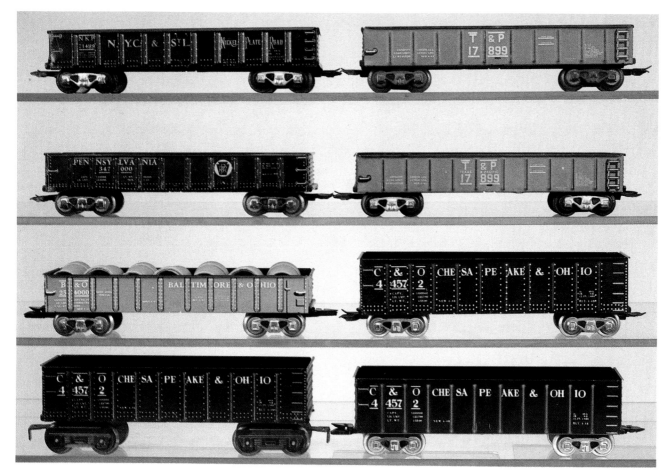

An assortment of scale gondolas. *Top shelf:* 71499 black "NYC & St. L"; 17899 blue-gray "T & P". *Second shelf:* 34700 black "P.R.R."; 17899 blue-gray "T & P" with "TEXAS & PACIFIC" written between the reporting marks. *Third shelf:* 254000 blue-gray "BALTIMORE & OHIO" with tile load; 44572 "CHESAPEAKE & OHIO" with rivet detail. *Bottom shelf:* Two variations of the 44572 "CHESAPEAKE & OHIO" high-sided gondolas. The one on the left has Type D trucks, tab and slot couplers, and rivet detail; the one on the right has Type B trucks and no rivet detail. L. Jensen Collection, B. Greenberg photograph.

	Gd	Exc
(C) Solid lithographed window panes; not illuminated; Type E trucks.	8	12
(D) Same as (C), but with Type F trucks.	8	12

3558 "NEW YORK CENTRAL": Silver body; blue lettering; "METEOR"; Type C trucks; plastic tilt automatic couplers.

	Gd	Exc
(A) White and gray Marx winged logo drumhead.	30	48
(B) Blue NYC winged oval herald.	30	48
(C) Same as (B), solid lithographed windows; not illuminated.	30	48

Metal Freight Cars

Boxcars

1950 "GAEX": Green roof, sides, end, and base; yellow lettering; black and yellow detail; plain green-painted door; Marx logo on one side; metal or plastic tilt automatic couplers.

	Gd	Exc
(A) "GAEX-DF" on yellow stripe; Type B trucks.	4	8
(B) Same as (A), but with Type D trucks.	4	8
(C) "DF" on yellow stripe; Type B trucks.	4	8

	Gd	Exc
(D) Same as (C), but with Type D trucks.	4	8
(E) Same as (C), but with Type D trucks; tab and slot couplers.	4	8

3200 "NEW YORK, NEW HAVEN AND HARTFORD": Brown roof and sides; black ends and base; white lettering; white and black detail; lithographed brown door detail; Marx wing logo on doors; Type B trucks; metal tilt automatic couplers.   6   12

9100 UNION PACIFIC: Black roof, end, and base; red sides with white lettering; white and black detail; lithographed red door detail; Marx wing logo on doors; Type B trucks; metal tilt automatic couplers.   10   15

70311 "PENNSYLVANIA": Brown roof and sides; black ends and base; white lettering; white, black, and yellow detail; lithographed brown door detail; Marx wing logo on doors; Type B trucks; metal tilt automatic couplers.   6   12

174580 NYC: Black roof, ends, and base; top half of side in red, bottom half of side in gray; white lettering; "Pacemaker FREIGHT SERVICE"; plain red-painted door; "MADE IN U.S.A." on one side; metal or plastic tilt automatic couplers.

	Gd	Exc
(A) No rivet detail; Type B trucks.	4	8
(B) Rivet detail on sides; Type B trucks.	4	8

An assortment of scale cars. *Top shelf:* Two (3550) "NYC" crane cars. Red plastic, "MARX" on boom; gray plastic. *Middle shelf:* Orange 652 "SHELL" tank car; silver 256 "NIACET CHEMICALS CORP." with black dome, ladder, and frame. *Bottom shelf:* Green 2532 "CITIES SERVICE; silver 256 "NIACET CHEMICALS CORP." with silve dome, ladder, and frame. L. Jensen Collection, B. Greenberg photograph.

	Gd	Exc
(C) Rivet detail on sides; Type D trucks.	4	8

Cabooses

20102 "NYC": Black roof; red top half, gray bottom half on sides; white lettering; black detail; (also made as six- and seven-inch cars with different bodies and similar lithography and numberings); Type B trucks; metal or plastic tilt automatic couplers. **3 5**

92812 "READING": Red body with white lettering; black detail; Marx wing logo; new date on car 9-41; Type B trucks; metal tilt automatic coupler. **3 5**

Flatcars

Note: *See text for load description. Add $5 for load and clamps, $3 for load only.*

2700 "NYC & St. L.": Black body; white lettering; white detail; "NKP"; Marx wing logo on side; metal or plastic tilt automatic couplers.

(A) No stakes or holes in the floor to attach stakes; Type B trucks.

	Gd	Exc
	20	30
(B) Three U-shaped stakes; Type B trucks.	15	20
(C) Three U-shaped stakes; Type D trucks.	15	20

	Gd	Exc

33773 "BOSTON & MAINE": Black body; white lettering; white detail; Marx wing logo on side; three U-shaped stakes; metal or plastic tilt automatic couplers.

(A) Type B trucks.	15	20
(B) Type D trucks.	15	20
(C) Type E trucks.	15	20

The three variations of the 44572 "C & O" black high-sided gondola. The left car has no rivet detail on the side, the right car does not have the Marx logo on the end and the center car has both rivet detail and logo. Note the lettering on the end at the lower left corner: BET87, BET87, BET86. L. Jensen Collection, B. Greenberg photograph.

Gd Exc

80410 "CHESAPEAKE & OHIO": Black body; white lettering; white detail; Marx wing logo; three U-shaped stakes; metal or plastic tilt automatic couplers.
(A) Type B trucks.	20	30
(B) Type D trucks.	20	30

Gondolas

17899 "T & P": Light blue-gray low-sided body; white lettering; white and black detail; Marx wing logo on ends; Type B trucks; metal or plastic tilt automatic couplers.
(A) "Texas & Pacific" written out between road name initials (T & P) and the car number.	5	10
(B) Texas & Pacific is not written out.	5	10

44572 "CHESAPEAKE & OHIO": Black high-sided body; white lettering; metal or plastic tilt automatic couplers.
(A) Gray rivets and detail; "Bet 86" on end; no Marx emblem; Type B trucks.	3	5
(B) Same as (A), but with Type D trucks.	3	5
(C) Same as (A), but with Type D trucks and tab and slot couplers.	3	5
(D) White rivets and detail; "Bet 87" on end; Marx emblem; Type B trucks.	3	5
(E) Same as (D), but with Type D trucks.	3	5
(F) Same as (A), but no rivet detail.	3	5

71499 "NYC & St. L.": Black low-sided body; white lettering and detail; "NICKEL PLATE ROAD" Marx wing logo on ends; Type B trucks; metal or plastic tilt automatic couplers. 5 10

254000 "BALTIMORE & OHIO": Light gray to light blue-gray low-sided body; white lettering; white and black detail; Marx wing logo on ends; metal or plastic tilt automatic couplers.
(A) Type B trucks.	3	5
(B) Type D trucks.	3	5
(C) Type G trucks.	3	5
(D) Type D trucks; tab and slot couplers.	3	5

347000 "PENNSYLVANIA": Black low-sided body; white lettering; white detail; Marx wing logo on ends; Type B trucks; metal or plastic tilt automatic couplers. 5 10

Hoppers

13079 "LNE": Black body; white lettering; Type B trucks; metal or plastic tilt automatic couplers.
(A) With end brace.	20	30
(B) With slot without end brace.	15	20
(C) Without slot for end brace.	15	20

Note: Only prewar LNE hopper cars have a strip of metal inserted on both ends to simulate end bracing. This piece was probably dropped to cut costs. Thus both pre- and postwar cars do not have this piece but do have the slots for the brace. Careful observation of the slot will show if paint is filling the slot. That means that no brace was ever put in the slot. Cars made last do not have the slot present in the end of the hopper, but the slot is still present in the frame (base). Most likely the dies to make the hopper end piece were either broken or replaced in later years.

Refrigerator Car

35461 "PACIFIC FRUIT EXPRESS": Brown roof; yellow sides; black ends and base; black lettering; black, yellow, and red detail; lithographed yellow door detail; Marx wing logo on doors; Type B trucks; metal tilt automatic couplers.
(A) Black ends and base.	10	15

(B) Red end and base. (Note: This car has been reported but not verified as a true variation.)

Stock Cars

13549 "A.T. & S.F.": Brown roof; orange sides; black ends and base; brown Santa Fe herald and lettering; black and yellow detail; lithographed brown door; Type B trucks; metal or plastic tilt automatic couplers. 10 15

53941 "PENNSYLVANIA: Brown roof and sides; black end and base; white lettering; white and black detail; lithographed brown door detail; Type B trucks; metal or plastic tilt automatic couplers. 150 175

Tank Cars

256 "NIACET CHEMICAL CORP.": "NIAX", silver body; red lettering; Marx wing logo under ladder; metal tilt automatic couplers.
(A) Silver frame and dome; Type B trucks.	5	10
(B) Black frame and dome; Type B trucks.	5	10
(C) Same as (B), but with type D trucks.	5	10

652 "SHELL": "S.C.C.X.", orange body with red lettering; no Marx logo; black frame and dome; metal or plastic tilt automatic couplers.
(A) Type B trucks.	6	12
(B) Type D trucks.	6	12

2532 "CITIES SERVICE": "C.S.O.X.", green body with white lettering; Marx logo on side at end; black frame and dome; metal or plastic tilt automatic couplers.
(A) Type B trucks.	5	10
(B) Type D trucks.	5	10
(C) Type D trucks; tab and slot couplers.	5	10

Work Cars

(3550) "NEW YORK CENTRAL": Plastic cab body and boom; die-cast hook; black lettering; black caboose base; "Marx" embossed on boom; metal or plastic tilt automatic couplers.
(A) Red body; Type B trucks.	25	35
(B) Gray body; Type B trucks.	5	10
(C) Gray body; Type D trucks.	5	10

(D) Same as (A), red base. Reader confirmation requested.

(3591A) SEARCHLIGHT: Red body; black flat or gondola base, Marx logo on plastic housing; Type B trucks; plastic tilt automatic couplers. 20 30

End view of three 13079 LNE black hoppers showing three variations. The left car has the end brace in place, on the middle car the brace is missing and the hole in the body is paint-filled indicating no brace was ever inserted, the right car does not have the body slot for the brace. The two left cars are prewar, the car on the right is postwar. L. Jensen Collection, B. Greenberg photograph.

An assortment of scale cars. *Top shelf:* 13079 "LNE" black hopper; 35461 "PACIFIC FRUIT EXPRESS" yellow refrigerator car with black ends. *Middle shelf:* Two stock cars. Orange 13549 "A.T. & S.F."; brown 53941 "PENNSYLVANIA". *Bottom shelf:* Two tank cars on Type D trucks. Orange 652 "SHELL" tank; silver 256 "NIACET CHEMICALS CORP." tank. L. Jensen Collection, B. Greenberg photograph.

Gd Exc

Metal Cross-Breed Cars

These are cars which use metal lithographed bodies from six-inch cars, but ride on Type B trucks with metal tilt automatic coupler except as noted.

554 "NORTHERN PACIFIC": High-sided gondola, green transition car; tab and slot coupler on one end, tilt automatic coupler on the other, six-inch base. **NRS**

567 "NEW YORK CENTRAL": Side-dump car; yellow body with black lettering; black caboose base; Marx logo on end of dump body; Type B trucks. **NRS**

(3550G) NYC: Crane car; orange body with black lettering; black caboose base, Marx logo on black boom; Type B trucks. **NRS**

(3559) FLOODLIGHT CAR: Black body; black caboose base; Marx logo on two floodlights; Type B trucks. **NRS**

(3561G) SEARCHLIGHT CAR: Back body; black caboose base; red and silver metal searchlight on red cone base; Type B trucks. **NRS**

71491 NKP: Side-dump car, black body with white lettering; "NICKEL PLATE ROAD", "Built date — '39"; black caboose base; Marx logo on end of dump body; Type B trucks. **NRS**

RAMP CAR: Olive drab ramp, body, and scale caboose base; tab and slot couplers. Note: This car does not have a six-inch body but was sold only in six-inch car sets. **NRS**

Gd Exc

Plastic Freight Cars

Note: *These cars are included here ONLY because they are on scale trucks. They are also in the Plastic Freight Car chapter since the bodies may come with other trucks.*

504 B & O: Caboose, light blue body; white lettering. **40 60**

2532 "CITIES SERVICE": Tank car; green body; white lettering; 6-3/4" in length; "C.S.O.X."; Marx logo under frame in center. **8 12**

(03563S) "ERIE": Flatcar; maroon body; yellow lettering; 7-1/4" in length; Marx logo on underside offset from center; Type B trucks; plastic tilt automatic couplers. **6 8**

(03556S) "SOUTHERN PACIFIC": Caboose; red body; white lettering; 6-1/8" in length; two Marx logos on same side (in sprue holes). **10 15**

13975 "A.T. & S.F.": Stock car; yellow body; black lettering; 7-3/8" in length; Marx logo under frame in center. **10 15**

347100 "PENNSYLVANIA": Gondola; gray body; red lettering; 7-5/8" in length; Marx logo on center underside. **6 8**

467110 "BALTIMORE AND OHIO": Boxcar; orange body; black lettering; 7-3/4" in length; Marx logo under frame in center. **8 12**

Chapter III

Seven-Inch Cars, 1950-1962

by Larry Jensen

When Louis Marx & Company perceived competition from Unique, their ability to rapidly conceive, develop and market a new toy resulted in the *seven-inch cars*. This characteristic made Marx the largest toy manufacturer of his time. Collectors have named these cars seven-inch cars because of the length of their base: 7-1/4 inches long. This distinguishes them from the metal lithographed six-inch cars of Volume I.

The seven-inch cars had four wheels, tab and slot couplers in the early years, and plastic dummy knuckle couplers in later production. The cabooses and old-time passenger cars were the exception: some had eight wheels and tilt-automatic or tab and slot couplers. Most seven-inch cars were mounted on a frame with axles secured at each end and were supported by four wheels. Exceptions were certain cabooses, when made for use with scale freight sets, such as the Atchison, Topeka & Santa Fe, Baltimore & Ohio, New York Central models, and the old-time passenger cars. The cabooses were produced with either B, D, or G trucks. Both tab and slot and tilt-automatic couplers were used. The Baltimore and Ohio and the New York Central Pacemaker cabooses came in both four- and eight-wheel versions. The Atchison, Topeka & Santa Fe caboose appeared in an eight-wheel version only.

HISTORY

Unique Art was a New Jersey toy manufacturing company owned by Sammy Bergman. Louis Marx and Sammy

had been close friends for many years. Marx sold toys for him and purchased Unique toys to resell. It was not uncommon for tools and dies for toy parts to be exchanged between the two plants. Imagine Marx's surprise when, in 1949, Unique Art introduced an O Gauge lithographed train set that would compete directly with the Marx line. Unique Art marketed their trains as boxed sets and individually. The circus animal cars were sold through the Jewel Tea Company. Another train in direct competition with Marx could have been the Unique Rock Island diesel, since Marx was producing a similar diesel, the 21 Santa Fe.

According to Chippy Martin, Unique Art's O Gauge set caused an uproar and a frantic rush on Marx's part to develop a competitive set. Marx began creating a line of seven-inch cars in January 1949.

The toy show was held each year in January with orders from the major buyers, like Sears and Wards, being placed in February. During the summer and fall of 1949 the manufacturing plant was busy making the trains for the 1949 Christmas season. Thus it seems likely that seven-inch trains were first introduced to buyers at the January 1950 toy show and were first sold in the fall of 1950 for that coming Christmas.

DESIGN MODELS

Seven-inch cars were derived from the scale train line. The Marx archives yielded several scale car bodies that were the beginning of the development of the seven-inch line. These first cars have the date "1-26-46" hand-painted on the underside. They were full length scale boxcars that had been modified by adding a six-inch base cut in half. These halves were put in place of the scale trucks to make a four-wheel car.

The goal was surely to make a less expensive car line. Only a new base and body were envisioned by its designers requiring a minimum tooling cost to start the new line. This new line would be less complex, requiring fewer parts and less time to assemble. This is evident when you look at the number of parts for the base including trucks and couplers used for a scale car verses a seven-inch car. A seven-inch car required 15 pieces of six different parts. In contrast, the scale car required 33 pieces of nine different parts.

It is presumed that these first design models did not track well on a curve because of the very long wheel base and the fixed nature of the axles on a four-wheel car. This created a dilemma for Marx designers. The scale length for a typical 40-foot boxcar was approximately eight inches, but an eight-inch car with a four-wheel base would not track well. To solve this problem, the designers borrowed a technique used by scale model railroaders called *foreshortening* which reduced a car's length and sacrificed *true scale accuracy*, but did not destroy the overall appearance of the model in relation to the rest of the scale models.

Marx had to invest in new tooling for the seven-inch bodies because scale bodies did not work out. Even though his designers had created many new cars, Marx limited the initial sets to a tender, gondola, boxcar, and caboose. There were later lithographic variations for these cars, but their variety seemed limited when compared to six-inch cars.

The designers did use the same base stamping for all the seven-inch cars, whereas the scale cars had many different bases. In fact, the only difference in the base for the seven-inch cars was the punching of the slots for the body tabs. The bases had only two different patterns for the slots. The boxcar and gondola used one pattern and the tender and caboose used the other pattern.

The Erie archives yielded several design models for the seven-inch line. Design models of the boxcar marked with the dates 3/3/49 and 3/4/49 used scale boxcar bodies with an inch cut out of the middle. At this same time seven-inch design models of a caboose and a gondola were made. The caboose was made by splicing a piece into a scale Reading caboose. The gondola was made from a Texas & Pacific scale gondola by shortening the sides and fastening the end into new slots. The base for these design models was a six-inch base with a piece spliced into the middle.

Design models dated May 1949 had handmade one-piece bases that were embossed with journal and spring detail, and almost certainly used six-inch dies. Since the spring detail was not complete, it is possible that broken dies removed from production were used. These design models included the Nickel Plate tender and caboose and Merchandise Service boxcar. All these design models were hand-painted: the tender body was handmade; and the caboose and boxcar were made from modified scale bodies.

A scale Shell tank car body dated August 1949 was mounted on a seven-inch base. The base had openings cut in

Two design models for seven-inch cabooses. *Top shelf:* Production car modified in the design department to produce a caboose for the seven-inch car line. Note the splice in the body just to the right of the cupola. The Marline herald is painted over. It has a handmade single-piece base. *Bottom shelf:* Another scale caboose body with splice. Used for the hand-painted Nickel Plate caboose design. B. Allan Collection, B. Greenberg photograph.

it to simulate the open frame work of a tank car. A design model of a flatcar was made and dated September 1949. It used cut-down scale sides mounted on a production seven-inch base that had the slots needed to attach the gondola body.

Production bodies for the NICKEL PLATE tender and caboose, WABASH gondola, and PENNSYLVANIA boxcar were all mounted on modified production seven-inch bases with scale trucks. These design models all had the same date, September 1949. Were the designers thinking of getting double duty from the new car bodies? We can only speculate.

In November 1949, a double-searchlight car was made by the designers. This car had large red plastic searchlights mounted on a low rectangular base fastened to a production caboose base. Several design models of flatcars were marked December 1949. These were a cable car, a timber load with the usual U-shaped stakes, and a flatcar with two plastic tractors.

A fascinating NICKEL PLATE caboose on scale trucks was designed in December 1949. It was illuminated with translucent plastic panes on the windows. A plastic brakeman was mounted on the rear platform. His arm was extended and reached around the right side of the body holding a lantern pointed forward. There was a light-tube through the man and his arm which enabled the lantern to light up!

Work on the new seven-inch line continued into 1950. In January, several different loads were designed and placed in production WABASH gondolas. There was a production NICKEL PLATE caboose with translucent plastic panes, an interior light bulb, and a pickup shoe like that used on six-inch cars. There was a hand-painted BORDENS gondola. A SOUTHERN cattle car was made in February. During the rest

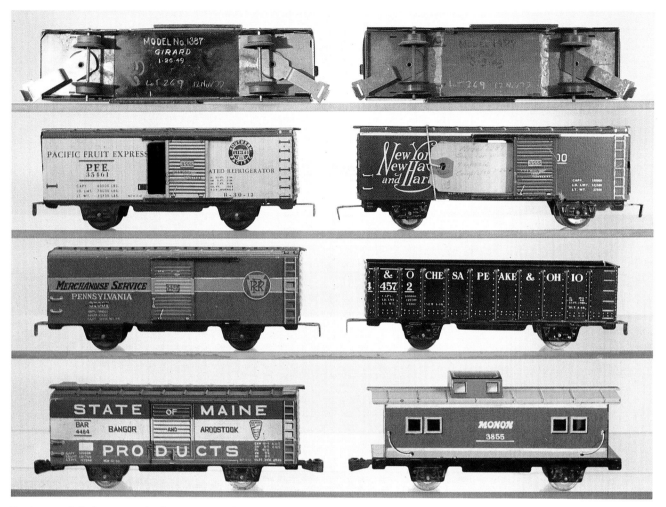

Design models for seven-inch cars. *Top shelf:* Bottoms of cars similar to those on second shelf. Right and left cars are reversed. *Second shelf:* Scale PFE reefer production body with piece cut out of middle. Notice that the word "EXPRESS" runs into the door jam and the roof ribs are close together where it has been spliced together. The base is made out of a production six-inch base with a piece spliced in. The car ends are cut from a production scale base but are fastened to the car body. Scale NYNH & H production boxcar with six-inch, four-wheel production base cut in half in place of the usual trucks. *Third shelf:* Handpainted PENNSYLVANIA boxcar that has a one-piece base and is made from a cut-down scale body. Note marked out 37007. C&O scale gondola that has been shortened. Notice the left side where the "C" and "4" are cut off. *Bottom shelf:* Handpainted "BANGOR AND AROOSTOOK" seven-inch on production boxcar body and base; handpainted "MONON" seven-inch on production caboose body and base. B. Allan Collection, B. Greenberg photograph.

of the year, there were several caboose designs made. An AT & SF 1951 and GREAT NORTHERN were hand-painted. The GN was on both a standard seven-inch base and a Type D truck base like the AT & SF. The NICKEL PLATE was put on Type D trucks with both slot and tab and tilt-automatic couplers. We are reasonably sure that it was never produced this way! A most interesting NICKEL PLATE operating caboose was designed. A shoe was rigged under the trailing D truck. When the caboose passed over an uncoupling ramp, the ramp would cause the shoe to lift up. Linkage was fastened to the shoe so that it caused a brakeman to swing out to the right past the side of the caboose as if to get off or to signal the engineer. Other designs included a MORREL REFRIGERATOR LINE reefer (boxcar) and the MARLINES brown cow gondola.

The MARLINES brown cow gondola came from the Erie archives. It was loaded with twelve plastic milk cans. The cans were red, yellow, white, or silver and were held in place by a cardboard insert with holes in it. The word "MARLINES" appeared in blue on the car sides with a drawing of a large brown cow. This car has been a mystery since its appearance. Recently, the author learned from someone living in the Girard area that Marx made products that were NOT for the consumer market. These may have been given to salesmen, store buyers, or sold to other groups for promotions. It seems most likely that the *dairy gondola* was made for such a reason and never sold to the general public. An example of this is the Bamberger Mack Truck. It was made by Marx for L. Bamberger & Company of Newark, New Jersey as a promotional special. When a patron made a large purchase Bamberger gave this toy to them in a carton marked "Merry Christmas".

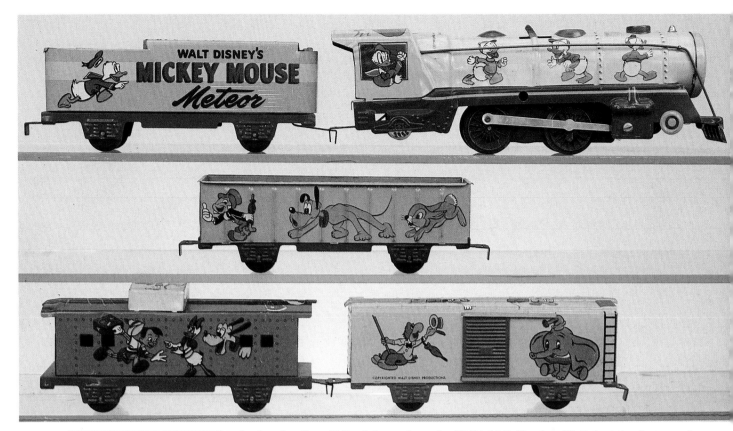

"MICKEY MOUSE METEOR" train showing Donald Duck in engine cab.   H. Diehl Collection, M. Feinstein photograph.

Apparently 1950 sales of the seven-inch line were so successful, or the competition did so poorly, that all development was suspended until 1955. The MONON caboose was designed early in the year. At the end of the year a MONON boxcar (which was never produced) and the BAR boxcar were designed. It is assumed that the C & O gondola, the solid door PRR boxcar, and the B & O, KCS, and NYC cabooses were also designed at this time, but we have no proof of this. The SP caboose, first appeared in the Sears Catalog in 1952, so it was probably designed in 1951. We also do not know when the Mickey Mouse train, and old-time passenger cars were designed.

The author would like to know if collectors can identify any other design models, especially ones that would fill in the gaps. For example, a hand-painted Wabash gondola design model would tell us when it was designed. Most likely it was developed in March, at the same time as the tender, boxcar, and caboose, but we would like to have evidence to this effect.

SETS

Scale Marx was *top of the line* and sold in 1949 for approximately $15 for a basic set. The six-inch cars were used in the *economy* sets which included the cheapest mechanical sets. These sold for from under $3 to about $6. The electric six-inch sets sold from $8 to $10. By adding extra cars, switches, or other accessories Marx could fill in any gaps in the price ranges. The seven-inch cars came in electric sets for

nearly $10 a set, with the steam engine, and went to nearly $15 a set with the diesel A-A engine. The 1950 Sears Catalog had a mechanical seven-inch set for $4.98 with the caption "Larger Engine — New Style Cars". One might surmise that this set would appeal to the father buying a set for his young son (for the father to play with!) who did not like the toylike quality of the six-inch cars. By comparison, the Unique Arts mechanical sets sold for around $4 to $6. The electrical sets sold for around $9 to $11.

One could speculate that the "MICKEY MOUSE METEOR" was created to meet the challenge of the Unique Art circus animal cars. The Walt Disney windup "MICKEY MOUSE METEOR" was the most colorful train Marx ever produced. The entire train was lithographed in bright colors and decorated with the familiar, zany Walt Disney comic characters. Today it is one of the most sought after sets by Marx collectors. As it turned out, the Unique Art toy train line was more of a tempest in a teapot than a full scale tinplate onslaught. In fact, Unique's toy typewriter proved to be a more serious competitor, which Marx overcame by producing a less expensive typewriter in the Orient.

In 1959, the William Crooks Civil War-period set was introduced. This passenger set had an old-time baggage and passenger car pulled by a plastic American-type engine with a plastic tender. The cars were manufactured using a modified stamping of the seven-inch caboose body. Both baggage and passenger car came in four- and eight-wheel versions. For the eight-wheel versions, the standard eight-wheel caboose base was modified by adding extra slots. In these slots plastic end

"MICKEY MOUSE METEOR" train showing Mickey Mouse in engine cab. This photograph shows the opposite side of the train as the previous photograph. H. Diehl Collection, M. Feinstein photograph.

railings and brakewheel were added to each end of the cars. A metal stamping that simulated truss rods was added to each side of the bottom of the base. For the four-wheel versions, the standard base was used with no end railings. The eight-wheel versions had plastic smokestacks at each end, the four-wheel versions had none. These were the only seven-inch passenger cars produced by Marx. They were marketed until 1962; the last cars were four-wheel versions for mechanical sets. The William Crooks locomotive and tender were re-introduced in Sears sets in the early 1970s; but with plastic deluxe freight cars.

Seven-inch cars, starting in 1950, were produced for nine years. The 1958 Sears Catalog was the last year that Sears advertised seven-inch freight cars. In 1959, the old-time passenger cars appeared in the Sears Catalog. Seven-inch cars did not abound in variations. We assume this was because Unique Art's train line suffered from an early demise; although another reason could have been the shift from metal to plastic cars in the early 1950s.

_____

Note: *Seven-inch, four-wheel, cars were made with both tab and slot or dummy plastic knuckle couplers. The wheels could be either metal or plastic, while the norm is for the tab and slot coupler to be with plastic wheels and the dummy plastic knuckle coupler to be with metal wheels, other combinations are also found. These variations are not significant except when specifically cited in the following descriptions. There is no discernible difference in their price. Since it is easy to change wheels or bodies, the listings represent what was actually manufactured and sold by Marx. Anything else should be questioned as to its authenticity.*

Boxcars

Gd Exc

1476 "MICKEY MOUSE TRAIN": 1950-51, yellow body and roof with Disney cartoon figures; Dumbo, Jiminy Cricket, etc.; tab and slot couplers only.   **50   75**

Note: *The Mickey Mouse Meteor cars were made with several different colors showing on the underside of the base. This is indicative of the way that the manufacturing plant would often use tin stock that had been prepared for one job but was taken and used for another. In the extreme case, this caused car bodies for one car to appear inside the body or on the bottom of the base for different cars. This creates*

4484 BAR boxcar in red, white, and blue. This car design was very popular with toy train companies and was used by Lionel and American Flyer as well as several of the HO manufacturers. Erie Archives, 1977.

A variety of seven-inch cabooses. *Top shelf:* C-513 "BALTIMORE & OHIO"; 980 "KANSAS CITY SOUTHERN". *Second shelf:* 1235 "SOUTHERN PACIFIC"; 3855 "MONON". *Third shelf:* C-514 "BALTIMORE & OHIO" on Type B trucks; 691521 Mickey Mouse train. *Bottom shelf:* 1951 "A.T. & S.F." on Type D trucks with tab and slot couplers; 20124 "NYC" on Type G trucks. B. Allan Collection, B. Greenberg photograph.

	Gd	Exc

interesting and sometimes unique cars, although they are more conversation pieces than collectible variations.

4484 "BANGOR AND AROOSTOOK": 1956-57, "STATE OF MAINE"; red, white, and blue body; blue roof; solid doors; white lettering; red details; plastic knuckle couplers only. **4 8**

Nos. 37950 through 37959 "PENNSYLVANIA": "MERCHANDISE SERVICE"; red and gray body; gray roof; black lettering; white details.

(A) 1950-58, catalogue number 955A; with sliding doors; "1427" on doors; tab and slot couplers. **3 6**

(B) 1956-58, catalogue number 945; with solid lithographed doors; plastic knuckle couplers. **3 6**

Cabooses

Nos. C-504 through C-518 "BALTIMORE AND OHIO": 1956-57, sky blue and black body with cut-out windows; gray roof; yellow lettering; B & O herald; white details.

(A) Plastic knuckle couplers. **10 15**

	Gd	Exc

(B) Plastic tilt coupler; Type B trucks. **5 7**

37958 P R R Merchandise Service Boxcar. Marx offered this car with ten different numbers from 37950 through 37959 by numbering each car on the lithography sheet with a different number.

Gd Exc

(C) Plastic tilt coupler; Type D trucks. 5 7

956 "NICKEL PLATE ROAD": 1950-58, red and gray body with cut-out windows; red roof; "Nickel Plate High Speed Service"; black lettering; white details. 4 8

969 through 980 "KANSAS CITY SOUTHERN": 1956-57, yellow, red, and black body with cut-out windows; black roof; black lettering; yellow details; plastic knuckle couplers. 15 25

Note: From the numbers found on the B & O and NYC cabooses, we know that there were 15 caboose bodies on each lithography sheet. However, we can confirm only seven numbers in the KCS series. We do not know if either 969 or 980 is an end number for a set of 15 numbers. We would like to know what numbers the readers of this book have to help to fill in the missing numbers. If there are indeed 15 numbers in the KCS series, then no one number should be any rarer than any other number; it is just that the author's access to the KCS caboose has been limited.

1235 "SOUTHERN PACIFIC": 1952-55, red and silver body with cut-out windows; maroon roof; white lettering; maroon details; Southern Pacific herald; tab and slot couplers only. 3 6

1951 "A.T. & S.F.": 1951-53, red body with black roof; white lettering; black details; Santa Fe cross herald; with and without end rivet detail; cut-out windows; Type D trucks. **Note:** This caboose was NOT made with a four-wheel base.
(A) Tilt automatic couplers. 5 10
(B) Tab and slot couplers. 5 10

3855 "MONON": 1956-57, red, gray, and white body; cut-out windows; gray roof; white lettering and details; plastic knuckle couplers only. 10 15

Nos. 20110 through 20124 "NYC": 1954-58, "Pacemaker", red and gray body with black roof; white lettering and details; cut-out windows.
(A) Tab and slot couplers. 3 6
(B) Plastic knuckle couplers. 3 6
(C) Type D trucks; tilt automatic couplers. 3 6
(D) Type G trucks; tilt automatic couplers. 3 6

691521 MICKEY MOUSE METEOR: 1950-51, orange body with cut-out windows; red roof with yellow cupola; with Disney cartoon figures; Pluto, Pinocchio, etc.; tab and slot couplers. 35 50

Gondolas

"Mickey Mouse Train": 1950-51, pale blue exterior, yellow interior; with Disney cartoon figures; tab and slot couplers only. 35 50

36000 "CHESAPEAKE & OHIO": 1956-57, brown exterior; white lettering; silver interior; C & O herald; plastic knuckle couplers only. 3 6

36000 C & O gondola with brown sides and white lettering, four metal wheels, and plastic knuckle couplers. Erie Archives, 1977.

80982 Wabash gondola with yellow sides and black lettering, four plastic wheels, and plastic knuckle couplers. Erie Archives, 1977.

Gd Exc

80982 "WABASH": 1950-58, yellow exterior; black lettering and details; black interior. 2 4

1 St. Paul & Pacific old-time baggage car with yellow body, black roof, and Type G trucks. H. Diehl Collection, M. Feinstein photograph.

Passenger Cars

1 "ST. PAUL & PACIFIC: 1959-60 or 1962, "BAGGAGE"; yellow body with black roof; brown lettering; black and white details.
(A) Plastic knuckle couplers only. 15 25
(B) Tilt automatic couplers; Type G trucks. 10 15

3 "ST. PAUL & PACIFIC": 1959-60 or 1962, coach, yellow body with black roof; brown lettering; balck and white details.
(A) Plastic knuckle couplers only. 15 25
(B) Tilt automatic couplers; Type G trucks. 10 15

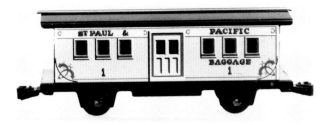

1 St. Paul & Pacific old-time baggage car with yellow body and black roof on the standard four-wheel base with plastic knuckle couplers. H. Diehl Collection, M. Feinstein photograph.

Chapter IV

Plastic Freight Cars

In 1945, plastic was an exciting new medium. Louis Marx realized its manufacturing potential, although it took him some time to reconcile the potential with the direct cost of converting his factories from metal to plastic production. Marx train designers first experimented with plastic molds in June 1948, and again in 1949. Research and design models which sold at the 1977 Marx auctions bear these dates. Plastic freight cars, however, did not appear until 1952. Always popular, they were manufactured through 1975 and were the last Marx trains.

By way of comparison, we note that Lionel began experimenting with plastic in 1940 when it made a phenolic plastic or Bakelite scale boxcar. In 1945 Lionel manufactured a new injection-molded gondola. They followed this with a 2454 Baby Ruth boxcar in 1946 when American Flyer introduced its line of plastic boxcars and tank cars.

The avid collector is both delighted and frustrated by the differences in color that is perceived when looking at plastic cars. Color differences within the same basic hue often arise unintentionally. A supplier may provide a different shade of plastic or paint even though it was ordered using the same catalogue number. Denoting these differences is often difficult: for example, several shades of what might be called *yellow* may be perceived as orange, yellow-orange, deep yellow, bright yellow, light-yellow, or even beige. If secondhand equipment has an unusual color, it may be sun-faded. In addition, adjacent colors, surface texture, and whether a car has been treated with a protective coating can distort psychological perception. For these reasons we have not listed variations based on subtle shadings in color.

As a medium, plastic was more versatile than metal in detailing a car body; it also required fewer tools to manufacture. Plastic molds were expensive, but in the final analysis the use of plastic for mass-produced toys reduced manufacturing costs substantially. At the same time other pioneering techniques such as sonic welding and air drills for blow-molding allowed Marx to replace less efficient equipment with newer, more sophisticated hardware.

Marx plastic cars are most readily differentiated by their wheel arrangement and their complexity. There are three categories: four-wheel, eight-wheel, and deluxe eight-wheel. *Four-wheel cars* (sometimes referred to as the lightweight class) were the first to be produced; they were also the simplest cars utilizing one-piece body molds with simulated trucks. *Eight-wheel cars* (sometimes referred to as the medium class) used the basic four-wheel car molds with the addition of a metal base and swivel trucks. They had few moving parts and little elaboration. The most complex, the *deluxe eight-wheel cars*, had numerous moving parts. They had the greatest amount of detail and today are the most desirable. Four-wheel cars were the least expensive, eight-wheel cars moderately priced, and deluxe eight-wheel cars the most expensive.

Although a plastic passenger car was designed in the Research and Development Department (as evidenced from the 1977 Marx auctions) Marx production plastic cars were all freight cars. There were boxcars, cabooses, cranes, flatcars, gondolas, hoppers, refrigerator cars, side dump cars, stock cars, and tank cars.

Of the three types of plastic cars, deluxe eight-wheel cars are among the most sought-after by collectors. The 1958 Sears Allstate set, for example, is very desirable. It came with orange diesel units, a deluxe green cattle car, an orange flatcar with green tractors, and an orange bay window caboose. Military plastic cars are another area of collector interest.

The Marx company later used different color plastic from the usual run, thus creating unusual pieces (as was done in the reversal of lithography colors in the metal six-inch series). Examples of this technique were the red Virginian hopper and the blue and yellow automobile carrier in the Champion freight set.

Colorful Mexican Marx set comprised of four-wheel plastic cars. R. MacNary Collection, M. Feinstein photograph.

Marx tried various sales techniques to promote plastic cars; one was to produce limited runs of Marline cars, such as the milk tank. The milk tank is very difficult to acquire today. Other limited-run cars are the Seaboard Air Line boxcar with double doors on each side (which no other toy manufacturer ever produced), the Rock Island boxcar in brown or tuscan, and the automobile carrier with a red base.

Both metal and plastic units were used for loads in plastic flatcars. Many metal tractor-trailer combinations and trailer-only units were used for loads on flatcars, as were plastic cars, panel trucks, and farm tractors. Marx also used cable drums, logs, lumber, pipes, and bridge girders, as well as military loads to dress up flatcars.

The following has been divided into three sections: plastic four-wheel, plastic eight-wheel, and deluxe cars. Under each section, the cars are listed numerically within categories.

Four-Wheel Cars

Introduced in 1952, four-wheel cars used a one-piece body mold cast with side frames which simulated four-wheel trucks. This design is referred to as *single-axle truck facade*. Four-wheel cars did not have moving parts (with the exception of the side dump car, crane, and dummy searchlight). They had no floor, and little ornamental color, other than stamped lettering or heralds. Their trucks consisted of a single axle with a metal wheel at each end. Some of the very late plastic four-wheel cars had a one-piece plastic axle and wheel set.

Variations exist of coupler mountings and coupler bars. Most cars had plastic knuckle couplers, but some came with metal tab and slot couplers. The later battery, mechanical, and low-priced electric (AC) sets came with plastic four-wheel cars. The cars were marketed later in different colors and in 1974, to enhance their attractiveness, many had their imitation truck side frames sprayed black. This later technique was

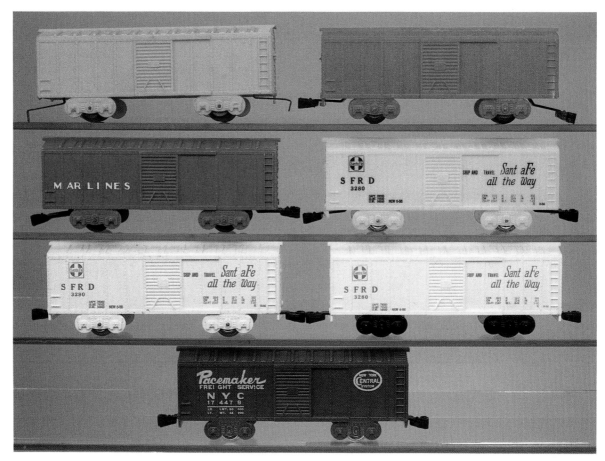

Top shelf: Two boxcars with no markings. The left came with decals to be applied by purchaser and were never used. The right is probably a car that was manufactured at the time that the factory closed down and was never finished. *Second shelf:* Blue Marlines boxcar, yellow 3280 S F R D. *Third shelf:* Two white S F R D boxcars. Note the black single-axle truck facade on the car on the right. *Bottom shelf:* Green 174479 NYC Pacemaker boxcar. H. Diehl Collection, M. Feinstein photograph.

utilized for the more expensive electric sets rather than battery and mechanical sets. Also, these plastic four-wheel cars were used in Mexican sets.

Note: Catalogue numbers refer to those used by Louis Marx & Company or Marx Toys. These numbers were used in Marx catalogues and also on the Marx order forms which were available from Girard until 1976.

Boxcars

	Gd	Exc
3280 "SFRD": Santa Fe cross herald, "SHIP AND TRAVEL Santa Fe all the Way"; plastic knuckle couplers.		
A) 1973, catalogue number 0965A, white body; red lettering.	2	5
B) 1974, catalogue number 0965H, white body; red lettering; black single-axle truck facade; plastic wheels.	2	5
C) Yellow body, black lettering.	2	5

161755 "NYC" 1952, yellow body; decals to be applied by purchaser; black letters and silver numbers; tab and slot couplers. **7 12**

174479 "NYC": Green body; white "Pacemaker FREIGHT SER-

	Gd	Exc
VICE"; NYC herald; white lettering; plastic knuckle couplers.	7	12
467110 "BALTIMORE & OHIO": 1950-75, "B & O"; black B & O capitol dome herald; black lettering; plastic knuckle couplers.		
(A) 1950s, yellow body.	3	5
(B) 1972, catalogue number 0955A, red body; white B & O capitol dome herald; white lettering; tin-plated metal or die-cast wheels.	3	5
(C) 1973, catalogue number 0955A, blue body; white B & O capitol dome herald; plastic knuckle couplers.	3	5
(D) 1974-75, catalogue number 0955A, orange body.	3	5
(E) Orange body with black single axle truck facade.	3	5
(F) Yellow body; decals to be applied by purchaser.	10	15
"MARLINES": 1952, blue body; white lettering; tab and slot couplers.	10	15

Cabooses

Note: All four-wheel cabooses with plastic knuckle couplers had only one coupler.

C-350 "MONON": Catalogue number 0956A, white lettering; plastic knuckle coupler.
(A) Tuscan brown body; white Monon "THE HOOSIER LINE" herald.
                                                                            10   15

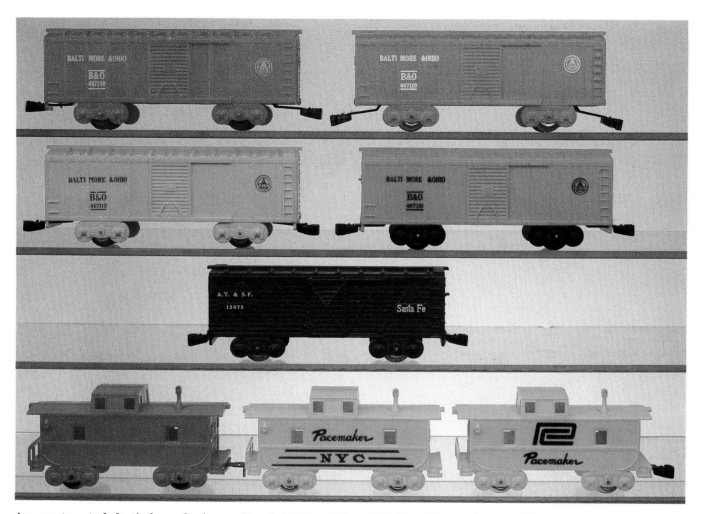

An assortment of plastic four-wheel cars. *Top shelf:* Two different shades of the red 467110 Baltimore & Ohio boxcar. *Second shelf:* Two orange 467110 Baltimore & Ohio boxcars. Note the one on the right has the black single-axle truck facade. *Third shelf:* 13975 brown A.T. & S.F. boxcar. *Bottom shelf:* Red caboose with no details, two yellow (18326) Pacemaker cabooses, the New York Central and the Penn Central. H. Diehl Collection, M. Feinstein photograph.

Gd Exc

(B) Red body. 10 15

504 "B & O": 1953, blue body; herald; yellow lettering; plastic knuckle coupler. 35 40

643 "W.P.": 1973, catalogue number 0956A, Western Pacific herald, green body; plastic knuckle coupler.
(A) Yellow lettering. 10 20
(B) Yellow lettering; black single-axle truck facade. 10 20
(C) Gold lettering; black single-axle truck facade. 5 10

969 "KCS": 1958, red body; "KANSAS CITY SOUTHERN LINE" herald; white lettering; plastic knuckle coupler. 10 15

1231 "M.P.": 1974, "MISSOURI PACIFIC SYSTEM"; plastic knuckle coupler.
(A) Catalogue number 0956/IH, blue body; white bird herald; white lettering; black single-axle truck facade; black metal wheels.
NRS
(B) Catalogue number 9056A, white body; black lettering, 10 15
(C) White body; blue herald; blue lettering; short stack; black single-axle truck facade; black metal wheels. 10 15

1977 "A.T. & S.F.": 1973-75, white lettering.
(A) 1973-74, catalogue number 0956B/1B, red body; tab and slot couplers. 2 4

Gd Exc

(B) 1974, catalogue number 0956H; red body; black single-axle truck facade; plastic knuckle coupler; black metal wheels. 2 4
(C) 1975, catalogue number 0956A; red body; plastic knuckle coupler. 2 4

1988 "B. & L.E.": 1974, catalogue number 0956H, "RADIO EQUIPPED"; orange body; black Bessemer rail logo; black lettering; black single-axle truck facade; black metal wheels; plastic knuckle coupler. 10 15

3900 "U.P.": 1974, catalogue number 04556, "UNION PACIFIC"; yellow body; black lettering; black single-axle truck facade; plastic knuckle coupler; metal wheels. 15 20

(4556) "SOUTHERN PACIFIC": 1952-75, plastic knuckle coupler.
(A) 1952, catalogue number 0956, tuscan brown body; decals to be applied by purchaser; gold letters and black numbers; metal tab and slot couplers. 2 3
(B) 1970, catalogue number 0956A; tuscan brown body; white lettering. 2 3
(C) Brown body; white lettering; number not on car. 2 3
(D) 1973, (Grant Department Store special), light orange body; black lettering. 2 3
(E) 1974, dark red body; white lettering; black single-axle truck facade. 2 3

An assortment of plastic four-wheel cabooses. *Top shelf:* White 1231 M.P. and red 1977 A.T. & S.F. with black single-axle truck facade; 1977 A.T. & S. F. with tab and slot couplers. *Middle shelf:* Orange 1988 B. & L.E. and yellow 3900 U.P. with black single-axle truck fac... red 17858 Rock Island. *Bottom shelf:* Black 18326 NYC with white and turquoise stripes; white 18326 NYC; red 95050 Lehigh Valley. Diehl Collection, M. Feinstein photograph.

An assortment of four-wheel plastic cars. *Top shelf:* Green Erie flatcar with yellow stake sides and tab and slot couplers. *Second shelf:* Two maroon Erie flatcars with maroon and yellow stake sides and plastic knucle couplers. The car on the left has yellow lettering, the one on the right has white lettering. *Third shelf:* Black NYC flatcar. This flat is not original but was made from a broken crane car. The car on the right is the Erie maroon flatcar with blue generator and gray dummy searchlight. *Bottom shelf:* Two NYC 967 side dump cars; blue and black. H. Diehl Collection, M. Feinstein photograph.

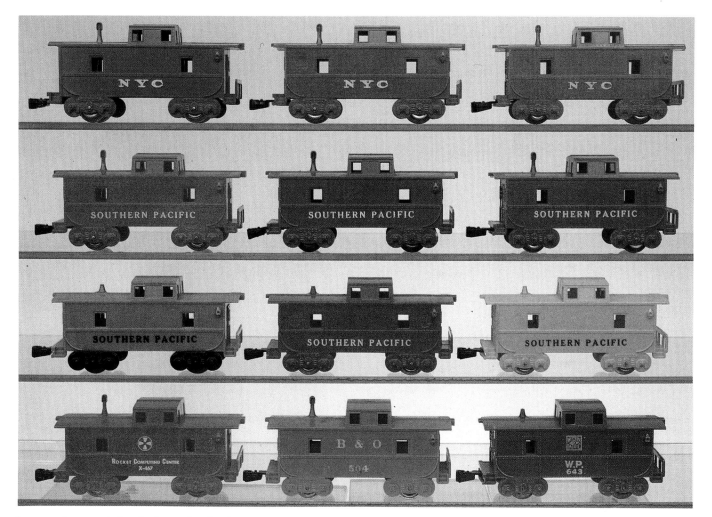

An assortment of plastic four-wheel cabooses. *Top shelf:* (18326) NYC in brown, tuscan brown, and orange. *Second shelf:* Southern Pacific in red, brown, and tuscan brown. *Third shelf:* Southern Pacific: green with black lettering and single-axle truck facade; tuscan brown; yellow. *Bottom shelf:* Red X-467 Rocket Computing Center, blue 504 B & O, green 643 W.P. with yellow lettering. H. Diehl Collection, M. Feinstein photograph.

	Gd	Exc
(F) Red body; white lettering.	2	3
(G) 1974, catalogue number 0956H, red body; white lettering; black single-axle truck facade.	2	3
(H) 1975, catalogue number 0956H, pea green body; black lettering; number not on car; black single-axle truck facade; plastic knuckle coupler.	2	3

17858 ROCK ISLAND: Red body; white lettering; Rock Island herald; plastic knuckle coupler. **2 3**

18326 "NYC": plastic knuckle coupler.

	Gd	Exc
(A) Catalogue number 0956A, white body; black lettering; "Pacemaker"; black stripes enclose "NYC"; number not on car.	12	20
(B) Same as A, but no stripes.	12	20
(C) White body; black lettering; "NYC"; NYC herald.	12	20
(D) Tuscan brown body; no herald; white lettering.	2	5
(E) Tuscan brown body; black herald; black lettering.	2	5
(F) Brown body; no herald; white lettering.	2	5
(G) 1970, orange body; no herald; white lettering.	2	5
(H) Yellow body; black lettering; "Pacemaker"; black stripes enclosed "NYC"; number not on car.	12	20

	Gd	Exc
(I) 1972, red body; "NYC" herald; black "Pacemaker"; white lettering.	2	5
(J) Black body with white strip above and turquoise stripe below; red lettering; NYC oval herald on white stripe; "NYC" and number on turquoise stripe; black single-axle truck facade..	10	15

18326 PENN CENTRAL: 1972-1974, Penn Central logo.

	Gd	Exc
(A) 1972, catalogue number 0956A, turquoise body; white lettering; plastic knuckle coupler.	2	5
(B) 1973, yellow body; black lettering; "Pacemaker"; number not on car; plastic knuckle coupler.	2	5
(C) 1974, catalogue number 0956B/1B, yellow body; black herald; black trim and lettering; number not on car; tab and slot couplers.	2	5
(D) Orange body; black lettering; "Pacemaker"; plastic knuckle coupler.	2	5

95050 "LEHIGH VALLEY": 1974, catalogue number 0956B/1B, red body; white diamond herald; "CUSHION UNDERFRAME"; white trim and lettering; black single-axle truck facade; plastic knuckle coupler. **2 5**

An assortment of four-wheel plastic flatcars with loads. *Top shelf:* Green Erie with two panel trucks; maroon Erie with two cars. The cars are not the original load but possibly came from a Marx playset. *Middle shelf:* Maroon Erie with white lettering and two panel trucks; blue Erie with black single-axle truck facade, one car and one panel truck. *Bottom shelf:* Blue Erie with black single-axle truck facade and two cars; maroon Erie with two red plastic farm tractors. H. Diehl Collection, M. Feinstein photograph.

An assortment of four-wheel plastic gondolas. *Top shelf:* Yellow Marlines with tab and slot couplers; blue 5532 Allstate with plastic knuckle couplers. *Middle shelf:* Blue 131000 S C L with knuckle couplers; black 1799 U.S.A.X. with three red missiles. *Bottom shelf:* Orange 347100 Pennsylvania; yellow 131000 S C L with tab and slot couplers. H. Diehl Collection, M. Feinstein photograph.

An assortment of four-wheel plastic gondolas. *Top shelf:* Two 347100 Pennsylvanias, red and blue. *Second shelf:* Blue 715100 NYC; gray 347100 Pennsylvania. *Third shelf:* Two shades of the blue 715100 NYC. *Bottom shelf:* Two 715100 NYC with black single-axle truck facade: blue with white lettering; green with black lettering. H. Diehl Collection, M. Feinstein photograph.

	Gd	Exc

Cranes

"NYC": Silver-gray body and boom, black base; white lettering; large "MARX" and "MADE IN USA" in circle cast on boom; die-cast hook; stack on roof; base length 7-3/16"; plastic knuckle couplers.

(A) Die-cast wheels; boom wires.	5	10
(B) No Marx logo on boom; no boom wires; tinplate metal wheels.	5	10

Flatcars

"ERIE": 1960, catalogue number 09521A, maroon body; yellow lettering; two red farm tractors; plastic knuckle couplers. 15 20

"ERIE": 1974, catalogue number 09528C, yellow stake sides; black lettering; square lumber stained brown; tab and slot couplers.

(A) Red body.		NRS
(B) Green body.		NRS

"ERIE": Catalogue number 09544A, maroon body; yellow lettering; plastic knuckle couplers.

(A) With one Sears turquoise and dark green trailer.	30	40
(B) With one white Walgreen trailer.	25	35
(C) With one white NYC trailer.	15	20
(D) With one Burlington trailer.	15	20

"ERIE": 1973, maroon body; square lumber stained brown; plastic knuckle couplers.

	Gd	Exc
(A) White lettering; maroon stake sides.	8	12
(B) White lettering; yellow stake sides.	8	12
(C) Yellow lettering; yellow stake sides.	8	12
(D) Yellow lettering; maroon stake sides.	8	12

"ERIE": 1974, catalogue number 0929A, automobile carrier (two vehicles, which varied in type and color, were placed on flatcars. Types included 1950 Fords, Chevrolets, Studebakers, and Dodge cars and panel trucks. Colors were red, yellow, green, blue, white, and silver; plastic knuckle couplers; metal wheels.

(A) 1974, blue body with white lettering; black single-axle truck facade.	10	15
(B) Green body; white lettering.	10	15
(C) 1974, maroon body; yellow lettering.	10	15
(D) 1974, maroon body; white lettering.	10	15

"NYC": Maroon body; white lettering; maroon stake sides; clip near one end for trailer load; plastic knuckle couplers. 10 15

Gondolas

5532 "ALLSTATE": 1962, catalogue number 0952A, blue body; white lettering; plastic knuckle couplers. 15 25

131000 "SCL": 1973, SCL herald.
(A) Catalogue number 0932C, yellow body; black lettering; tab and slot couplers. 2 4

An assortment of four-wheel plastic 21913 L.V. hopper cars with plastic knuckle couplers. *Top shelf:* Two black with yellow lettering. *Second shelf:* Black with orange lettering; green with white lettering. *Third shelf:* Light blue with white lettering; dark blue with white lettering. *Bottom shelf:* Two with black single-axle truck facade. Orange with black lettering; red with white lettering. H. Diehl Collection, M. Feinstein photograph.

	Gd	Exc

(B) Catalogue number 0952/6A, blue body; white lettering; plastic knuckle couplers. 2 4

347100 "PENNSYLVANIA": 1952-73, PRR keystone herald.
(A) 1952, gray body; no keystone, decals to be applied by purchaser; black lettering; tab and slot couplers. 2 4
(B) 1971, catalogue number 0952A, orange body; black keystone herald; black lettering; tab and slot couplers. 2 4
(C) 1971, same as (B), but with plastic knuckle couplers. 2 4
(D) 1972, catalogue number 0952A, gray body; red keystone herald; red lettering; plastic knuckle couplers. 2 4
(E) 1972-73, yellow body; black lettering; plastic knuckle couplers. 2 4
(F) 1973, red body; white lettering; plastic knuckle couplers. 2 4
(G) 1973, blue body; white lettering; plastic knuckle couplers. 2 4
(H) Yellow body; plastic knuckle couplers; decals to be applied by purchaser. 2 4
(I) Blue body; plastic knuckle couplers; decals to be applied by purchaser. 2 4

715100 "NYC": 1970-74, NYC herald.
(A) 1970-74, catalogue number 0952A or 0952H, blue body; white lettering; plastic knuckle couplers. 3 6
(B) Same as (A), but with black single-axle truck facade. 3 6
(C) 1973-74, catalogue number 0952H, red body; black lettering;

black single-axle truck facade; plastic knuckle couplers. 3 6
(D) 1974, catalogue number 0952B, light green body; black lettering; black single-axle truck facade; plastic knuckle couplers. 3 6

GONDOLA: 1962, red body; catalogue number unknown; plastic wheels; Marxtronic special couplers. 8 12

"MARLINES": 1952, yellow body and frame; black heat-stamped lettering; tab and slot couplers. 10 15

Hopper Cars

21913 "L.V": 1965-74, Lehigh Valley herald; plastic knuckle couplers. (Note: There is no period after the V on the car.)
(A) 1970, catalogue number 0454A, green body; yellow diamond herald; yellow lettering. 2 5
(B) 1973-74, catalogue number 0954H, green body; white diamond herald; white lettering. 2 5
(C) 1970-72, catalogue number 0954A, black body; yellow diamond herald; yellow lettering. 2 5
(D) 1974, catalogue number 0954H, orange body; black diamond herald; black lettering; black single-axle truck facade. 2 5
(E) 1974, catalogue number 0954H, blue body (two distinct shades); white diamond herald; white lettering. 2 5
(F) 1974, catalogue number 0954B, red body; white diamond herald; white lettering; black single-axle truck facade. 2 5

Top shelf: Two green 2532 C.S.O.X. tank cars. *Bottom shelf*: X-246 Chemical Rocket Fuel; (9553) Gulf Oil Corp. H. Diehl Collection, M. Feinstein photograph.

Military Cars

Gd Exc

X-246 "CHEMICAL ROCKET FUEL": Tank car; one dome; "DANGER", "HIGHLY FLAMMABLE"; white star herald; red lettering; plastic knuckle couplers.
(A) Catalogue number 09553A; cream body and base. 5 10
(B) White body and base. 5 10

X-467 "ROCKET COMPUTING CENTER": Caboose, red body; white herald; white lettering; catalogue number 0956A; plastic knuckle coupler. 30 40

1796 "ROCKET LAUNCHER": 1959-60, flatcar; Cape Canaveral set, white body with blue star herald; blue lettering; red missile launcher with three missiles; plastic knuckle couplers. 30 40

1799 "U.S.A.X.": 1959, gondola; "DANGER HIGH EXPLOSIVES", "MISSILES" white star herald, white lettering; rocket missile load consisting of three red plastic rockets; plastic knuckle couplers.
(A) Blue body. 35 45
(B) Black body. 35 45

Searchlight Cars

"ERIE": 1962, catalogue number 09571, maroon body; yellow lettering; plastic knuckle couplers.
(A) Black dummy searchlight and generator. 20 30
(B) Gray dummy searchlight and blue generator. 20 30

Side Dump Cars

Gd Exc

967 "NYC": 1957-58, white oval herald; white lettering; tilt body pivots on frame brackets.
(A) Catalogue number 0957A, black body and frame; tab and slot couplers. 35 50
(B) Black body and frame; plastic knuckle couplers. 35 50
(C) Blue body and frame; plastic knuckle couplers. 35 40

Stock Cars

13975 "A.T. & S.F.": Stock car, "Santa Fe", catalogue number 0975, body measures 7-3/8" long instead of usual 7-3/4"; brown body with white lettering; plastic knuckle couplers. 2 5

Tank Cars

2532 "C.S.O.X.": 1966-70, catalogue number 09553A; green body; white lettering; one dome; "CITIES SERVICE"; Cities Service herald; plastic knuckle couplers. 3 5

(9553) "GULF OIL CORP": 1974, catalogue number 09553A; orange body; black Gulf herald; black lettering; one dome; black single-axle truck facade; plastic knuckle couplers. 25 35

(9553) "ALLSTATE MOTOR OIL": One dome; white lettering.
(A) Light blue body; plastic knuckle couplers. 5 10
(B) Dark blue body; plastic knuckle couplers. 5 10

Two Allstate Motor Oil tank cars in two different shades of blue. H. Diehl Collection, M. Feinstein photograph.

Eight-Wheel vs. Deluxe

The following chart is presented to assist the reader in identifying eight-wheel and deluxe plastic cars. Generally, the eight-wheel car is shorter than the deluxe, however, there are many other identifiable characteristics.

	Eight-Wheel Cars	Deluxe Cars
Boxcars	One-piece molded plastic. Marx used the same mold as the plastic four-wheel cars, leaving off the simulated trucks.	Doors open, some have automated door with blue plastic man.
Cabooses	Plastic railings and ladders.	Metal railings and ladders. All bay window cabooses are deluxe.
Cranes	Plastic cab, platform, and fixed boom. Hook crank only.	5590 crane only. Comes with or without searchlight. Two hand-wheels on one side of the cab.
Flatcars	Shorter base than deluxe. Same body molding as plastic four-wheel. It has seven stake pockets. This category includes stake sides, log unloader, or automobile carrier.	Has nine stake pockets. Most have brake wheel. All depressed-center flatcars are deluxe.
Gondolas	Same molding as plastic four-wheel car. No movable drop ends brake wheel.	Movable drop ends. Side mounted brake wheel molded into plastic on one side near right-hand top.
Hoppers	21913 L.V. only. Same mold as plastic four-wheel car.	21429 Lehigh Valley or 28236 Virginian.
Refrigerator Cars	None.	Doors open, some have automated door with blue plastic man.
Searchlight Cars	(05571) A.T. & S.F. or military only.	Searchlights are mounted on depressed-center flatcars or extra deck flatcars.
Stock Cars	13975 A.T. & S.F. only. One-piece molded plastic. Same mold as plastic four-wheel car.	54099 Missouri Pacific only. Doors open, some have automated door with plastic cow.
Tank Cars	Single-dome single-tank only. Same mold as plastic four-wheel car.	Three-dome single-tank or twin tanks.
Work Cabooses	None	All

An assortment of eight-wheel plastic cars with tilt automatic couplers. *Top shelf:* Two red 467110 B & O boxcars. The one on the right is the early glossy car. *Second shelf:* Orange 467110 B & O boxcar; yellow 13975 A.T. & S.F. stock car. *Third shelf:* Two 13975 A.T. & S.F. stock cars. Left is brown, right is tuscan brown. *Bottom shelf:* Two 13975 A.T. & S.F. stock cars, left has Type F trucks, right has Type G trucks. H. Diehl Collection, M. Feinstein photograph.

Eight-Wheel Cars

Plastic *eight-wheel cars* were first manufactured during the mid-1950s. In developing these cars, Marx used the same molds as the four-wheel cars, with the addition of a metal floor to which two sets of four-wheel pivoting trucks were mounted. In examining a four-wheel car from this same period the slots for the metal floor are evident. These cars were a medium size and price, one-and- seven-eighth inches wide and six-and-three-eighths inches long. Boxcars came in two lengths: Seven-and-three-eighth inches as in the 13975 AT & SF stock car and seven-and-three-fourth inches as in the 34178 GN boxcar. Handrails and doors were cast as part of the body

shell. Most had tilting automatic plastic couplers, although a few had dummy plastic knuckle couplers. Most eight- wheel cars were sold in moderate-priced sets, yet during the mid-1970s they were sold in Marx's last top-of-the-line sets.

Note: Marx made some plastic cars that were fitted with 3/16th scale trucks. The car itself was not manufactured as a 3/16" scale car and for the convenience of the reader is listed in this chapter in a separate listing as well as in Chapter II. All tilt automatic couplers listed are plastic except those marked "tilt automatic metal."

An assortment of eight-wheel plastic boxcars. *Top shelf*: Two 467110 B & O. Note the slight shade differences. *Second shelf*: 34178 dark green Great Northern; 467110 B & O in a third shade of blue possibly caused from sun-fading. *Third shelf*: Two 3280 S F R Ds. Yellow with Type G trucks; orange with Type F trucks and plastic knuckle couplers. *Bottom shelf*: 34178 light green Great Northern; white S F R D.   H. Diehl Collection, M. Feinstein photograph.

Boxcars

	Gd	Exc
3280 "SFRD": Santa Fe cross herald; "SHIP AND TRAVEL Santa Fe all the Way"; tilt automatic couplers.		
(A) 1956, catalogue number 04555; orange body; black lettering; Type G trucks.	2	5
(B) 1962, same as (A), but with Type F trucks.	2	5
(C) 1970, white body; red lettering; Type F trucks.	2	5
(D) Same as (C), but Type G trucks.	2	5
(E) Yellow body; black lettering; Type G trucks.	2	5

34178 "GREAT NORTHERN": 1961, 1975, catalogue number 04555, "GN"; white GNR goat herald, white lettering; tilt automatic couplers.

	Gd	Exc
(A) 1961, dark green body; Type F trucks.	3	6
(B) 1961, dark green body; Type G trucks.	3	6
(C) 1975, light green body; Type G trucks.	3	6

467110 "BALTIMORE & OHIO": 1958-73, catalogue number 04555, "B & O"; white B & O capital dome herald; white lettering; tilt automatic couplers.

	Gd	Exc
(A) 1960, red body; black B & O herald; Type F trucks.	3	5
(B) 1964, blue body, Type G trucks.	3	5
(C) 1972, red body; plastic knuckle couplers; Type F trucks.	3	5
(D) 1973, red body; Type G trucks.	3	5
(E) 1973, red body; black B & O capitol dome herald; Type G trucks.	3	5
(F) 1973, orange body; black lettering; Type D trucks.	3	5
(G) Same as F, Type G trucks.	3	5

Cabooses

C-350 MONON: White lettering; Monon "THE HOOSIER LINE" herald; Type G trucks; tilt automatic couplers.

	Gd	Exc
(A) Tuscan brown body.	5	10
(B) Red body.	5	10

564 "ALLSTATE": 1959, catalogue number 04556, tuscan brown body; white lettering; Allstate United States map herald; Type F trucks.

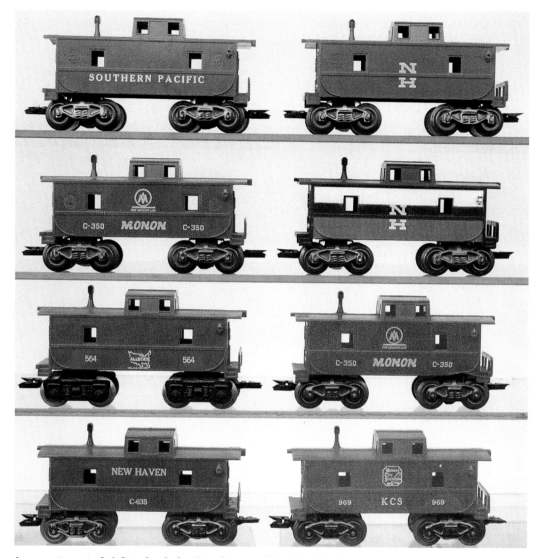

An assortment of eight-wheel plastic cabooses. Note the plastic railing which differentiates these cabooses from the deluxe cabooses. *Top shelf:* Tuscan brown (4556) Southern Pacific; brown (C-635) New Haven. *Second shelf:* Tuscan brown C-350 Monon; black C-635 New Haven with white and orange stripes. *Third shelf:* Tuscan brown 564 Allstate; red C-350 Monon. *Bottom shelf:* Tuscan brown C-635 New Haven; red 969 KCS. H. Diehl Collection, M. Feinstein photograph.

Gd Exc

(A) Tilt automatic couplers. 5 10
(B) Plastic knuckle couplers. 5 10

C-635 "NEW HAVEN": Catalogue number 04556, white lettering; Type G trucks; tilt automatic couplers.
(A) Tuscan brown body. 3 6
(B) 1962, tuscan brown body; New Haven NH logo; no number on car. 3 6
(C) 1962, same as (B), but with Type F trucks. 3 6
(D) Same as (B), but with Type E trucks. 3 6
(E) 1959, brown body; New Haven NH logo; no number on car. 3 6
(F) Black body with white top band and orange band on bottom; New Haven NH logo; no number on car. 5 10

C-678 "NEW HAVEN": Brown body; white lettering; New Haven NH logo; Type G trucks; tilt automatic couplers. 3 6

969 "KCS": Catalogue number 04556; red body; white lettering;

Gd Exc

Kansas City Southern Lines herald; tilt automatic couplers; Type G trucks. 10 15

01500 "RIO GRANDE": 1974, catalogue number 04556; orange body; black lettering; black stripe; "RADIO EQUIPPED", "Rio Grande the ACTION road"; Type G trucks; tilt automatic couplers. 25 35

(1972) "SANTA FE": 1974, Type G trucks; tilt automatic couplers.
(A) Tuscan brown body. 3 6
(B) Red body. 3 6

1977 "A.T. & S.F.: Catalogue number 04556; white lettering; Type G trucks.
(A) Tuscan brown body; tilt automatic couplers. 2 4
(B) Tuscan brown body; plastic knuckle couplers. 2 4
(C) 1974, red body; plastic knuckle couplers. 2 4
(D) Red body; tilt automatic couplers. 2 4
(E) 1973, gray body with yellow top band and red bottom band; gray

An assortment of eight-wheel plastic cabooses. *Top shelf:* White (18326) NYC (possibly faded by mold powder contamination in the plastic); white (18326) Penn Central. *Middle shelf:* Tuscan brown (4556) Southern Pacific; red (4556) Southern Pacific. *Bottom shelf:* Tuscan (1972) Santa Fe; green (4556) Southern Pacific. H. Diehl Collection, M. Feinstein photograph.

An assortment of eight-wheel plastic cabooses. *Top shelf:* Two 18326 Penn Centrals: left is tuscan brown, right is turquoise. *Middle shelf:* Two 18326 NYCs: left is tuscan brown; right is black with white and turquoise stripe and plastic knuckle couplers. *Bottom shelf:* Two 18326 NYCs: left is red with plastic knuckle couplers, right is brown. H. Diehl Collection, M. Feinstein photograph.

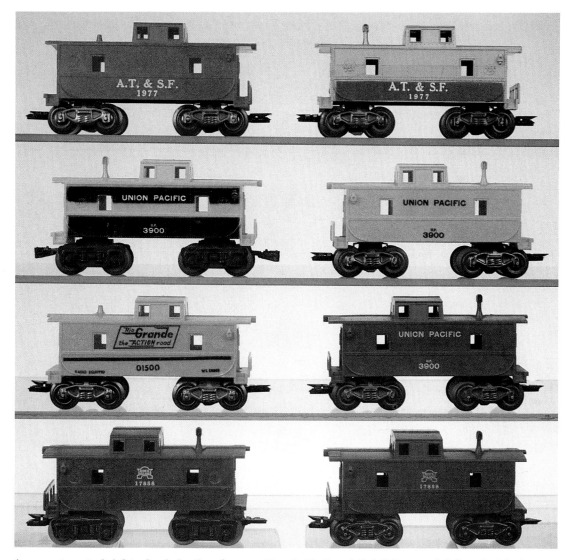

An assortment of eight-wheel plastic cabooses. *Top shelf:* Two A.T. & S.F. cars: left is red, right is gray with red and yellow stripes. *Second shelf:* Two 3900 Union Pacific: orange with black stripes and Type F trucks; orange with Type G trucks. *Third shelf:* Orange 01500 Rio Grande; brown 3900 Union Pacific. *Bottom shelf:* Two 17858 Rock Islands: left is tuscan brown, right is brown. H. Diehl Collection, M. Feinstein photograph.

	Gd	Exc
roof and cupola; plastic knuckle couplers.	2	4
(F) Same as (E), tilt automatic couplers.	5	10

3900 "UNION PACIFIC": 1974-75, catalogue number 04556; Type G trucks; tilt automatic couplers.

	Gd	Exc
(A) 1975, orange body; herald with black top and bottom band; white lettering.	3	6
(B) Same as (A), Type F trucks.	3	6
(C) Orange body; black lettering; no top or bottom black bands.	5	10
(D) Yellow body with black lettering.	15	20
(E) Tuscan brown body with white lettering.	2	5
(F) Brown body; white lettering.	2	5

(4556) "SOUTHERN PACIFIC": 1953-73, tilt automatic couplers.

	Gd	Exc
(A) Tuscan brown body; white lettering; Type F trucks.	2	3
(B) Same as (A), but Type G trucks.	2	3
(C) Red body; white lettering; Type F trucks.	2	3
(D) 1972-73, red body; white lettering; Type G trucks.	2	3
(E) Green body; white lettering; Type G trucks.	2	3

	Gd	Exc
(F) Same as (D), with plastic knuckle couplers.	2	3

17858 ROCK ISLAND: White lettering; Rock Island herald; Type F trucks; tilt automatic couplers.

	Gd	Exc
(A) Tuscan brown body; Type F trucks.	2	3
(B) Brown body; Type G trucks.	2	3

18326 "NYC": White lettering; New York Central herald; Type G trucks; tilt automatic couplers.

	Gd	Exc
(A) Red body.	2	5
(B) Red body; plastic knuckle couplers; Type F trucks.	2	5
(C) Red body; no number on car; plastic knuckle couplers.	2	5
(D) Red body; no number on car; plastic knuckle couplers; Type F trucks.	2	5
(E) Tuscan brown body.	2	5
(F) Tuscan brown body; plastic knuckle couplers.	2	5
(G) Tuscan brown body; Type F trucks.	2	5
(H) White body; "Pacemaker"; black horizontal stripes enclose "NYC"; no number on car.	2	5
(I) Same as (H), Type F trucks.	2	5

An assortment of deluxe and eight-wheel cranes. *Top shelf:* Two deluxe 5590 NYC cranes. The left is black with a searchlight; the right has a charcoal gray cab and boom. *Second shelf:* 5590 deluxe NYC crane; eight-wheel NYC gray crane. *Third shelf:* Two eight-wheel plastic cranes. The left is 1020 IC; the right is the NYC gray crane on a scale caboose base. *Bottom shelf:* Two eight-wheel plastic cranes. NYC black on left and gray on right. H. Diehl Collection, M. Feinstein photograph.

	Gd	Exc
(J) Yellow body; black horizontal stripes enclose "NYC"; no number on car.	2	5
(K) Brown body; Type G trucks; tilt automatic couplers.	2	5
(L) Black body; white and turquoise stripes; Type F trucks; plastic knuckle couplers.	2	5

18326 "PENN CENTRAL": "Pacemaker"; PC logo; black lettering; Type G trucks.

	Gd	Exc
(A) 1973, white body; tilt automatic couplers.	2	5
(B) Red body; tilt automatic couplers.	2	5
(C) 1973-74, turquoise body; tilt automatic couplers.	2	5
(D) 1974, tuscan brown body; plastic knuckle couplers.	2	5
(E) Same as (D); Type F trucks.	2	5

Cranes

CRANE: No catalogue number; boom wires; die-cast hook; gray plastic cab and platform; black plastic short base; tilt automatic couplers.

	Gd	Exc
(A) Type G trucks.	5	10
(B) Type F trucks.	5	10

	Gd	Exc

1020 "I.C.": Orange plastic cab and platform; brown plastic boom; black "X35" on cab; black lettering; black base; base length 8-3/8"; die-cast hook; boom wires; Type G trucks; tilt automatic couplers. **15 20**

"NYC": Black base; white lettering; New York Central herald on cab; "MARX" embossed on boom; Type G trucks; tab and slot couplers.

	Gd	Exc
(A) Silver-gray plastic platform, cab, and boom.	8	12
(B) Silver-gray plastic cab, and boom; tilt automatic couplers.	8	12
(C) Black plastic platform, cab, and boom.	8	12
(D) Black plastic platform, cab, and boom; tilt automatic couplers.	8	12

CRANE: Silver-gray body and boom; "MARX" embossed on boom; New York Central herald on cab; base length 8-3/8"; small die-cast hook type with boom wires; tilt automatic couplers; Type F trucks. **5 10**

Flatcars

Note: Regular eight-wheel plastic flatcars can be distinguished from

An assortment of Erie log cars. *Top shelf:* Two maroon flatcars with manual unload trip; left has white lettering, right has yellow lettering. *Bottom shelf:* Blue with manual unload trip; maroon with remote unload trip. H. Diehl Collection, M. Feinstein photograph.

	Gd	Exc

deluxe flatcars in two ways. First,· and most obvious, is the fact that regular eight-wheel plastic flatcars have seven stake pockets on each side, as opposed to deluxe flatcars which have nine. Second, regular eight-wheel plastic flatcars are shorter when compared to the deluxe flatcars.

56 WILLIAM CROOKS: 1973, catalogue number 04563, for William Crooks set; maroon body; yellow stake sides; lumber load (six pieces of square lumber); white lettering; Type G trucks.
(A) Tilt automatic couplers.   20   30
(B) (Sears 1973 William Crooks set); plastic knuckle couplers.
                                                  20   30

(586) "ERIE": Catalogue number 04563; maroon body; stake sides; yellow lettering.
(A) Tilt automatic couplers; Type G trucks.   2   4
(B) Plastic knuckle couplers; Type G trucks.   2   4
(C) Tilt automatic couplers; Type F trucks.   2   4

(0929) "ERIE": Catalogue number 0929, automobile carrier; blue body; white lettering; tilt automatic couplers; Type G trucks.
                                                  10   15

(05594) "ERIE" LOG CAR: 1957-58, catalogue number 05594; maroon body; white lettering; manual unload trip with five logs; Type G trucks.
(A) Tilt automatic couplers.   10   15
(B) Plastic knuckle couplers.   10   15
(C) Yellow lettering; tilt automatic couplers.   10   15

(D) Yellow lettering; tilt automatic couplers; Type F trucks. 10 15
(E) Yellow lettering; plastic knuckle couplers.   10   15
(F) Blue body; white lettering; black plastic dump bin for track side dumping; Type G trucks.   10   15
(G) Same as (F), but Type F trucks.   10   15
(H) 1957, maroon body; yellow lettering; electric remote-control unload trip with five logs; special track; tilt automatic couplers; Type G trucks.   10   15
(I) 1958, same as (H), but Type F trucks.   10   15

"ERIE": 1974, maroon body; white lettering; tilt automatic couplers; Type G trucks.
(A) Two red plastic farm tractors.   12   18
(B) Two gray plastic farm tractors.   12   18
(C) Two yellow plastic farm tractors.   12   18
(D) "SEARS" tractor trailer.   30   40
(E) "ALLSTATE" tractor trailer.   30   40
(F) "WESTERN AUTO" tractor trailer.   30   40
(G) "WALGREEN" tractor trailer.   30   40

Gondolas

5532 "ALLSTATE": 1959, catalogue number 04572, white lettering; tilt automatic couplers.
(A) 1959, turquoise body; Type G trucks.   5   10
(B) 1959, turquoise body; Type F trucks.   5   10

Two maroon Erie eight-wheel flatcars with Sears tractor trailer. H. Diehl Collection, M. Feinstein photograph.

An assortment of eight-wheel gondolas. *Top shelf:* 1799 U.S.A.X.; 5532 blue Allstate. *Second shelf:* 5532 turquoise Allstate. *Third shelf:* Subtle shade differences of the blue 5532 Allstate. *Bottom shelf:* Blue 5532 (another shade difference); 347100 Pennsylvania. H. Diehl Collection, M. Feinstein photograph.

	Gd	Exc
(C) 1959, blue body; Type G trucks.	5	10
(D) 1959, blue body; Type F trucks.	5	10

347100 "PENNSYLVANIA": 1952-73, catalogue number 04572; "PRR" keystone herald.
(A) 1956, gray body; red herald; red lettering; tilt-automatic couplers; Type F trucks. 2 4
(B) 1958, same as (A), but with Type G trucks. 2 4
(C) 1965, orange body; black herald; black lettering; tilt automatic couplers; Type G trucks. 2 4
(D) 1965, red body; black herald; black lettering; tilt automatic couplers; Type G trucks. 2 4
(E) 1970, blue body; white herald; white lettering; Type F trucks. 2 4
(G) 1971, red body; black herald; black lettering; plastic knuckle couplers; Type G trucks. 2 4
(H) Red body; white herald; white lettering; Type G trucks. 2 4
(I) Same as (H), but plastic knuckle couplers. 2 4
(J) 1971, gray body; red herald; red lettering; plastic knuckle couplers; Type G trucks. 2 4
(K) Same as (J), but Type F trucks. 2 4

715100 "NYC": 1973, catalogue number 04572; green body; NYC herald; black lettering; tilt automatic couplers; Type G trucks. 3 6

Hopper Cars

21913 "L.V": 1970-71, catalogue number 05554; LV herald; Type G trucks; tilt automatic couplers.
(A) 1970, black body; orange diamond herald; orange lettering. 2 5
(B) 1970, black body; yellow diamond herald; yellow lettering. 2 5
(C) 1970, blue body; white diamond herald; white lettering; plastic knuckle couplers. 2 5
(D) 1970, orange body; black diamond herald; black lettering. 2 5
(E) 1970, red body; white diamond herald; white lettering. 2 5
(F) 1971, blue body; white diamond herald; white lettering. 2 5
(G) Green body; white diamond herald; white lettering. 2 5

An assortment of eight-wheel plastic cars. *Top shelf:* Two 347100 Pennsylvania cars. Car on left has black lettering, Type G trucks; car on right has white lettering, Type F trucks. *Second shelf:* Two red 347100 Pennsylvania cars. Car on left has tilt automatic couplers; car on right has plastic knuckle couplers. *Third shelf:* Two gray 347100 Pennsylvania cars: left has Type F trucks, right has Type G trucks. *Bottom shelf:* Two black 21913 LV hoppers with orange lettering. H. Diehl Collection, M. Feinstein photograph.

Gd Exc

Military Cars

234 "U.S. ARMY": 1957, caboose; catalogue number 04556; olive drab body; white herald; white trim and lettering; tilt automatic couplers.
(A) Type F trucks.   15   25
(B) Type G trucks.   15   25

246 "CHEMICAL ROCKET FUEL": Tank car; catalogue number 09553; red lettering; one dome; white star herald with red field and "DANGER"; Type G trucks; tilt automatic couplers.
(A) White body and base.   5   10
(B) Cream body and base; cream star herald.   5   10
(C) Same as (B), but with plastic knuckle couplers.   5   10

X-467 "ROCKET COMPUTING CENTER": Caboose; red body; white lettering; catalogue number 04556, Type G trucks; tilt automatic couplers.   30   40

1796 "ROCKET LAUNCHER": 1959-60; flatcar; white body with blue star herald; blue lettering; red missile launcher and missile rack; Type G trucks; tilt automatic couplers.   30   40

Gd Exc

1799 "U.S.A.X.": 1959, gondola; "DANGER HIGH EXPLOSIVES"; "MISSILES"; red body; white star herald; white lettering; rocket missile load; Type G trucks; tilt automatic couplers.   35   45

2236 "U.S.A.": 1957, gondola; catalogue number 04572, olive drab body; white star herald; white lettering; tilt automatic couplers.
(A) Type G trucks.   30   40
(B) Type F trucks.   30   40

"U.S.A.F.": 1959, flatcar; "MISSILE LAUNCHER"; white body; blue star herald; blue lettering; missiles on each side of deck and one in incline launcher; Type G trucks; tilt automatic couplers.   50   100

(05571) SEARCHLIGHT: 1959, searchlight car; catalogue number 05571/1, red body; white star herald; white lettering; blue generator and white searchlight; Type G trucks; tilt automatic couplers.
(A) "U.S.A.F.".   20   30
(B) "ATOMIC LIGHT GENERATOR"; dark blue generator.   25   35

(9553) "ALLSTATE ROCKET FUEL": 1959-74, catalogue number 09553, one dome; white body and base; red lettering, Type G trucks; tilt automatic couplers.
(A) Type G trucks.   5   10
(B) 1960, Type F trucks.   5   10

An assortment of eight-wheel plastic cars. *Top shelf*: 21913 LV hopper. Left is blue with white lettering; right is black with yellow lettering. *Second shelf*: Two 21913 blue LV hoppers. Note the shade differences. *Third shelf*: (9553) orange Gulf tank with black lettering. *Bottom shelf*: Two (9553) blue Allstate tanks. Right has plastic knuckle couplers. H. Diehl Collection, M. Feinstein photograph.

Searchlight Cars

	Gd	Exc
(05571)"A.T. & S.F.": 1965, maroon body; black generator and searchlight; Type G trucks; tilt automatic couplers.	20	30

Stock Cars

13975 "A.T. & S.F.": 1955, stock car; catalogue number 0975, "Santa Fe"; 7-3/8" long instead of usual 7- 3/4"; white lettering; tilt automatic couplers.

	Gd	Exc
(A) Brown body; Type F trucks.	2	5
(B) Brown body; Type G trucks.	2	5
(C) Tuscan brown body; Type G trucks.	2	5
(D) Tuscan brown body; Type F trucks.	2	5
(E) Red body; Type F trucks.	2	5
(F) Yellow body; black lettering; Type F trucks.	2	5

Tank Cars

2532 "C.S.O.X.": 1966-70, catalogue number 09553; one dome;

green body and base; white Cities Service herald; white lettering; tilt automatic couplers.

	Gd	Exc
(A) 1966, Type F trucks.	3	5
(B) 1968, Type G trucks.	3	5
(C) 1968, Type F trucks; plastic knuckle couplers.	3	5
(D) 1970, Type G trucks; plastic knuckle couplers.	3	5

(9553) TANK: 1959-74, catalogue number 09553, one dome; tilt automatic couplers.

	Gd	Exc
(A) 1959, "ALLSTATE", light blue body and base; white Motor Oil herald; white lettering; Type F trucks.	5	10
(B) 1959, same as (A), but Type G trucks.	5	10
(C) Same as (A), but Type G trucks; plastic knuckle couplers.	5	10
(D) 1959, same as (A), but with turquoise blue body and base.	5	10
(E) 1974, "GULF", orange body and base; black herald; black lettering; Type F trucks.	30	35
(F) Same as (E), but with Type G trucks.	30	35

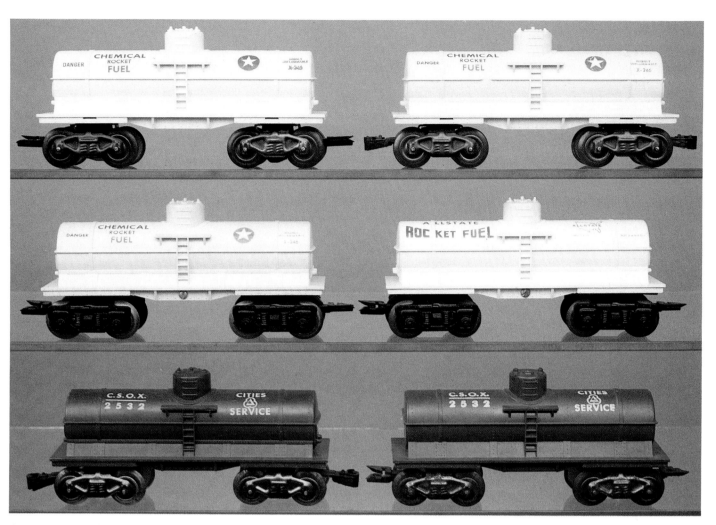

An assortment of eight-wheel plastic tank cars. Note that these are all one-tank, single-dome cars. *Top shelf:* Two X-246 Chemical Rocket Fuel cars. Right has plastic knuckle couplers. *Middle shelf:* X-246 Chemical Rocket Fuel; (9553) Allstate Rocket Fuel. *Bottom shelf:* Two 2532 green C.S.O.X. cars. Left car has plastic knuckle couplers. H. Diehl Collection, M. Feinstein photograph.

Plastic "Scale" Cars

Gd Exc

Note: Marx fitted some of the plastic cars with Type B trucks. There are eight known to exist. All of these cars had heat-stamped lettering with the exception of the crane and tank car. Because bases can be easily changed, this is an important feature in determining the authenticity of a plastic "scale" car.

204 "B & O": Caboose; blue; white heat-stamped lettering; Type B trucks.   **40   60**

2532 "C.S.O.X.": 1966-70, tank car; catalogue number 09553; one dome; green body and base; white Cities Service herald; white lettering; Type B trucks; tilt automatic couplers.   **5   10**

(4556) "SOUTHERN PACIFIC": 1953, caboose; tilt automatic couplers; red body; white heat-stamped lettering; Type B 3/16" scale trucks.   **2   3**

(035635) ERIE: Flatcar; maroon body; yellow lettering; length is 7-1/4"; seven stake pockets; maroon stake sides; plastic tilt couplers;

Gd Exc

Type B trucks.   **10   15**

13975 "A.T. & S.F.": 1955, stock car; catalogue number 0975, "Santa Fe"; 7-3/8" long instead of usual 7-3/4"; white Santa Fe herald; yellow body; black heat-stamped lettering; Type B trucks; tilt automatic couplers.   **10   15**

347100 "PENNSYLVANIA": 1953, gondola; catalogue number 04572; "PRR" keystone herald; gray body; red heat-stamped herald and lettering; tilt-automatic couplers; Type B trucks.   **2   4**

467110 "BALTIMORE & OHIO": 1958, boxcar; catalogue number 04555, orange body; "B & O"; white B & O capitol dome herald; black heat-stamped lettering; Type B trucks; tilt-automatic couplers.
                                                         3   5

CRANE: No catalogue number; boom wires; die-cast hook; dull black steel base with square corners; base length 6-1/8"; "MARX" embossed on boom; Type B trucks; tilt automatic couplers.
(A) Gray plastic crane cab and boom.   **5   10**
(B) Red plastic crane cab and boom.   **25   35**

Deluxe?

Webster defines deluxe as "elaborate," or something "especially elegant." Although they were very appealing, I am not sure I would categorize some of the trains manufactured by the Louis Marx & Company as "especially elegant." Nevertheless, the term deluxe, as used in the vernacular of most Marx train collectors, has been terribly abused.

In the early 1950s Marx advertisements, along with other company literature, began to mention the word "deluxe" quite frequently, mostly in reference to some of the more detailed sliding door, 8-1/2" boxcars. These boxcars had, in addition to more exciting graphics, four-wheel black plastic overlay trucks with large journal boxes and die-cast wheels which, of course, added more heft or weight to the car. Soon other cars began sporting the same plastic overlay trucks, such as the 5590 deluxe crane, as well as some of the 11" silver passenger cars, which were truly deluxe with interior lighting and gleaming exterior.

Eventually things became a little confusing when the plastic overlay trucks began showing up on all sorts of eight-wheel plastic cars, and not just cars labeled "deluxe." These included many of the medium solid door boxcars, smaller hoppers, gondolas, tank cars, and just about everything else that could accommodate the larger trucks.

It is uncertain if Marx ever referred to some of the middle-weight cars that came in some sets as deluxe. However, most of us, as collectors, began to refer to the trucks on the cars as deluxe and therein the confusion was wrought.

Sometime later Marx made another plastic overlay truck (Type E) with smaller journal boxes. They were not nearly as prominent or as appealing as the Type F trucks, but lo and behold, these, too, were called deluxe.

What evolved out of all this, was a rather undisciplined use of the word "deluxe" by most collectors and operators who generally used the term to describe *any* car having a large journal box, and plastic overlay trucks with the die-cast wheels. However, this use of the word "deluxe" is incorrect, and the word should only be ascribed to those cars that are truly large, top-of-the-line, deluxe cars.

Paul Gailey

Deluxe Plastic Cars

Deluxe plastic cars measure about eight-and-one-half inches long and two inches wide. They have sliding doors, metal railings and ladders and separately cast parts. These cars were sold in Marx's best sets destined for Sears, Wards, and other distributors. They were also sold separately. From about 1955 to the mid-1960s, youngsters and their parents could choose from a handsome deluxe assortment. Some of these deluxe freight cars were included on the Marx order list until the early 1970s, about the time that Quaker Oats acquired Marx. In 1955, Marx offered a depressed-center flatcar with cable reels, an operating boxcar with pop-out man, a revolving searchlight car, or an operating milk car, followed in 1956 and 1957 by a Seaboard Air Lines pipe flatcar, a twin-tank flatcar, an operating wrecker crane, an operating stock car, and a well-proportioned bay window caboose.

Boxcars

                                                                              Gd Exc

18918 "GREAT NORTHERN": Catalogue number 05555, sliding doors; brown body; white lettering; Type F trucks; tilt automatic couplers.   **25   35**

20053 "SEABOARD": 1957, 1959, double sliding 20-foot side doors; Seaboard Airline Railroad herald, white lettering; tilt automatic couplers. Note: The prototype Seaboard boxcar was designed for loading lumber using a forklift. Seaboard was the only railroad that used this car. They contracted with Marx to manufacture this car and

                                                                              Gd Exc

even paid for the tooling!

(A) 1957, catalogue number 04560, dark red body; Type G trucks.
                                                                              40   60

(B) 1959, catalogue number 05560, tuscan brown body; Type F trucks.
                                                                              35   50

77003 "B & M: 1952, 1955, 1957, catalogue number 05555; Boston

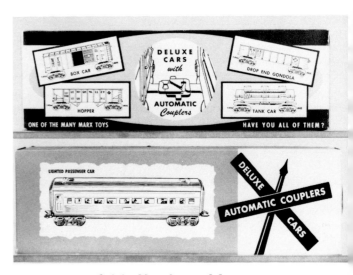

Original box from a deluxe car.

An assortment of deluxe cars. The cars on the right have the automated door with the blue plastic man. *Top shelf:* Two white 5955 S.E.R.X. refrigerator cars. *Second shelf:* Two white 43461 PFE refrigerator cars. *Third shelf:* Two white 249319 Marlines boxcars. Bottom shelf: Two red 249319 Marlines boxcars. H. Diehl Collection, M. Feinstein photograph.

	Gd	Exc

& Maine herald; sliding doors; black door; white and black lettering; tilt automatic couplers.

(A) 1952, turquoise body and frame; Type F trucks.	10	15
(B) 1955, light blue body; Type G trucks.	10	15
(C) 1957, dark blue body; Type F trucks.	10	15

147815 "RI": 1952-59, sliding doors; white Rock Island herald; Type G trucks; tilt automatic couplers.

(A) 1952, catalogue number 04555, red body; white lettering.	10	15
(B) 1952, same as (A), but with Type E trucks; short tilt automatic metal couplers.	10	15
(C) 1956, catalogue number 05555, tuscan brown body; white lettering.	20	30
(D) Same as (C), but with Type F trucks.	20	30
(E) 1959, catalogue number 05555, red body; white lettering; Type F trucks.	10	15

176893 "NYC": Catalogue number 05555, sliding doors; green body; NYC System oval herald; white lettering; tilt automatic couplers.

(A) Type F trucks.	7	12
(B) Type G trucks.	7	12

Two 147815 R.I. boxcars. Top car is tuscan brown, bottom car is red. H. Diehl Collection, M. Feinstein photograph.

Top shelf: Two red 249319 Marlines boxcars. The left has automated door with blue plastic man. The right is not automated. *Bottom shelf:* Two green 176893 NYC boxcars. The left has Type F trucks, the right has Type G trucks. H. Diehl Collection, M. Feinstein photograph.

An assortment of deluxe boxcars. *Top shelf:* 18918 brown Great Northern; 186028 tuscan brown U.P. *Second shelf:* Two 20053 Seaboard cars. This car was not made to carry automobiles, but rather lumber. The left is tuscan brown, the right is red. *Third shelf:* Two 77003 B & M. cars. The left is turquoise, the right is light blue. *Bottom shelf:* Dark blue 77003 B & M; tuscan brown 259199 Canadian Pacific Railway. H. Diehl Collection, M. Feinstein photograph.

An assortment of deluxe cabooses. *Top shelf:* Tuscan brown 4427 A.T. & S.F. with Type E trucks; 45 William Crooks. *Middle shelf:* Red 4427 A.T. & S.F.; 2366 Canadian Pacific. *Bottom shelf:* Tuscan brown 4546 NYC; red 4546 NYC with no number. H. Diehl Collection, M. Feinstein photograph.

	Gd	Exc
186028 "U.P.": 1955, catalogue number 05555, "UNION PACIFIC", "ROAD OF The Streamliners"; sliding doors; tuscan brown body; white lettering; tilt automatic couplers.		
(A) Type F trucks.	20	30
(B) Type G trucks.	20	30
249319 "MARLINES": 1955, 1959, catalogue number 05595, boxcar with sliding doors; platform; tilt automatic couplers.		
(A) 1955, Red body; white lettering; Type D trucks.	12	18
(B) 1955, Red body; white lettering; Type F trucks.	12	18
(C) Same as (B), but with automated door and blue man.	15	20
(D) 1959, catalogue number 05555, white body; red lettering; Type D trucks.	12	18
(E) White body; red lettering; automated door and blue man; Type G trucks.	15	20
(F) Same as (E), but with Type F trucks.	15	20
259199 "CANADIAN PACIFIC RAILWAY": Tuscan brown body; sliding doors; Type G trucks.	50	75

Cabooses

	Gd	Exc
45 WILLIAM CROOKS: 1973, catalogue number 05556; no road name; for 1973 William Crooks sets; brown body; metal rails and ladder; white lettering; simulated wooden sides; Type G trucks; plastic knuckle coupler.	25	35
643 "W.P.": 1957, catalogue number 05596/1, Western Pacific herald; green with bay window; stripe above and below yellow lettering; antenna on roof; metal rails and ladder; tilt automatic couplers.		
(A) Type F trucks.	35	50

	Gd	Exc
(B) Type G trucks.	35	50
(2225) "ALLSTATE": 1958-59; bay window; no number on car; Type F trucks; antenna on roof; metal rails and ladder.		
(A) 1958, orange body; black Allstate United States map herald; black lettering.	18	25
(B) 1959, medium blue body, white Allstate United States map herald; white lettering.	18	25
2225 "SANTA FE": 1958-1966, catalogue number 05596/1; bay window; "RADIO EQUIPPED"; white lettering; antenna on roof; metal rails and ladder; tilt-automatic couplers.		
(A) Red body; Type F trucks.	18	25
(B) 1966, tuscan brown body; Type G trucks.	18	25
2366 "CANADIAN PACIFIC": Catalogue number 04556; dark red body; Canadian Pacific herald; white lettering; metal rails and ladder; Type G trucks; tilt automatic couplers.	35	50
3824 "U.P.": 1956, catalogue number 05596/1; tuscan brown body with bay window; antenna on roof; ladder and wire handrails on each end; Type F trucks; tilt automatic couplers.	25	35
4427 SANTA FE: 1952-59, catalogue number 05556; red body; metal rails and ladder; Type F trucks; tilt automatic couplers.		
(A) 1954, "SANTA FE"; white lettering.		NRS
(B) 1957, 1959, "A.T. & S.F."; white lettering.	10	15
(C) 1955-56, "A.T. & S.F."; black lettering; tilt automatic metal couplers.	10	15
(D) 1955-56, "A.T. & S.F.", black heat-stamped lettering; Type G trucks.	10	15
(E) 1957, same as (D), but black lettering.	10	15
(F) 1957, "A.T. & S.F."; tuscan brown body; Type G trucks.	15	20

An assortment of deluxe bay window cabooses. *Top shelf:* Orange 2225 Allstate. *Second shelf:* Two 2225 blue Allstate cars. The left appears like new, the right shows the typical discoloration from age and chemicals in the air common to blue cars. *Third shelf:* Tuscan brown 2225 Santa Fe; green 643 W.P. *Bottom shelf:* Tuscan brown 17858 Rock Island with Type E trucks; tuscan brown 3824 U.P. with Type F trucks. H. Diehl Collection, M. Feinstein photograph.

	Gd	Exc
(G) Same as (F) but Type E trucks.	15	20

(H) 1952, catalogue number 09642 (Sears set); tuscan brown body; black heat-stamped lettering; tilt automatic metal short couplers. — 15 20

4546 "NYC": Tuscan brown body; white lettering; metal rails and ladder; Type G trucks; tab and slot couplers.
(A) Type F trucks. 20 30
(B) Type G trucks. 20 30
(C) Red body; black lettering; "NYC"; no number on car; Type G trucks. 20 30

17858 ROCK ISLAND: 1958-59, catalogue number 05596/1, white Rock Island herald; bay window; white lettering; antenna on roof; metal rails and ladder.
(A) Dark red body; Type F trucks; plastic knuckle couplers. 8 15
(B) Same as (A), but with Type G trucks. 8 15
(C) Same as (A), but with tilt-automatic couplers. 8 15
(D) 1959, catalogue number 04556, tuscan brown body; Type F trucks; plastic knuckle couplers. 8 15

(E) Tuscan brown body; tilt automatic couplers, Type G trucks. 18 25
(F) Tuscan brown body; tilt automatic couplers, Type E trucks. 18 25

Cranes

5590 "NYC": Black body; black die-cast base; base length 7-1/4"; white oval herald; white lettering; Marx logo on cab; two handwheels on side of cab; die-cast hook, aluminum pulley; green boom strings; Type F trucks; tilt automatic couplers.
(A) Searchlight on roof; grayish-white lettering. 30 40
(B) Without searchlight on roof. 20 30
(C) Charcoal gray cab and boom; without searchlight on roof. 20 30

Flatcars

1024 "IC": 1974, catalogue number 05563; black body; white herald;

An assortment of deluxe and eight-wheel flatcars. *Top shelf:* Deluxe blue 4566 C.W.E.X. with two gray cable reels; deluxe maroon 39520 S.P. with two yellow cable reels. *Second shelf:* Deluxe orange 4528 Erie with two green farm tractors; deluxe maroon 4528 Erie with two gray farm tractors. *Third shelf:* Two deluxe maroon 4528 Erie with two red tractors. The left has yellow lettering, the right has white lettering. *Bottom shelf:* Two eight-wheel maroon flatcars. The left has yellow lettering with two gray farm tractors; the right has white lettering with two red farm tractors. H. Diehl Collection, M. Feinstein photograph.

Gd Exc

white lettering; yellow stake sides; lumber load; Type G trucks; tilt automatic couplers. 10 15

4528 "ERIE": 1956, catalogue number 05521; Type F or G trucks.
(A) Maroon body; yellow lettering; two red tractors. 15 30
(B) Maroon body; white lettering; two gray tractors. 15 30
(C) Maroon body; yellow lettering; maroon stake sides. 15 30
(D) Maroon body; white lettering; maroon stake sides. 15 30
(E) Maroon body; white lettering; yellow stake sides. 15 30
(F) Orange body; black lettering; two green tractors. 35 55

4538 "ERIE": Maroon body; yellow lettering; type F trucks; tab and slot couplers. NRS

4566 "C.W.E.X.": 1955, catalogue number 05566; depressed-center; blue body (light, medium or dark blue); white lettering; two gray cable reels; tilt automatic couplers.
(A) Type F trucks. 25 30
(B) Type G trucks. 35 45
(C) Type D trucks. 25 30
(D) Two yellow cable reels; Type F trucks. 75 100

(05544) "ERIE": 1960, 1962, catalogue number 05544/1; maroon

Gd Exc

body; yellow lettering; Type F trucks; plastic tilt automatic couplers.
(A) "SEARS ROEBUCK AND CO." tractor trailer; dark green cab and turquoise trailer. 30 40
(B) "BURLINGTON" tractor trailer; blue cab and white trailer. 15 20
(C) Same as (A), but red cab. 30 40
(D) "ALLSTATE" tractor trailer; blue cab and orange trailer; silver ramp; die-cast wheels. 30 40
(E) Same as (D), but red cab; no ramp. 30 40
(F) "MONTGOMERY WARDS" tractor trailer; gray cab and gray trailer. NRS

5545 "C.B. & Q": 1957-60; catalogue number 05545; maroon body; white lettering; Type F trucks; tilt automatic couplers.
(A) 1959, with two orange "ALLSTATE" trailers. 50 75
(B) 1957, with two white "BURLINGTON" trailers; end unloading ramp. 18 25
(C) 1958, with two red "BURLINGTON" trailers; no ramp. (Lithographed trailers bear Line-Mar Trademark.) 18 25
(D) 1958, with "ERIE" bridge girder. 12 18

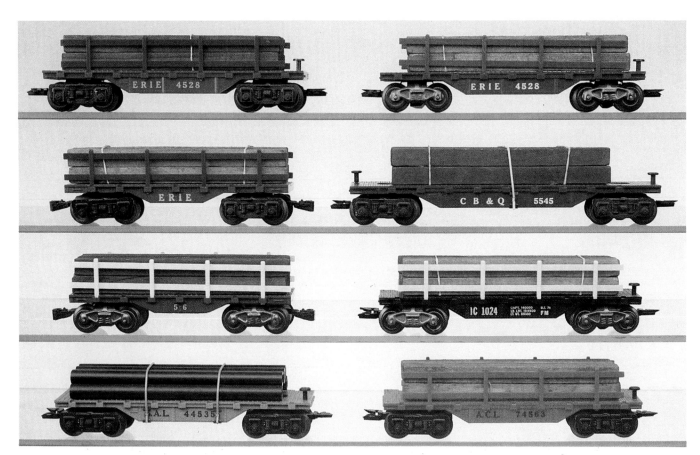

An assortment of deluxe and eight-wheel flatcars. *Top shelf*: Two deluxe 4528 maroon cars with maroon stake sides and lumber load. The left has yellow lettering and Type F trucks, the right has white lettering and Type G trucks. *Second shelf*: Eight-wheel maroon (586) Erie with maroon stake sides.; deluxe 5545 maroon C B & Q. This car is shown with the incorrect load. It should have the girder on it. *Third shelf*: Eight-wheel brown 56 William Crooks with yellow stake sides and lumber load; deluxe black 1024 with yellow stake sides and lumber load. *Bottom shelf*: Deluxe gray 44535 S.A.L. with blue lettering and pipe load; deluxe red 74563 A.C.L. with black lettering, red stake sides, and lumber load. H. Diehl Collection, M. Feinstein photograph.

Top shelf: Two deluxe maroon C B & Q flatcars with two trailers. *Bottom shelf*: Deluxe maroon 5545 C B & Q with two orange Allstate trailers; eight-wheel maroon Erie flatcar with tractor-trailer load. H. Diehl Collection, M. Feinstein photograph.

Top shelf: Two deluxe 5545 C.B. & Q. cars with girder bridge. The left has the marked girder bridge, the right is unmarked. *Bottom shelf:* Two deluxe 4566 flatcars with cable reels. The left is light blue, the right is medium blue. H. Diehl Collection, M. Feinstein photograph.

	Gd	Exc
(E) 1958, with "ERIE" bridge girder; Type G trucks.	12	18
(F) 1958, with unmarked bridge girder; Type G trucks.	12	18
(G) 1960, with two silver "BURLINGTON" trailers and one tractor; Type G trucks.	18	25
(H) With two "WALGREEN" trailers.	50	75
(I) With two "NYC" trailers.	25	35
(J) With two "WESTERN AUTO" trailers.	45	65

39520 "S.P.": 1958; depressed-center body; two yellow cable reels; tilt automatic couplers.

	Gd	Exc
(A) Catalogue number 05568; maroon body; yellow lettering; Type F trucks.	25	35
(B) Catalogue number 05538, black body; white lettering.	25	35
(C) 1958, (Sears set), same as (B), but with gray generator in center; Type G trucks.	25	35
(D) 1958, same as (C), Type F trucks.	25	35

44535 "S.A.L.": Catalogue number 04535 (05535); gray body; blue lettering; eight pieces of black pipe; tilt automatic couplers.

	Gd	Exc
(A) Type F trucks.	25	35
(B) Type G trucks.	25	35

51100 "SOU.": 1955-73; catalogue number 05585; automobile carrier whose automobiles were randomly placed on flatcars in terms of car type and color. Types included 1950 Ford, Chevrolet, and Studebaker cars and panel trucks. Colors were red, yellow, green, blue, dark blue, turquoise, white, and silver; automobile rack; tilt automatic couplers.

(A) 1955, maroon base; gray automobile rack; yellow lettering; Type

	Gd	Exc
F trucks.	15	20
(B) Same as (A), but with orange lettering.	20	30
(C) 1973, catalogue number 05584; same as (A), but with Type G trucks; plastic knuckle couplers.	15	20
(D) 1955, red base; yellow lettering; Type F trucks.	15	20
(E) 1958, brown base; yellow lettering; Type F trucks.	15	20
(F) 1957-73, blue base; yellow automobile rack; white lettering; Type G trucks.	20	30

74563 "A.C.L.": 1961, catalogue number 05563; red body; red stake sides; lumber load; tilt automatic couplers.

	Gd	Exc
(A) 1961, white lettering; Type F trucks.	20	25
(B) Black lettering; Type G trucks.	20	25
(C) Black lettering; Type F trucks.	20	25

"ERIE": 1973, catalogue number 05528; maroon body; yellow lettering; stake sides; tilt automatic couplers.

	Gd	Exc
(A) Type F trucks.	10	15
(B) Type G trucks.	10	15

"ERIE": Catalogue number 05538; black body; white lettering; orange cable reel; Type F trucks; tilt automatic couplers. **NRS**

Gondolas

Note: All deluxe gondolas have movable drop ends.

20309 "L & N": 1959, 1961, movable drop ends; seven sewer tiles (cardboard); tilt automatic couplers; Type F trucks.

Deluxe 51100 Southern maroon flatcar with gray automobile carrier. H. Diehl Collection, M. Feinstein photograph.

Deluxe 51100 Southern blue flatcar with yellow automobile carrier. H. Diehl Collection, M. Feinstein photograph.

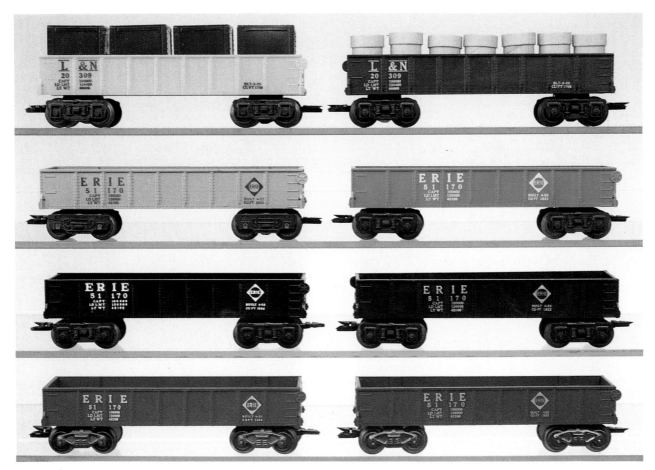

An assortment of deluxe gondolas. *Top shelf:* Two 20309 L & N cars, left is yellow with four plastic boxes, right is brown with seven cardboard sewer tiles. Normally these tiles are laying down, but have been set up for the reader to view. *Second shelf:* Two 51170 Erie cars, left is gray, right is blue. *Third shelf:* Two black 51170 Erie cars. Note the differences in the lettering and the placement of the lettering. *Bottom shelf:* Two blue 51170 Erie cars. Once again, note the difference in the lettering and its placement on the car. H. Diehl Collection, M. Feinstein photograph.

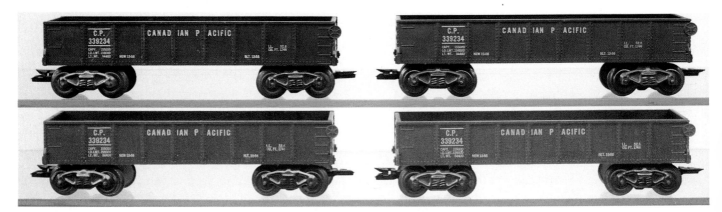

Top shelf: Two brown 339234 Canadian Pacific cars; note the slight shade differences. *Bottom shelf:* Two 339234 Canadian Pacific; left is tuscan brown, right is red. H. Diehl Collection, M. Feinstein photograph.

Two deluxe 51170 Erie gondolas. The left is orange with black lettering and Type G trucks. The right is black with gray lettering and Type D trucks. Two characteristics of the deluxe gondolas are the movable drop ends and the brakewheel that is cast into the plastic mold. It is noticeable on the top right side of each of these gondolas. H. Diehl Collection, M. Feinstein photograph.

Gd Exc

(A) 1959, catalogue number 05536, brown body; white lettering.
50 75

(B) 1961, catalogue number 05572; yellow body; no sewer tile load; black lettering.
35 50

51170 "ERIE": 1952-70, catalogue number 05572, movable drop ends; Erie diamond herald; tilt automatic couplers. Note: The Erie diamond herald came in two variations: an outline of the diamond and circle around "ERIE", and a solid diamond around "ERIE".

(A) 1952, black body; white heat-stamped herald and lettering; Type E trucks.
5 10

(B) 1954, catalogue number 05539, black body; white lettering; four black plastic removable containers; Type F trucks.
35 50

(C) 1956, black body; gray herald; gray lettering; Type D trucks.
5 10

(D) Black body; blue lettering; Type E trucks.
5 10

(E) 1958, orange body; black herald; black lettering; Type G trucks.
30 40

(F) 1959, red body; black lettering.
12 18

(G) 1959, gray body; black lettering.
12 18

(H) 1959, blue body; white lettering; Type E trucks.
8 12

(I) Same as (H) but Type F trucks.
8 12

(J) Same as (H) but Type G trucks.
8 12

(K) 1970, 1975, catalogue number 04572, black body; white heat-stamped herald and lettering; Type G trucks.
5 10

(L) 1959, catalogue number 05572/2; gray body; blue lettering; Type E trucks.
12 18

(M) Gray body; blue lettering; Type F trucks.
8 12

339234 "CANADIAN PACIFIC": 1957, 1960-62, catalogue number 05572; movable drop ends; Canadian Pacific herald; white lettering; tilt automatic couplers; Type G trucks.

(A) 1957, tuscan brown body.
20 30

(B) 1960, black body.
25 35

(C) 1962, red body.
20 30

(D) 1960, tuscan brown body; Type F trucks.
20 30

Hopper Cars

21429 "LEHIGH VALLEY": 1965-76, catalogue number 04554; black body; tilt automatic couplers.

(A) 1974, yellow diamond herald; yellow lettering; Type F trucks.
7 12

(B) 1965, same as (A), but with metal tilt automatic couplers.
7 12

(C) 1966, orange diamond herald; orange lettering; Type D trucks.
7 12

(D) 1970, same as (C), but with Type G trucks.
7 12

28236 "VIRGINIAN": 1955, 1974; two heralds; white lettering; tilt automatic couplers.

(A) 1955, catalogue number 04554, maroon body; Type G trucks.
15 20

Gd Exc

(B) 1955, catalogue number 05554, brown body; Type F trucks. (Three shades of brown known to exist.)
15 20

(C) 1974, red body; Type G trucks.
75 100

Military Cars

586 "U.S.A.": 1957, flatcar; catalogue number 04563; olive drab body; white star herald; white lettering; plastic army tank load (one of five different gray plastic army loads, two per car); tilt automatic couplers.

(A) Type F trucks.
25 35

(B) Type G trucks.
25 35

1796 "MISSILE LAUNCHER DANGER": 1959-60; flatcar; blue body with white star herald; white lettering; missile on mounts, one in vertical launcher; Type F trucks; tilt automatic couplers.
30 40

1963 "U.S.A.X." 1963, work caboose; red cab; blue base; "FUEL CONTROL CENTER", Missile Express herald; white lettering; white tank with "ROCKET FUEL"; Type G trucks; tilt automatic couplers.
12 15

2130 "U S A": Work caboose; olive drab body; star herald; white lettering; tank on deck with black metal ladders; olive drab cab on rear; Type G trucks; tilt automatic couplers.
75 100

2246 "U.S.A.": 1957, flatcar; catalogue number 05563; olive drab body; white star herald; white lettering; jeep or army truck load (one of five different gray plastic Army loads, two per car); Type G trucks; tilt automatic couplers.
40 50

2824 "U.S.A.": 1957; flatcar; catalogue number 05563; depressed-center; olive drab body; missile on incline launcher with two extra missiles and man standing at one end; tilt automatic couplers.

(A) Type F trucks.
50 75

(B) Type G trucks.
50 75

2824 GONDOLA: 1961-62, gondola; catalogue number 05592; movable drop ends; missile launcher with operating rocket inside; Type F trucks; tilt automatic couplers.

(A) 1961, "USAF", yellow body; gray trim; opening top door over body; red lettering.
25 35

(B) 1962, "USA", olive drab body; top opening door over body; white lettering.
25 35

2858 "UNITED STATES ARMY": "BUREAU OF ORDNANCE"; boxcar with sliding doors; olive drab body and frame; USAX herald; white lettering; Type G trucks; tilt automatic couplers.
150 175

"MISSILE LAUNCHER & CARRIER": Flatcar; long blue body; white lettering; "EXPLOSIVES", "DANGER"; gray racks and white vertical launcher; tilt automatic couplers.

(A) Type G trucks.
50 100

(B) Type F trucks.
50 100

An assortment of deluxe hoppers. *Top shelf:* Two 28236 Virginian cars: left is red with Type G trucks, note the stud-mounted trucks; right is brown with Type F trucks. *Second shelf:* Two brown 28236 Virginian cars. Combined with the brown car above, this photograph shows the three variations of brown that are known to exist. *Third shelf:* Two black Lehigh Valley cars with yellow lettering. Left has Type E trucks, right has Type G trucks. *Bottom shelf:* Two black 21429 Lehigh Valley cars with orange lettering. Left has Type D trucks, right has Type F trucks. H. Diehl Collection, M. Feinstein photograph.

Top shelf: Two deluxe 4581 B.K.X. searchlight cars. The left has Type F trucks, the right has Type G trucks. *Bottom shelf:* Two deluxe searchlight cars. The left is 24 searchlight with yellow generator, the right is 4563 G.E.X. H. Diehl Collection, M. Feinstein photograph.

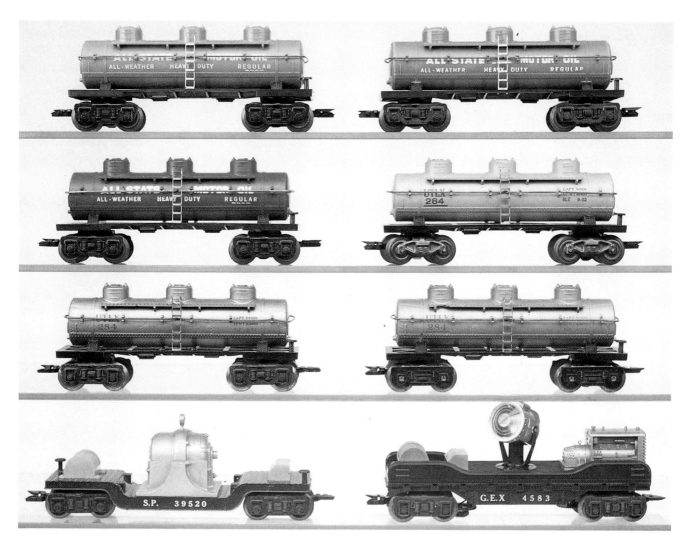

An assortment of deluxe cars. *Top shelf:* Two blue (5553) triple dome tanks. Note the shade differences. *Second shelf:* The left is the blue (5553) Allstate triple dome tank, a third shade difference. The right is the gray 284 UTLX triple dome tank. *Third shelf:* Two silver-gray 284 UTLX triple dome tank cars. *Bottom shelf:* 39520 S.P. depressed-center flatcar with gray generator; 4583 GEX searchlight car with extra deck. H. Diehl Collection, M. Feinstein photograph.

	Gd	Exc

Refrigerator Cars

Note: The following cars are listed as refrigerator cars due to the markings on the car. However, Marx used the same car mold as the boxcar.

5595 "S.E.R.X.": 1959, catalogue number 05595; "FARM MASTER BRAND"; sliding doors; white door guides; white body; red lettering; "DAIRY PRODUCTS"; automated door and blue man; maroon plastic loading platform; tilt automatic couplers.

	Gd	Exc
(A) White body; Type F trucks.	5	10
(B) White body; Type G trucks.	5	10
(C) White body; Type F trucks; automated door with blue man.	5	10
(D) Cream body; Type F trucks.	5	10
(E) Cream body; Type G trucks.	5	10
(F) Cream body; Type F trucks; automated door with blue man.	5	10

43461 "P.F.E.": 1955, "PACIFIC FRUIT EXPRESS", sliding doors

and white door guides; white body; red lettering; Southern Pacific herald, "VENTILATED REFRIGERATOR"; tilt automatic couplers.

	Gd	Exc
(A) Catalogue number 05565, Type F trucks.	4	8
(B) Catalogue number 05595, operating car with automated door and blue man that slides out when door opens; Type F trucks.	4	8
(C) Type G trucks.	4	8
(D) Cream body, Type F trucks.	4	8
(E) Cream body, Type G trucks.	4	8

Searchlight Cars

24 "ICG": 1974, catalogue number 05571, no road name (in ICG sets), depressed-center, searchlight; black body, gray searchlight and yellow generator; Type G trucks; tilt automatic couplers. **20 30**

4528 "ERIE": 1957; catalogue number 05583, maroon body; yellow lettering; extra deck; gray generator, searchlight, and equipment; Type F trucks; tilt automatic couplers. **15 30**

4571 "W.E.C.X.": 1955-65, depressed-center flatcar; red body; white

An assortment of deluxe cars. *Top shelf:* Two maroon 5545 C B & Q flatcars with two trailers. *Second shelf:* Two 54099 Missouri Pacific stock cars. The left is yellow with brown door, the right is orange. *Third shelf:* Two 54099 Missouri Pacific stock cars. The left is green with Type F trucks, the right is red with Type G trucks. *Bottom shelf:* Two 54099 Missouri Pacific stock cars with automated door and cow that slides out when the door opens. Notice the slight shade differences. H. Diehl Collection, M. Feinstein photograph.

Gd Exc

lettering; gray generator and searchlight; tilt automatic couplers.
(A) 1955, Type F trucks.   8   12
(B) Type D trucks.   8   12
4581 "B.K.X.": Catalogue number 05581; depressed-center flatcar

Deluxe red 5561 W.E.C.X searchlight car with depressed center and gray searchlight. H. Diehl Collection, M. Feinstein photograph.

Gd Exc

with searchlights at each end; red body; white lettering; gray generator in center; tilt automatic couplers.
(A) Type F trucks.   15   20
(B) Type G trucks.   15   20
4583 "G.E.X.": 1955, catalogue number 05583; black body; white lettering; extra deck section; gray or black generator, searchlight and equipment; tilt automatic couplers.
(A) Type E trucks.   18   25
(B) Type F trucks.   18   25
5561 "W.E.C.X.": Red body; white lettering; depressed-center; gray searchlight; Type F trucks; tilt automatic couplers.   8   12

Stock Cars

54099 MISSOURI PACIFIC: 1956-57, 1960, 1974, sliding doors; white Missouri Pacific herald; "I-GN 54099"; white lettering; tilt automatic couplers. Note: Operating car has automated door and

An assortment of deluxe tank cars. *Top shelf:* Two maroon (5543) green Cities Service twin tank cars. The left has Type G trucks, the right has Type F trucks. *Second shelf:* Blue (5543) Gulf with orange twin tanks; maroon (5543) Allstate with white twin tanks. *Third shelf:* Two blue (5553) Allstate triple dome tank cars. Note the slight shade differences. *Bottom shelf:* White (5553) Milk triple dome tank car; white (5553) Exxon triple dome tank car. H. Diehl Collection, M. Feinstein photograph.

                                                                    Gd Exc

plastic cow that slides out when door opens, loading ramp, and platform.

(A) 1956, catalogue number 05570, red body; operating; Type F trucks.   **5   10**

(B) Red body; operating; Type G trucks.   **5   10**

(C) 1956, catalogue number 05575, red body; non-operating; Type F trucks.   **5   10**

(D) 1957, red body; non-operating; Type G trucks.   **5   10**

(E) 1956, catalogue number 05570, green body; operating; Type F trucks.   **25   35**

(F) Green; non-operating; Type F trucks.   **5   10**

(G) Catalogue number unknown (Sears set), orange body; black lettering; operating; Type F trucks.   **NRS**

(H) 1960, orange body; non-operating; Type G trucks.   **100   125**

(I) 1974, catalogue number 05575, yellow body and brown door; black lettering; non-operating; Type G trucks.   **75   100**

                                                                    Gd Exc

Tank Cars

284 "U.T.L.X.": 1954, 1964, three dome; gray tank with black base; red lettering; wire handrail around tank; metal ladders; tilt automatic couplers.

(A) 1954, catalogue number 04553 (05553); Type E trucks.   **4   8**

(B) Silver-gray tank; heat-stamped lettering; Type E trucks. **4   8**

(C) 1964, catalogue number 05553; Type G trucks.   **4   8**

(D) Same as (A), but Type F trucks.   **4   8**

(5543) TWIN TANKS: 1955-74, catalogue number 05543; twin tanks; white lettering; metal ladders, wire handrails on ends; tilt automatic couplers.

(A) 1958, "ALLSTATE"; white tanks with maroon base; Type F trucks.   **35   50**

(B) 1959, same as (A), but with Type G trucks.   **35   50**

(C) 1955, no number on car; "CITIES SERVICE"; green tanks with maroon base; Cities Service herald; white lettering; Type F trucks.   **18   25**

An assortment of deluxe work cabooses. *Top shelf:* Brown (4587) A.T. & S. F. with two slant top toolboxes positioned lengthwise; tuscan brown (4588) Allstate with black illuminated searchlight. *Second shelf:* Tuscan brown (4589) NYC with gray tank on deck and felt track sweeper pads; tuscan brown 586 R.I. with two slant top toolboxes. *Third shelf:* Black 1015 ICG with orange cab and white tank; tuscan brown 4586 U.P. with black illuminated searchlight. *Bottom shelf:* Tuscan brown 5586 W.P. with yellow lettering and two slant top toolboxes. H. Diehl Collection, M. Feinstein photograph.

	Gd	Exc
(D) 1974, "GULF"; orange tanks with blue base; Gulf herald; black lettering; Type G trucks.	75	100

(5553) THREE DOME TANK: 1960, 1974, catalogue number 05553; three dome; metal ladders, wire handrail around tank; tilt automatic couplers.

	Gd	Exc
(A) 1974, "EXXON", white tank with blue base; red lettering; Type G trucks.	65	90
(B) "ALLSTATE MOTOR OIL"; blue tank with black base; white lettering; "ALL WEATHER", "HEAVY DUTY", "REGULAR"; Type G trucks.	10	15
(C) 1960, "MILK", cream tank and base; small milk bottle and Glass Lined Tank herald, "LD.Wt. 45500 BLT.4- 60" on sides; red lettering; metal ladders and wire handrails around tank.	200	300
(D) Same as (B), but with Type F trucks.	200	300
(E) Same as (D), but with Type G trucks.	200	300

Work Cabooses

586 "ROCK ISLAND": Catalogue number 05586/1; tuscan brown body; white lettering; two slant top toolboxes; short rear cab; tilt automatic couplers.

	Gd	Exc
(A) Type F trucks.	7	12
(B) Type G trucks.	7	12

1015 "ICG": 1974, catalogue number 05580, orange cab; white tank with metal ladders; black base; white Illinois Central Gulf herald and black "X325" on cab; white lettering, Type G trucks; tilt automatic couplers.   **15   20**

3824 "U.P.": 1956, 1962, catalogue number 05556; tuscan brown body; white lettering; black illuminated searchlight; short rear cab; Type F trucks; tilt automatic couplers.   **25   35**

4586 "U.P.": 1957-58, catalogue number 05596; tuscan brown body; white lettering; short rear cab; Type G trucks; tilt automatic couplers.

Two deluxe red 4590 A.T. & S.F. work cabooses. The left has Type D trucks, the right has Type F trucks. H. Diehl Collection, M. Feinstein photograph.

	Gd	Exc
(A) Black illuminated searchlight.	18	25
(B) Two slant top toolboxes positioned lengthwise on the base.	18	25

(4587) "AT & SF": 1962, catalogue number 05596; tuscan brown body; white lettering; black illuminated searchlight; short rear cab; Type G trucks; tilt automatic couplers.
	Gd	Exc
(A) Black illuminated searchlight.	15	20
(B) Two slant top toolboxes positioned lengthwise on the base.	15	20

(4588) "ALLSTATE": 1955, tuscan brown body; short rear cab; black illuminated searchlight; tilt automatic couplers.
	Gd	Exc
(A) Yellow lettering; Type G trucks.	25	35
(B) Same as (A), but Type F trucks.	25	35
(C) White lettering.	25	35
(D) Same as (C), but Type F trucks.	25	35

(4589) "NYC": 1957, catalogue number 05580; tuscan brown body;

gray tank with black metal ladders on deck; felt track sweeper pads; white lettering; short rear cab; tilt automatic couplers.
	Gd	Exc
(A) Type G trucks.	35	50
(B) Type F trucks.	35	50

(4590) "AT & SF": 1955-62, catalogue number 05586/1; tilt automatic couplers; wire railing on front and back; brakewheel.
	Gd	Exc
(A) 1958, tuscan brown body and base; white lettering; Type G trucks.	10	15
(B) 1958, red body and base; black lettering; Type F trucks.	10	15
(C) 1959, same as (B), but with Type D trucks.	10	15
(D) 1962, same as (B), but with Type G trucks.	10	15

5586 "W.P.": 1957, catalogue number 05586/1; tuscan brown body; yellow lettering; two slant top toolboxes lengthwise; short rear cab; tilt automatic couplers.
	Gd	Exc
(A) Type F trucks.	12	18
(B) Type G trucks.	12	18

Chapter V

Accessories

The same techniques employed to manufacture Marx trains were used to produce Marx accessories. Extra parts from one accessory were incorporated into newer items. In the case of the 1931 enameled steel truck with an operating cannon, the cannon was reused in a 1938 Army train set. In another case, the metal searchlight which had illuminated the 410 floodlight, the 436 floodlight tower, and six-inch, four-wheel searchlight cars began its Marx career as part of a battery-operated toy truck (similar to the cannon truck). When Marx progressed from metal to plastic, the first accessories were all metal. Later they were usually a mixture of both plastic and metal.

Dating accessories is difficult. Some early accessories reappeared in different colors after an extended absence. Accessories were first catalogued in 1936, although some were manufactured in 1935. The only labeled Joy Line accessory is the power station which bears "The Girard Model Works" label, but the early three-light block signal and a few other accessories were also produced during the late Joy Line period. The later profusion of Marx accessories gave rise to the slogan on the Marx accessory box: "One of the many Marline Accessories, have you all of them?" Hopefully, all of them have been listed!

General dating of first production accessories can sometimes be achieved by comparing their bases. *Small, flat bases* were utilized in the later 1930s and into the 1940s. These were produced simultaneously with three-inch *rounded metal painted bases* into the early 1950s which made the accessories heavier and slightly taller. *Chrome bases* appeared in the 1950s and were followed later by the *larger square bases* produced both in metal and plastic. Although most accessories can be dated using these guidelines, exceptions can be expected.

Large illustrations on accessory cartons graphically advertised the accessories inside. The cartons served another

practical purpose: they provided a surface for displaying installation instructions. Many Joy Line accessories were battery-operated and probably were used with mechanical sets. With the introduction of electric Joy Line trains from 1932 to 1934 Marx began producing electric accessories.

Metal accessories were usually green- or red-enameled or brightly lithographed. After scale cars and locomotives were introduced into the Marx line, the colors of the accessories became more subtle. Prewar accessory catalogue numbers were three-digit numbers with an occasional suffix "A" to note a variation. After the war, a zero was placed before the catalogue number to designate plastic; then it was changed to a four-digit number and during the late Quaker Oats period, the suffix "C" was sometimes added; perhaps indicating the type of packaging.

Best-selling accessories were colorful and brightly lit, although Marx also marketed low-cost, plastic, non-operating

This is one of five train set boxes where the box was lithograph to be a building that could be used with the train set. The box lithographed in red and green on brown corrugated stock. T end of the box shows two trucks backed into two bays. L. Jens Collection, G. Stern photograph.

Left to right: 464 block signal; 434 block signal, single target type; 439 automatic semaphore; 312 manual semaphore; 1404 block signal, position light, metal type; 1404A block signal, position light, plastic type; 311 manual semaphore; 311 manual semaphore; 404 block signal, two lights; 404 block signal, three-light. E. Matzke Collection, G. Stern photograph.

items. After the Colber Company dropped out of the train accessory business Marx used some of the Colber dies, i.e. 1303 girder bridge. Marx occasionally resorted to a printed cardboard, self-assembled accessory which accompanied less expensive price-leader sets, such as those sold by J. C. Penney.

Variations in some accessories seem endless, such as the 1305 girder bridge produced both before and after World War II. Utilizing the same metal bridge, Marx continually changed its color combination and road name heralds so as to market many variations throughout the years and to accommodate its large-volume customers. It should be noted that the majority of accessories do not have an item number printed on them. The accessory carton bears the item number (usually on the box end flap) which in many cases is also the instruction number, since instructions are printed on the box.

Accessories are divided into the following ten categories. Each item is listed numerically within its category.

Block Signals and Semaphores

Buildings, Automated

Buildings, Miscellaneous

Crossing Signals and Gates

Lamps and Poles

Miscellaneous Items

Sets of Signs and Figures

Stations

Towers and Lights

Tunnels, Derricks, Trestles, and Bridges

Note: Where items overlap as in sets, they are listed in several places. Also, some items are listed more than once if they logically fall into several categories.

Block Signals and Semaphores

	Gd	**Exc**

063 SEMAPHORE: Plastic, non-operating, simulated jewel semaphore lights; movable blade, manual; 6" high. **2 5**

0211 SEMAPHORE: Plastic, manual. **2 5**

311 MANUAL SEMAPHORE: Metal round base with metal flat-fluted size-reducing stepped pole with slot for wire handle to control signal; upper quadrant red semaphore arm; red and green balls with head shield; 9-1/2" high.
(A) Black base and pole. **2 5**
(B) Red base and pole. **2 5**

312 MANUAL SEMAPHORE: Green round metal base; flat-fluted size-reducing stepped pole with slot for wire handle to control signal; upper quadrant red semaphore arm with red and green balls; not equipped with a head shield as is the 311; pole point is more pronounced; 9-1/2" high. **5 10**

321 CROSSING SET: Four-piece manual metal set: semaphore, telltale hazard warning fixture, caution sign, and crossing gate. **15 25**

403 MARKER LIGHT: Circa 1955, plastic illuminated low dwarf signal; black plastic hood with red lens; mounted on rectangle with track connector blades. **15 20**

404 AUTOMATIC BLOCK SIGNAL, THREE LIGHTS: Metal body, pole, base, and head; battery-operated on/off switch on base; control lever on rear of head, 6-1/2" high.
(A) Red body, pole, base, and head (no lever on base). **5 10**
(B) Black base with three numbered screw connectors; black face on head. **4 8**
(C) Green body, pole, and head; black base and head face. **4 8**
(D) All black. **4 8**
(E) Black body and head face; silver pole and head. **4 8**
(F) Black with chrome base, face, ladder, and body top; numbered screw connectors on base; control lever and rheostat to control speed on right side of base; "AUTOMATIC SIGNAL" decal; no control lever on rear of head. **4 8**

Gd Exc

(G) Same as (F), but no numbered screws; screw terminals on left; control lever and rheostat control on right fiber side of body. **4 8**

404 BLOCK SIGNAL, TWO LIGHTS: Metal square base, pole, and head; three numbered screw connectors on base; control lever on rear of head, 6-1/2" high.
(A) Dull black body base, pole, and head. **3 6**
(B) Same as (A), except three numbered solder connectors on base; hooded bulbs; rheostat control on right side. **3 6**
(C) Red body, pole and head; black head faces and body top. **3 6**
(D) Black base, post, and head; chrome body top and head faces; ladder; hooded bulbs. "AUTOMATIC SIGNAL" decal on body; control lever on side of body; 6-1/2" high. **3 6**
(E) Same as (D), but chrome base; black visors over bulbs. **3 6**

405 BLOCK SIGNAL, THREE LIGHTS: Black metal body, head, and hoods; chrome base, ladder, head face, and body top; decal on front of body; control lever and rheostat on side of body.
(A) No decal or ladder. **4 8**
(B) With decal and ladder. **4 8**

0430 SIGNAL SET: Plastic, 29 pieces: 12 railroad signs, 12 telephone poles, one semaphore, one crossing signal, one street lamp, one crossing gate, and one road grade crossing. **8 12**

434 BLOCK SIGNAL, SINGLE TARGET TYPE: 1952, black with chrome ladder and light housing; four wires from base of ladder to track clip and connector; 8" high; red target changes to green by solenoid operation.
(A) "A" on board on pole, rectangular die-cast base. **4 8**
(B) Same as (A), but with "74" on board on pole. **4 8**
(C) Same as (A), but with rectangular plastic base. **4 8**

434 BLOCK SIGNAL, THREE LIGHTS: Black metal body, pole, and head; chrome head faces, ladder, and hoods; die-cast black base with three screw connectors; hooded red, amber, and green bulbs; "AUTOMATIC SIGNAL" decal on body; control lever on rear of body; 6-1/2" high. **5 10**

439 AUTOMATIC SEMAPHORE WITH ILLUMINATED INDICATIONS: 1949, 1952-58, black plastic and metal with three-position yellow upper quadrant semaphore arm; chrome ladder and lamp housing; "74" on board on pole, four wires from base of ladder to track clips and connectors; red, yellow, and green plastic lens 9-1/4" high. (Solenoid-operated.)
(A) Rectangular die-cast base. **8 10**
(B) Plastic rectangular base. **8 10**
(C) 1949, with rounded pressed-metal base. **8 10**
(D) Plastic rectangular base; no numberboard. **8 10**

454 BLOCK SIGNAL, TWO LIGHTS: 1952, black body, pole, head, and rectangular base; chrome ladder and hoods over bulbs; "AUTOMATIC SIGNAL" decal on body; control lever on rear of body, 7" high.
(A) Die-cast base; metal body and pole. **3 6**
(B) Plastic base; metal body and pole. **3 6**

464 BLOCK SIGNAL, DOUBLE TARGET TYPE: Circa 1957 plastic with hooded red and green lights; control switch in front of base; three wires from base of pole to track connectors.
(A) Circa 1957, gray base, pole, and head. **5 10**
(B) Black base, pole, and head. **5 10**

1402 BLOCK SIGNAL, TWO LIGHTS: Black metal body, pole, and head; chrome body top, head faces, and ladder; hooded bulbs, "AUTOMATIC SIGNAL" decal on body, 6-1/2". **4 8**

1404 BLOCK SIGNAL, POSITION LIGHT TYPE: All metal; face with five lights to show "proceed" by vertical and "stop" by horizontal lights; silver fenced platform on black round-holed or crisscross tower; chrome base with three screw connectors, permanently attached by wire to remote-control unit; 9" high.
(A) Black metal face with five red lights. **35 50**

Gd Exc

(B) Chrome face with two horizontal red lights, two vertical green lights, and one center (caution) yellow light; flat-type bulbs; crisscross tower. **45 60**

1404 BLOCK SIGNAL, POSITION LIGHT TYPE: Plastic round face mounted off-center; no platform; with five yellow plastic lens lights to show "PROCEED" by vertical or "STOP" with horizontal display by use of an internal slotted disk in head; chrome ladder to rectangular elevated base; wire from bottom of ladder to lights and coil in base to operate aspects, 8-3/4" high.
(A) Gray. **10 15**
(B) Black. **15 20**

1405 BLOCK SIGNAL, THREE-LIGHT "TRAINMASTER": Black metal body, pole, and head; base integral with section of track; chrome body top; black hoods over bulbs; "TRAINMASTER" decal on body; four-button control panel connected to base; rheostat on body, three screw connectors on base, 6-1/2" high. **25 30**

Buildings, Automated

Note: *Some of these buildings are also found under other headings.*

0218 CROSSING WATCHMAN SHED: 1956, plastic, red base; blue watchman actuated by weight of train on track lever. **7 15**

1420 CROSSING SHANTY AND MAN, AUTOMATIC: Circa 1957, lithographed metal shanty; actuated blue watchman on swinging door and plastic crossing gate. **12 18**

1434 OVERHEAD DOUBLE TRACK SIGNAL BRIDGE: Plastic and metal; two movable targets; light changes as train approaches. **12 18**

1439 CROSSING SHANTY AND MAN, AUTOMATIC: Same as 1420. **12 18**

1440 CROSSING SHANTY AND MAN: Same as 1420, except illuminated with plastic windows. **20 30**

1450 FUELING STATION: Automated, illuminated station with moving man and light; two fuel pumps; shanty in center of platform. **25 35**

1456 BARREL LOADER: Automated plastic barrel loading platform with man on forklift and one man at top of ramp; with yellow barrels. **25 40**

1460 GANTRY CRANE: 1955-57, plastic black cab, metal four-leg tower gantry on four wheels, boom and hook; manually-operated pivoted cab.
(A) Electric light under frame top. **150 175**
(B) No electric light. **150 175**

1614 AUTOMATIC DUMP UNIT: Yellow-lithographed shack with slanted roof and open front to permit two arms to extend when electrically-operated; NYC 567 side dump car; with single-button control panel, number 1603; extension of shack to lock under track section; 3-3/4" high; with metal track side pan for dumping cars. **50 70**

1615 AUTOMATIC DUMP UNIT: Same as 1614, but reportedly sold with black-coated, ball-like candy for simulated coal. **35 50**

Buildings, Miscellaneous

0225 BILLBOARD: Plastic; not illuminated.
(A) Yellow. **3 6**
(B) Green. **3 6**

Top shelf: 3861 barn; 3851 church. *Middle shelf:* Original boxes for the buildings on the top shelf. *Bottom shelf:* 3881 railroad station with original box; 3872 ranch house with original box. B. Liebno Collection, B. Greenberg photograph.

	Gd	Exc
0226 BILLBOARD: Plastic; illuminated.		
(A) Yellow.	10	15
(B) Green.	10	15

304 CATTLE RUNWAY: Metal; black-enameled or painted aluminum. 5 10

3721 POLICE STATION: 1952 and earlier, plastic with accessories. 8 15

3741 ARMY BARRACKS: 1952 and earlier, plastic with accessories. 20 30

3771 DINER: 1952 and earlier, plastic, also catalogued as 477. 8 15

3781 FIREHOUSE: 1952 and earlier, plastic with accessories. 8 15

3792 RANCH SET: 1952 and earlier, plastic with accessories. 8 15

3802 HOUSE: 1952 and earlier, plastic colonial house with accessories. 10 20

	Gd	Exc

3812 FACTORY: 1952 and earlier, plastic with accessories. 20 30

3822 SCHOOL: 1952 and earlier, plastic with accessories. 10 20

3832 AIRPORT: 1952 and earlier, plastic with accessories. 25 35

3841 MARKET: Plastic supermarket with accessories including five people, baggage truck, station wagon, etc. 8 15

3842 MARKET: Same as 3841. 8 15

3851 CHURCH: Plastic with five people, fence, two trees. 8 15

3852 CHURCH: 1952, same as 3851. 8 15

3856 CHICKEN COOP: Plastic. 8 15

3861 BARN: Plastic barn and silo with accessories. 8 15

3862 BARN: 1952, same as 3861. 8 15

3871 RANCH HOUSE: Plastic house with four people, garden table and chairs, fence, 9" long, 4" wide, 4" high. 8 15

Top shelf: 3891 service station with original box. **Middle shelf:** 3812 factory; 3832 airport. **Bottom shelf:** The original boxes for the buildings on the middle shelf. B. Liebno Collection, B. Greenberg photograph.

	Gd	Exc

3872 RANCH HOUSE: 1952, same as 3871.   8   15

3881 RAILROAD STATION: Yellow plastic.
(A) Red roof and platform.   8   15
(B) Brown roof and platform.   8   15

3891 SERVICE STATION: 1952 or earlier, plastic with accessories including two pumps, four people, two cars, lift, etc.   25   35

3892 SERVICE STATION: 1952, same as 3891.   25   35

(6105) TRUCK: Four-wheel plastic baggage truck.   3   6

(6106) SCALE: Four-wheel plastic platform scales.   3   6

(6107) TRUCK: Two-wheel metal freight hand truck.   5   10

(6107B) BENCH: Stamped steel; 2-1/8" x 1" x 1-1/2" high.   3   5

(6108) SHOVEL: Tin-plate scoop shovel supplied with 1615 dump unit and 567 car.   10   15

(6109) TRUNK: Lithographed metal steamer trunk; lithographed travel stickers and opening lid.
(A) Black with orange bands.   15   20
(B) Black with yellow bands.   15   20

(6109A) SUITCASE: Lithographed metal, tan with lithographed travel stickers and opening lid; similar to 6109, but smaller.   20   30

(6110) CARDBOARD BUILDING SET: Barber shop / candy store, shed, watchman's house, one-car garage, two-story house, firehouse, railroad station, one-story modern house.   5   10

(6111) FENCE AND RAMP: Plastic fence and stock unloading platform with ramp — came in sets with stock car.   3   5

(6112) ROCKET ACCESSORIES: Plastic Cape Canaveral set: rocket fixtures and figures.   NRS

(6114) FIGURE SET: Lithographed metal farm animals (sheep, cow, and pig) on sheet metal silhouettes with bottom bent at 90 degrees to provide stand. For use with 304 cattle runway and six-inch cattle car; came with "Station Box" train sets.   NRS

NEWSSTAND: Gray plastic (usually came in sets); catalogue number unknown.   2   3

Items that were available direct from Marx factory:
Plastic automobiles for flatcar load — offered until 1970.
Metal dump truck for flatcar load — offered until 1965.
AET 261 round lumber for flatcar load — offered until 1970.
AET 492 square lumber for flatcar load — offered until 1970.
PL 950 W space rocket with fins for flatcar load — offered until 1968.
AET 1312 pipe assembly for gondola car load — offered until 1968.

Left to right: 1438 crossing gate, automatic; 428 crossing gate, automatic; 428 crossing gate, automatic; (unidentified); 438 crossing signal, automatic gate; 317 manual crossing gate; 438 crossing signal, automatic gate. E. Matzke Collection, G. Stern photograph.

Crossing Signals and Gates

	Gd	Exc

064 CROSSING GATE: Plastic, movable gate arm, manual.

	Gd	Exc
	1	2

066 GRADE CROSSING: Brown plastic with slots for rails; white "RR" on roadway.

(A) Single lane. .50 1
(B) Double lane. .50 1
(C) Similar to (A), but made of wood painted brown, no marking on roadway. 2 3

067 CROSSING SIGNAL: Plastic, non-operating, simulated jewel lights; white/black crossbuck; red stand; 6" high. 1 2

(0214) CROSSING SIGNAL: Plastic, crossing warning; crossbuck with swinging banjo; actuated by weight of train. 3 5

0217 CROSSING GATE: Gray plastic; actuated by weight of train on track lever. 1 2

0218 CROSSING WATCHMAN SHED: 1956, plastic, red base, blue watchman; watchman comes out of shanty when actuated by weight of train on track lever. 4 8

0221 AUTOMATIC SIGNAL SET: Circa 1951, plastic crossing gate; cross sign with crossbuck; swinging banjo and semaphore; all actuated by weight of train. 5 10

314 CROSSING SIGN: Round metal base, flat-fluted stepped size-reducing pole with T-shaped white sign with red "CAUTION" and black "HIGH SPEED TRAINS", 7-1/2" high.

	Gd	Exc
(A) Red base and pole.	2	4
(B) Green base, pole with slot for handle like 311 semaphore.	2	4
(C) Black base and pole.	2	4

317 MANUAL CROSSING GATE: Metal body and base; black and white diagonally striped; jointed, with street stop and jewel; gate arm; hand crank on side of body, 8" high.

(A) Red body and base. 2 4
(B) Black body. 2 4

321 CROSSING SET: Four-piece manual metal set: semaphore, telltale hazard warning fixture, caution sign, and crossing gate.

	10	15

406 SINGLE BULL'S-EYE CROSSING SIGNAL: Metal with black body top and black square base; 4-1/2" high; white illuminated drum sign with red lettering "RAILROAD CROSSING"; red celluloid inserts; with two screw connectors.

217 crossing gate with the original box. H. Diehl Collection, M. Feinstein photograph.

Boxtop from railroad grade crossing set. H. Diehl Collection, M. Feinstein photograph.

Left to right: 067 crossing signal; 314 crossing sign; 421 crossing signal with flashing lights; 314 crossing sign; 418 crossing signal with bell; 417 crossing caution sign; 421 crossing signal with flashing lights; 409 crossing blinker; 417 crossing caution sign. E. Matzke Collection, G. Stern photograph.

	Gd	Exc
(A) Red body.	3	6
(B) Black body.	3	6
(C) Green body with green square base.	5	10

(D) Same as (C), except no screw connectors and operates on internal battery; on/off switch.   5   10

(E) Black body; insulated copper rail overlay clip to provide flashing operation.   5   10

(F) Black body; chrome base; black illuminated drum sign with white lettering.   5   10

(G) Silver-painted body.   5   10

409 CROSSING BLINKER: Rectangular base with three screw connectors and body top; white T-shaped sign on top of post with red "CAUTION" and black "HIGH / SPEED / TRAINS"; two alternately flashing red lights integral to T-shaped sign; instructions on box; 7-1/2" high.

(A) Black body and pole; chrome base and body top.   8   12

(B) Red body and pole; black base and body top.   8   12

414 CROSSING CAUTION WITH RINGING BELL: Red metal round black base; flat-fluted stepped size-reducing pole with T-shaped white sign with red "CAUTION" and black "HIGH SPEED TRAINS"; ringing chrome bell; 7-1/2" high.   6   10

417 CROSSING CAUTION SIGN:
(A) Red metal, round black base; flat-fluted stepped size-reducing pole with T-shaped white sign with red "CAUTION" and black "HIGH SPEED TRAINS"; ringing chrome bell and swinging white banjo sign with red pointer and black "STOP"; single-prong rail connector, 1-3/8" long copper track overlay contact; instructions on box, number FB-736; 7-1/2" high.   6   12

(B) Same as (A), but with round chrome base.   6   12

(C) Circa 1957, (box labeled "Bell Ringing Crossing Signal"); black plastic elevated base with two screw connectors and ringing bell; black pole with single red bulb; black crossbucks; white "RAILROAD CROSSING" and black octagonal sign; white-printed "STOP ON RED SIGNAL", 6- 3/4" high.   6   12

(D) Same as (C), except gray base and pole; white crossbucks; black "RAILROAD CROSSING" and white octagonal sign.   6   12

418 CROSSING SIGNAL WITH BELL: 1952, black metal body and round pole; white crossbuck with "RAILROAD CROSSING" in black letters; chrome bell with clapper. Marlines decal on body: "STOP — DO NOT CROSS TRACKS WHILE BELL IS RINGING"; two screw connectors on base; 7-1/2" high.

(A) Black square base.   4   8

(B) Chrome square base.   4   8

Gd Exc

421 CROSSING SIGNAL WITH FLASHING LIGHTS:
(A) Plastic black base with three screw connectors; vertical pole with crossarms and lights attached; neon red "RAILROAD", and white "CROSSING" on crossbucks; octagonal black sign with white-printed "STOP ON RED SIGNAL" under alternately flashing red lights.   4   8

(B) Same as (A), except white "RAILROAD" and "CROSSING".   4   8

(C) Same as (A), except plastic gray base, white crossbucks; black-printed "RAILROAD CROSSING"; octagonal white sign; black-printed "STOP ON RED SIGNAL"; 7" high.   4   8

423 TWIN LIGHT CROSSING FLASHER: 1952, black metal, with three screw connectors; black pole with white sign "STOP ON SIGNAL"; twin alternately flashing lights in black crossarm with black light background; white crossbucks with black "RAILROAD CROSSING"; three wires from base; 7-1/2" high.

(A) Black oval base.   5   10

(B) 1952, black square base, box number 432A.   5   10

(C) Same as (B), except chrome square base and crossarm.   5   10

428 AUTOMATIC CROSSING GATE: Plastic base with two screw connectors; gate crossarm with two translucent reflectors and rolling counterweight; 7" high (also 6438 and 428(C)).

(A) Black base with diagonally striped black/white gate crossarm.   2   4

(B) Gray base with striped black/gray gate crossarm.   2   4

430 CROSSING SET: Three-piece set: wood roadway/track grade crossing with three notches for rails; crank-operated metal crossing gate; short metal crossing sign with crossbuck and one red jewel on post.   5   10

0430 SIGNAL SET: Plastic, 29 pieces: 12 railroad signs, 12 telephone poles, one semaphore, one crossing signal, one street lamp, one crossing gate, and one road grade crossing.   8   12

438 AUTOMATIC CROSSING GATE: 1952, black metal body and base with two screw connectors; black or red flat-fluted stepped size-reducing pole with white crossbucks, "RAILROAD CROSSING" in black; red jewel at pole top; diagonally black/white striped-jointed, with street stop and jewel, gate arm; 8" high.   4   8

1420 CROSSING SHANTY AND MAN, AUTOMATIC: Circa 1957, metal lithographed shanty with blue man fixed on door that swings out when actuated, crossing gate descends (plastic arm).   12   18

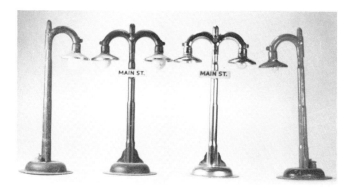

Left to right: 419 single light lamp post; 429 street lamp; 429 street lamp; 419 single light lamp post.

Gd Exc

1426 CROSSING SIGNAL, FLASHING LIGHTS AND BANJO: Base with three screw connectors, pole and arm for swinging banjo sign; white on black with "STOP"; black crossarm with two alternately flashing lights; black crossbucks on pole with white "RAILROAD CROSSING"; white "1 Track" sign on crossarm.
(A) Gray plastic base.   5   10
(B) Black plastic base.   5   10

1438 CROSSING GATE: 1952, double crossing gates, one roadway, one pedestrian, die-cast black motor case box, steel base, white and black-striped arms; red light in cast housing on top of motor box, lantern on arm.   10   15

1439 CROSSING SHANTY AND MAN, AUTOMATIC: Same as 1420.   12   18

1440 CROSSING SHANTY AND MAN: Same as 1420, except illuminated with plastic windows.   18   22

(6103) GRADE CROSSING: Brown plastic, two lanes wide; rubber-stamped "RR Crossing" on each side.   1   2

Lamps and Poles

061 TELEPHONE POLE SET: Brown plastic, double crossarm poles; 12 to a set (also 6072 and 6061 when sold as individual items).   2   4

062 LAMP POST: Plastic, non-illuminated dummy with shade; 6" high; gooseneck style.   1   2

068 HIGH TENSION POWER POLES: Brown plastic power poles; H-type fixture for transmission lines; two poles each fixture; 7-1/2" high, six to a set.   4   8

072 LAMP POST: 1952, 1955, plastic shade; large base; 6" high. (also 0672); gooseneck style.
(A) Gray octagonal post; gray illuminated shade.   2   4
(B) Black post; gray shade.   2   4

073 LAMP POST SET: Three plastic, illuminated boulevard lamps with fire call box, mailbox, and police call box on posts; three two-prong track connectors (box numbered 073/3 and instructions on box FB-734); 6-1/4" high.   5   10

074 LAMP POST: 1955, plastic, round gray base; octagonal post; enclosed translucent milk-white boulevard-type globe, 6-1/4" high, (also 6074).   2   4

078 LAMP POST: Plastic round gray base with octagonal post; boulevard arms with two upright bulbs and downward pointing finials; 6-1/2" high. Same as 426.   4   8

0161 POWER POLE SET: Plastic, double crossarm type, 12 poles. (Later number 1974.)   2   4

Gd Exc

308 STREET LAMP: Metal body, black body top; black base with switch for internal battery operations; 7" high, (possibly a Joy Line item).
(A) Green body, pole, and crossarms; square base.   15   30
(B) Same as (A), but with red body, pole, and crossarms.   10   25
(C) Red body, gooseneck arm; round elevated base; access by door in body.   10   25

408 STREET LAMP: Metal with black body top and square base with two screw connectors, milk-white twin globes mounted downward.
(A) Red body, pole, and crossarms.   4   8
(B) Black body with silver pole and crossarms.   4   8
(C) Silver body, pole, and crossarms.   4   8

419 SINGLE LIGHT LAMP POST: Metal pole, arm, and round base; bulb downward, with two screw connectors; 7-1/2" high.
(A) Black pole, arm, and base; chrome shade.   4   8
(B) Red pole and arm; black base and shade.   4   8

426 STREET LAMP: Plastic round gray base, octagonal pole; crossarms with two upright bulbs with finials pointed downward; 6-1/2" high.   4   8

429 STREET LAMP: 1952, metal pole and round black base with two screw connectors; black on white sign "MAIN STREET" on pole; 7-1/2" high.
(A) 1952, black pole and arms; chrome (or black) shades.   5   10
(B) Chrome pole, arms, and shades.   7   15

0430 SIGNAL SET: Plastic, 29 pieces: 12 railroad signs, 12 telephone poles, one semaphore, one crossing signal, one street lamp, one crossing gate, and one road grade crossing.   8   12

Miscellaneous Items

307 TRACK LOCK: Metal clip to hold track together.   .10   .15
308 TRACK LOCK: Box of 12 metal clips to hold track together.   .50   1
309 TRACK SEPARATORS: Box of 12 wooden separators to keep parallel O27 and O34 tracks properly spaced.   3   5

333F SMOKE REFILL:
(A) Green glass bottle; "1 liquid ounce".   1   3
(B) 1970, plastic tube.   1   3

409 CIRCUIT BREAKER: Black plastic, rectangular base with two spring clip connectors; marked "25 WATTS"; 1-1/2" x 2-1/4".   1   2

415 CIRCUIT BREAKER: 50 watt model, all-black body with red reset button with spring clip connectors.   2   4

419 CIRCUIT BREAKER: Same as 409 circuit breaker, except "30 WATTS".   2   4

Left to right: 420 circuit breaker with decal; 406 railroad crossing signal; 406 railroad crossing signal; 420 circuit breaker without decal.

Top shelf (left to right): 425 circuit breaker; 061 telephone pole; 408 street lamp; (unidentified); 313 low clearance hazard telltale; 0605 bumper; 410 searchlight on square pedestal; 419 street lamp, black with chrome shade; 1405 block signal, three-light "TRAINMASTER". *Bottom shelf (left to right):* 505 bumper; 406 single bull's-eye crossing signal; 316 fence; 304 cattle runway; 420 circuit breaker with decal; 406 single bull's-eye crossing signal. E. Matzke Collection, G. Stern photograph.

	Gd	Exc

420 CIRCUIT BREAKER: Metal body and open-sided drum on top of base with red celluloid inserts with lighted "SHORT CIRCUIT"; two screw connectors on square base; reset button "AUTOMATIC SIGNAL" decal; 4-1/2".

(A) All black; reset button on left side. 3 6

(B) Black body and face of drum, all else chrome; reset button on right side. 3 6

(C) Black body and face of drum, all else chrome; flat fiber reset lever on right side. 3 6

420A CIRCUIT BREAKER: Same as 420(C), but with revised instructions and recommendation to use 12-volt bulb only. (Previous instructions allowed 10- or 12-volt bulb.) 3 6

421 RHEOSTAT: Sliding control/contact arm with red wooden handle; "stop" to "fast" control; lever depresses to change direction; perforated top on case; four feet on base; 2" x 2-1/2" x 1/2" high.

(A) Chrome. 4 8

(B) Black. 4 8

422 RHEOSTAT: Chrome finish. 4 8

425 CIRCUIT BREAKER: Black metal body and oval base; jewel in opposite sides of body; lighted "SHORT CIRCUIT"; two screw connectors on base; reset button under decal; "Marline" decal with "CIRCUIT BREAKER" in red on yellow background; 4-1/2". 4 8

464/C TRACK CONNECTION PACKAGE: One straight track section, one curved track section, two black track clips. 1 2

500 KEY: For windup mechanical locomotives. 3 4

505 BUMPER: Non-illuminated bumper.

(A) Black metal; spring-loaded bumping bar; square body with jewel on top; 2-1/4" high. 1 3

(B) Same as (A), except red. 1 3

(C) Gray plastic body with red lens on top. 1 3

	Gd	Exc

605 BUMPER: Spring-loaded bumping bar; connecting wire and spring clip to track; black drum with black/white stripes and red celluloid inserts, illuminated; 4" high.

(A) Black metal. 3 6

(B) White or cream. 3 6

0605 DEAD END BUMPER: Gray, white, or black plastic body with red lens on top; illuminated. 1 3

700 WHISTLE: Metal two-tone mouth whistle. 8 12

701 WHISTLE: Metal two-tone mouth whistle. 8 12

724 UNCOUPLING TRACK UNIT: 3 6

1601 COUPLER ADAPTER: Die-cast knuckle and bronze slip nut to permit use of the 21 diesel having tab and slot couplers with Lionel knuckle coupler cars. 3 5

1605 REMOTE CONTROL UNCOUPLER UNIT: 1-1/2" x 2-3/4", with clip at each end. 1 3

(6101) CONTROLLER: Black plastic with metal control box panel, with two knife edge tabs to be inserted in underside of track rail; two control buttons for battery set: green for "forward" and red for "reverse"; two spring clip connectors on base; 6-1/3" x 2-3/4" x 1/2". 1 2

(6102) BATTERY BOX: Black metal "sleeve" for battery container to hold six D-type flashlight dry cells; one end with two spring clip connectors; 7-3/4" x 2-3/4" x 1-1/2". 6 8

X-10 LUBRICANT: Tube of train lubricant. .50 1

X-5 BULB KIT: Replacement bulbs, 12-volt: two clear and one each of red, amber, and green. 2 4

B-25 LIGHT: Utility light extension, chrome spotlight with two-prong track connector; spring clip for attachment to large, through truss bridge (instructions on box FB-148). 3 6

Top shelf: 2970 Girard whistling station with original box. *Middle shelf:* 2979 Oak Park station; 2900 Glendale Depot. *Bottom shelf:* 5424 freight station. F. Pauling Collection.

Sets of Signs and Figures

	Gd	Exc

316 FENCE: Stamped black-enameled sheet metal or painted aluminum, price per section: **2 3**

348 RIGHT OF WAY SIGN SET: 1953-55, five-piece metal railroad sign set; 2-1/2" high. **8 12**

0430 SIGNAL SET: Plastic, 29 pieces: 12 railroad signs, 12 telephone poles, one semaphore, one crossing signal, one street lamp, one crossing gate, and one road grade crossing. **8 12**

782 FIGURE SET: Plastic railroad figures. **2 4**

1136 "MINIATURE SCALE ACCESSORY SET": Seven metal lithographed railway signs. **2 4**

1180 "HIGHWAY SIGNS": Twelve plastic railroad signs. **3 5**

1182 "RITE-O-WAY": Twelve plastic railroad signs. **3 5**

1281 "RITE-O-WAY": Twelve plastic railroad signs. **3 5**

1282 SIGN SET: Twelve plastic right-of-way signs. **3 5**

1624 SIGN: Lithographed metal; small black and white "UN-COUPLE HERE". **1 2**

54/119 FIGURE SET: Set of 35 pieces including six railroad figures. **NRS**

Stations

	Gd	Exc

1430 UNION STATION: Lithographed metal; hand-operated crossing gate; crossing warning; depression for track; 6-3/4"x 12".
(A) Blue with red roof; clock on front of station. **50 90**
(B) Same as (A), but without clock. **50 90**
(C) Yellow with red roof; clock on front of station. **50 90**
(D) Same as (C), but without clock. **50 90**

1600 GLENDALE DEPOT: Lithographed metal freight station with crossing gate actuated by train's weight; roof overhangs each end; clock on front; included red or blue handcart and six cardboard boxes.
(A) Red base. **35 50**
(B) Green base. **35 50**

1830 UNION STATION: Blue-lithographed; red roof and light base 13-5/8" x 10"; building 5" high; "UNION STATION"; hand-operated crossing gate; crossing warning; depression for track; 6-3/4" x 12". Similar to 1430.
(A) Clock on front of station. **50 90**
(B) Without clock. **50 90**

1900 GLENDALE DEPOT: Station with crossing actuated by train's weight; battery-operated warning signal.
(A) Red base. **35 50**
(B) Green base. **35 50**

Gd Exc

2890 WHISTLING RAILROAD STATION WITH CANOPY: Lithographed metal with front canopy length of station; flat roof with simulated lithographed skylights; whistle control on right side; on plain raised platform.   **15   25**

2898 and 2899 STATION: Similar to 2890 without canopy; whistling lithographed metal station, battery-operated by button; sometimes comes with plastic roof.   **15   25**

2900 GLENDALE DEPOT: Lithographed metal station with crossing gate activated by train's weight; battery-illuminated crossing signal and lamp; roof overhangs each end; clock on front, "GLENDALE DEPOT"; with loose metal bench, baggage hand truck, and two suitcases.
(A) Red base; battery-illuminated crossing signal end lamp.
                                                                          45   75
(B) Red base; two screw connectors; illuminated crossing signal and lamp.   **45   75**
(C) Same as (A), but green base.   **45   75**
(D) Same as (B), but green base.   **45   75**

2940 GRAND CENTRAL STATION: Circa 1939, buff-yellow lithographed station with swinging doors; illuminated interior; removable yellow-blue-gray shingled roof; mounted on base with lithographed steps, grass, and two travel signs, 10-3/4" x 17".
                                                                          100 125

2959 GIRARD WHISTLING STATION: Lithographed metal red brick station; gray shingled roof with "GIRARD"; with remote-controlled, steam-type whistle and remote button unit; 5-1/4" x 9".   **15   20**

2960 GIRARD WHISTLING STATION: Same as 2959, but catalogue number changed.   **15   20**

2970 GIRARD WHISTLING STATION: Same as 2959, but with light.   **20   25**

2979 OAK PARK STATION: Circa 1951, lithographed metal yellow brick station with yellow-green shingle roof; "OAK PARK"; with remote-controlled diesel-type horn and remote-control button, 5-1/4" x 9".   **35   50**

2980 OAK PARK STATION: Same as 2979, but catalogue number changed.   **25   35**

2990 OAK PARK STATION: Same as 2979, but with light.
                                                                          50   75

3381 STATION AND ACCESSORY SET: Circa 1952 and earlier, plastic.   **5   10**

3880 GLENDALE STATION: Plastic, hip roof station, "Glendale".   **3   6**

3881 STATION: Same as 3880, but with people and accessories.
                                                                          5   10

3882 STATION: Same as 3881.   **5   10**

4116 GLENDALE STATION KIT: (Sold unassembled in box.) Lithographed metal red brick platform; yellow brick walls; gray roof and brick chimney; with six light gray plastic figures, four different type hand trucks, and bench; illuminated with track connector, bulb, and instructions.   **25   35**

4412 GLENDALE STATION: Lithographed metal station with solid lithographed windows.   **20   30**

4416 GLENDALE STATION: Same as 4412, but with light and accessories, cut-out windows.   **30   40**

4418 GLENDALE STATION: Same as 4412, but with voice box crank-operated.   **100 125**

5420 FREIGHT STATION: 1952, lithographed metal station with two trucks and other freight handling equipment; 29" x 11" x 9".   **20   35**

Gd Exc

5424 FREIGHT STATION: 1953-54, same as 5420, but many more accessories.   **25   45**

(6104) STATION PLATFORM: Plastic, with hip roof cover and four silver posts; with six unpainted standing plastic people (may have only come in sets). Found in 52850 "BIG RAIL" work train set.
                                                                          3   5

GRAND CENTRAL STATION: Small; tan and red lithography; catalogue number unknown.   **25   35**

GRAND CENTRAL STATION: Small; blue and yellow lithography; catalogue number unknown.   **25   35**

Towers and Lights

065 WATER TOWER WITH SPOUT: 1952-53, gray plastic round tank 3-1/2" high, 4-1/4" diameter; four plastic supports with square black feet; gray movable spout; black plastic ladder 8-1/4" long.
(A) Red supports; gray tank and spout.   **5   10**
(B) Yellow supports; red tank and spout.   **8   12**
(C) Green supports; yellow tank and spout.   **15   20**
(D) Gray supports; yellow tank and spout.   **15   20**
(E) White supports; red tank and spout.   **15   20**
(F) Black supports; black tank and spout.   **15   20**

0165 WATER TANK: Gray plastic round tank; 14" high, 4" diameter on black square base; no ladder, spout, or piping.   **3   6**

310 SEARCHLIGHT: Green square metal pedestal stand; battery-operated with on/off switch.   **6   12**

0405 SPOTLIGHT: Plastic, mounted on small, low wheel-like stand; black and red.   **4   8**

410 SEARCHLIGHT ON SQUARE PEDESTAL: Metal body and base with two screw connectors, black pedestal top; red support arms to hold red light housing, chrome ventilator on top of light and chrome lens retaining ring; solid chrome cap with red handles on rear of housing; up/down movable head with 360-degree circle; 5-1/4" high.
(A) Red body and black base; with no on/off switch.   **4   8**
(B) Green body and base; on/off switch in base for battery operation.   **15   25**

Left to right: 413A switchman tower;   409 crossing blinker; 413A switchman tower.

Top shelf (left to right): 416 floodlight tower; 416A floodlight tower; 0436 searchlight tower; 454 block signal; 0416 floodlight tower; 423 crossing signal with flashing lights, oval base; 436 searchlight tower. *Bottom shelf (left to right):* 429 street lamp; 074 lamp post; 308 street lamp; 078 lamp post; 420 circuit breaker; 429 street lamp; 418 crossing signal with bell; 423 twin light crossing flasher; 419 single light lamp post. E. Matzke Collection, G. Stern photograph.

Gd Exc

413A SWITCHMAN TOWER: Circa 1952, metal cabin on crisscross tower; black square base with two screw connectors; chrome ladder; lithographed tower cabin: telegrapher, leverman, one open side with red celluloid in window, lighted; 9-1/4" high.
(A) Cream lithography with green trim; red tower. 5 10
(B) Cream lithography with red trim; black tower. 5 10
(C) White lithography with green trim; red tower. 5 10

416 SEARCHLIGHT TOWER, TWIN LIGHTS: Metal tower with crisscross tower on top of body and base; rectangular fenced platform with two adjustable lights; hand switch for battery; 10-1/2" high.
(A) Green platform, tower, body, and base. 6 12
(B) Red platform, tower, and body; black base. 4 8
(C) Same as (B), but with two screw connectors. 4 8
(D) Chrome platform and tower; black body and base. 4 8

(E) Chrome platform, green tower, body, and base. 6 12
(F) Black platform; red tower and body; black base; no hand switch. 4 8
(G) Black platform and base; green tower and body. 4 8

416A FLOODLIGHT TOWER, TWIN LIGHTS: Metal tower with round-holed tower on square base; rectangular fenced platform with two adjustable lights; two screw connectors; 11-1/2" high.
(A) Black platform, tower, and base. 5 10
(B) Chrome platform, tower, and base. 5 10
(C) Chrome platform, and tower; black base. 5 10
(D) Red platform, tower, and base. 5 10
(E) Chrome platform; black tower and base. 5 10

0416 FLOODLIGHT TOWER, FOUR LIGHTS: 1952-53, gray plastic crisscross tower with four adjustable metal chrome floodlights

Left to right: 0436 searchlight tower with box; 0416 floodlight tower with box; 436 searchlight tower. R. LaVoie Collection, G. Stern photograph.

	Gd	Exc

in two banks on black platform; chrome ladder; instructions on box, number FB-187; 13-1/2" high. **12 18**

424 RADIO TRAIN CONTROL TOWER: Metal cabin on crisscross or round-holed tower; various-type bases with two screw connectors.
(A) Green and cream cabin; red crisscross tower on square red body with square black base. Cabin has solid lithographed windows on two sides, "RADIO TRAIN CONTROL" on third; fourth side with punched-out window mullions backed by a plastic sheet connected to a breath-operated butterfly switch; thumb switch under cabin side with number "7" on it; 11-1/2" high. **5 10**
(B) Same as (A), except red and cream cabin, black round-holed type tower on black rectangular die-cast base; 13-1/2" high. **5 10**
(C) Gray and brown cabin; black crisscross tower on black square base. Cabin has "RADIO TRAIN CONTROL, STATION No. 7" on fourth side, and backed by black sheet metal; "6" on switch side of cabin; chrome ladder; gray lithographed roof; 9-1/4" high. **20 30**

436 SEARCHLIGHT TOWER: Black metal round-holed tower with pressed oval base; chrome rings and ventilator on chrome-fenced rectangular platform; with two screw connectors; 13-3/4" high. **8 17**

0436 FLOODLIGHT TOWER: 1952-53, gray plastic crisscross tower with two red plastic adjustable lights on fenced black platform; black square base; chrome ladder; 13-1/4" high. **15 20**

0446 REVOLVING BEACON TOWER: Gray or black plastic crisscross tower; ladder from base to octagonal black fenced platform; with dimpled bulb for rotation of plastic and metal ventilated beacon head; instructions on box, number FB-189; 12-1/2" high. **15 20**

0456 SEARCHLIGHT TOWER: Catalogue number unknown; silver and black plastic with single light mounted on rubber foot vibrator (similar to that of searchlight car) on black circular platform. **25 30**

465 WATER TOWER: Gray plastic crisscross tower with bubbling tube heated by bulb; square black base, chrome ladder; 14-1/2" high. **20 25**

1379 WATER TOWER: Same as 0165. **20 25**

2920 SWITCHMAN TOWER: Plastic cream clapboard-sided cabin with maroon roof and trim on four cream stilt legs with bases; maroon two-piece steps hook into walkway around tower cabin; 7-1/2" high.
(A) Illuminated. **35 45**
(B) Non-illuminated. **25 35**

	Gd	Exc

2939 SWITCHMAN TOWER: Same as 2940, but illuminated. **15 20**

2940 SWITCHMAN TOWER: 1952-58, same as 2939, but two moving blue men activated by train and track diagram board, instructions on box FB-247.
(A) Illuminated. **35 45**
(B) Non-illuminated. **25 35**

Tunnels, Derricks, Trestles, and Bridges

299 TRACK TRESTLE SET: Circa 1940, steel over/under track trestle set consisting of eight black-enameled trestle frames with track holding tab; upper and lower cross member (same as 412 derrick frames); eight pieces of O34 curved track; unnumbered instructions with picture of assembled set; packaged in plain tan pasteboard box. **12 18**

309 TUNNEL: Two-piece lithographed metal, mottled red and green patches on yellow, (similar to army tanks). **20 30**

313 LOW CLEARANCE HAZARD TELLTALE: Wire mast and arm on metal round pressed base, with fiber fringe warning device; 7" high (reference date 1940 — included with lithographed 897 locomotive set).
(A) Black base. **5 10**
(B) Chrome base. **7 10**
(C) Silver base. **10 15**

390 TUNNEL: 1939-53.
(A) 1939-53, metal; two-piece collapsible; lithographed farm scene on sides. **2 4**
(B) 1950, molded fiber; 15" long x 12" wide x 9" high. **3 6**

390C RAILROAD ACCESSORY SET: One 390 tunnel and two 313 warning telltales. **20 25**

392 TUNNEL: 1950, collapsible two-piece metal; with coal mine tipple lithographed on side, box number FB-782. **3 6**

399 RAILROAD ACCESSORY SET: One 390 tunnel, two 313 warning telltales, and one 1305 girder bridge. **25 30**

412 DERRICK: Black metal elevated platform; red boom; black rounded roof on cab with lithographed door on back and window on front; frame has five ladder step holes.

390 tunnel.

1303 Erie girder bridge

1305 girder bridge with box

Gd Exc

(A) Orange and black cab with "WRECKER" and "NEW YORK CENTRAL LINES"; oval Marx herald and trademark on rear; orange color varies. 5 15

(B) Same as (A), but with red-orange cab. 5 15

(C) Similar to (A), but "WRECKER" not printed on cab sides, white roof (early version). 15 20

(D) Similar to (A), but no Marx trademark on rear, "WRECKER" printed on cab sides, orange color varies. 5 15

422 DERRICK: Metal elevated platform, A-shaped pitched roof with lithographed shingles; six ladder step holes.

(A) Red boom and platform; red cab with blue trim; white and black details. 8 12

(B) Black boom and platform; red cab with gray trim, gray and black details. 8 12

0442 DERRICK: 1952, gray plastic crane on gray plastic four- leg platform with red plastic footings; plastic crank in boom to move hook; "MARX" cast on boom; black NYC system herald on cab. 5 8

Gd Exc

611 TRESTLE ELEVATOR: Black-enameled stamped-steel; adjustable with wing nuts. 4 8

611A TRESTLE ELEVATOR: Black-enameled stamped-steel; adjustable with base bar. 4 8

612 TRESTLE: Black-enameled stamped-steel trestle; frame fitted for lower and upper track to snap in. 2 5

615 TRESTLE: Black-enameled stamped steel. 2 5

1303 BRIDGE: Plastic black plate girders with cast-in detail; metal deck plate; 9-3/4" long; "ERIE" and diamond heralds on girder sides. 2 4

1305 BRIDGE: Metal girder bridge 12" long, 5-1/8" wide, 2" high; metal floor and sides; no Marx emblems; various road names. (See accompanying chart.) 5 15

1320 BRIDGE: Short version through-truss metal bridge; "ROCK ISLAND", "ILLINOIS CENTRAL", or "WABASH" herald over end portals; 18" long.

1305 Girder Bridge

Railroad	With RR name - two small decals				Without RR name - two large decals					One large decal
	Red	Black	Blue	Yellow	Red	Black	Blue	Yellow	Silver	Silver
NEW YORK CENTRAL	X	X			X		X	X	X	X
PENNSYLVANIA		X		X	X	X	X	X	X	X
ROCK ISLAND	X	X	X		X		X	X	X	X
ILLINOIS CENTRAL		X			X	X	X	X	X	X
GREAT NORTHERN	X	X	X							
WABASH	X	X								

Courtesy R. Jackson

	Gd	Exc
(A) Silver.	5	15
(B) Blue.	5	15
(C) Red.	5	15

1324 BRIDGE: 18" long version through-truss metal bridge; "ROCK ISLAND", "ILLINOIS CENTRAL", "WABASH", or "P.R.R." herald over end portals; beacon light.

(A) Silver.	12	25
(B) Blue.	12	25

1340 FOOT BRIDGE: Silver metal overhead foot bridge, two stairways on each side. **Note:** The foot bridges shown in accessory catalogues for 1952 and 1955 do not show the usual Marx foot bridge. The pictures appear to be of the Minitoy foot bridge, No. FB-3, made by Minitoys, Inc., Irvington, New Jersey.

(A) P.R.R. herald.	5	10
(B) U.P. herald.	5	10

1350 BRIDGE: 24" long version; silver through-truss metal bridge.
8   12

1379 and 1380 BRIDGE: 24" long version; silver through-truss metal bridge with snap-on light (RA-29). Made as 1379 in 1951.
15   25

1392 LIFT BRIDGE: Plate girder lift bridge; silver with red; Illinois Central herald; manual crank and worm gear to raise and lower track and frame.
8   15

1412 RAILROAD TRESTLE SET: Plastic, 24-piece set, graduated.
5   10

1414 TRESTLE AND BRIDGE SET: Graduated plastic trestle in figure eight and bridge set.
5   10

1434 OVERHEAD SIGNAL BRIDGE: Plastic bridge with two black dual signal lights on silver frame; lights controlled by two track

1350 Trestle Bridge with box

	Gd	Exc

contactors and two track overlay contactors, (instruction sheet IS-240).
25   35

1460 GANTRY CRANE: 1955-57, plastic black cab; metal four-leg tower gantry on four wheels with boom and hook; manually-operated pivoting cab, electric light under frame top.
50   75

(6113) TRESTLE AND BRIDGE SET: Plastic bridge/tunnel and set of trestles.
4   8

Chapter VI

Train Toys

TROLLEY AND HANDCARS

The Marx trolley and early handcars were made as mechanically-operated floor toys. The windup Marx *12th St. trolley*, about nine inches long, was lithographed with double-entry doors at each end of the sides. On each side it had eight lithographed windows with passengers. There was also a motorman on duty in a wide front window. The front wheels pivoted to permit the use of flanged wheels for windup track or floor use. The wheels could be locked to permit the car to run in a circular path. The trolley would not, however, operate on three-rail electric track since the center rail interfered with the bell striker mechanism. The trolley appeared in the late 1920s or early 1930s and was shown in the 1934 Sears Fall Catalog.

The trolley's windup motor was similar to that used by Marx in the early army tanks and in the 1936 M10003 stream-lined floor sets. Regrettably, these windup motors had gears fashioned from metal that did not endure. The trolley was produced either with or without a light. The lighted one had a battery holder in the body and an electric headlight bulb under the front window. Unlighted variations may or may not have a slot in the roof.

Handcars have always been popular. Perhaps Marx's earliest handcar was the 1933 *Girard handcar* made by the Girard Model Works. It boasted two lithographed metal men in work clothes who pumped tirelessly while the car's windup spring motor ran on large, stamped flangeless metal wheels. Marx next focused on well-known comic characters from the mid-1930s as themes. One of the most popular cars had little Kayo, standing on a box marked "DYNAMITE", pumping the handcar opposite Moon Mullins. Popeye and Olive Oyl, popular in the 1930s, also shared a handcar. In the late 1950s and 1960s, Marx used comic strip notables such as Mickey Mouse and Donald Duck or Barney Rubble and Fred Flintstone to pump his handcars.

200 "12TH ST." trolley. H. Diehl Collection, M. Feinstein photograph.

Standard Gauge floor toy. *Top shelf:* Red locomotive with battery-operated headlight with black tender. *Bottom shelf:* Light green gondola; red passenger coach. L. Jensen Collection, B. Greenberg photograph.

FLOOR TOYS

Marx Standard Gauge

Although some of Marx's floor toys approximated Standard Gauge size, the *Standard Gauge floor train* was not designed to operate on Standard Gauge track but meant to be pulled or pushed by hand. Standard Gauge floor train sets were first manufactured in 1933. Locomotives came with a battery- operated or a dummy copper headlight. The instruction sheet accompanying the locomotive with the battery-operated headlight read "Girard Model Works" rather than "Girard Manufacturing Company" which indicated that it was manufactured prior to 1935. The locomotive, constructed of three sheet steel stampings, was painted red. Conventional tab and slot fasteners held the stampings together. The largest stamping (boiler/cylinder/frame/cab), was joined to the front stamping (boiler-front/cylinder head/pilot/steps) and the rear stamping (cab floor/steps/coupler pin), which had a gong-type bell attached. The locomotive was fitted with stamped-steel, tin-plated drivers with flanges, similar to the eight-spoked drivers used on the Joy Line locomotive. Unlike the Joy Line locomotive, the floor toys did not have side rods. A stamped-copper or tin-plated smokestack, a dummy metal bell, and three embossed domes adorned the boiler. Cab windows were cut out on each side and there were two embossed hatches on the roof. The locomotive was 9 inches in length, 3- 1/2 inches high, and 2-7/8 inches wide. The rear axle had a crank in the middle which, when the locomotive was pulled, activated a clapper which struck the gong. The train was well constructed and designed for the rigors of tough floor play.

Painted in gleaming black enamel, the tender consisted of two sheet metal parts; it measured 6-1/4 inches long, 2-5/8 inches high, and 2-3/4 inches wide. The largest part combined the body, side frames, simulated coal top, and front coupler loop. The second part formed the rear of the tender and included the coupler slot. The tender was fitted with four, eight-spoked drivers and a Joy Line rear coupler. Its body was embossed with a three by one- inch panel on both sides. The front end swept down gracefully in a curved arc.

The only Standard Gauge freight car was a light green gondola, 7-3/4 inches long, 2-3/8 inches high, and 2-3/4 inches wide. It consisted of three sheet metal pieces; two sides and a floor/end piece fastened together with tabs and slots. The gondola had four eight-spoked wheels and Joy Line couplers.

The largest car of the series was a red sheet steel passenger coach. It measured 7-3/4 inches long, 3-3/8 inches high, and 2-3/4 inches wide. It was formed from three sheet metal pieces, the roof/sides/frame and two end pieces. Its windows were cut out, reminiscent of the early Marx passenger cars. The side panel was embossed with a one-quarter by two-inch indentation. At each end the doors were similarly embossed. The car was fitted with eight-spoked driver wheels and Joy Line couplers. Enhancing its appearance were a shallow raised monitor roof and steps at each end under the doors.

Lumar Lines

The term "Lumar Lines," derived from Louis Marx's name, was used in the 1930s for many toys and trains. Marx produced the *Lumar Lines floor train* from 1939 through 1941 and after World War II. The train had wooden wheels and was similar in construction to the earlier Standard Gauge floor train, although it was narrower and sleeker. Car bodies were blue or red with white or black letttering and the frame was of a contrasting color. An army train came in olive drab. The locomotive was a one-piece Commodore Vanderbilt-type

Lumar Lines floor toy. *Top shelf:* Red locomotive. *Middle shelf:* Blue gondola on red frame; red gondola on blue frame. *Bottom shelf:* Original box for the above set. H. Diehl Collection, M. Feinstein photograph.

locomotive/tender combination. When first offered in 1939, it came with two passenger coaches, two gondolas, and a caboose, packaged in a box for use as an attractive freight and passenger station. In 1941, the same locomotive was sold, but this time with only two gondolas and a caboose. This version was packaged in an interesting box that could be used as a freight terminal.

Marx was always quick to adapt existing dies to new needs. In 1940, when the country was defense-minded, military toys were eagerly bought at dime store counters. Marx, consequently, brought out an army floor train set using an olive drab version of the Commodore Vanderbilt, a hybrid derived from many existing parts. To attract attention, a bell was added to the locomotive. The gondola was fitted with a cardboard insert holding a dozen gold-colored, wooden shells. The military floodlight car was derived from the Glendale plant's spotlight truck. The large spotlight was mounted on a floor train frame and, without cut-out side truss rods, improvised a proper military aura. The cannon, previously part of the Army train set, was re-established completing Marx's new military set.

After World War II, this train was made with gondola cars lettered "FRIENDSHIP". This was in honor of a special train

pulling 48 boxcars loaded with goods sent from the United States in 1947 to war-torn Europe.

Marx made many other floor trains in various sizes. These can be found in the listings at the end of the chapter.

CHANNEL TRACK TRAINS

Mercurys

In 1937, Marx brought out an unusually small electric train set referred to as the *Mercury*. It ran on U-shaped channel track, which provided a one-inch gauge runway for its flangeless wheels. This may have been Marx's answer to OO or HO sets which had just begun to appear. It is also likely that Marx developed this miniature electric line to complement the very interesting electrically-powered small automobile set which ran on the same U-shaped track.

The figure eight, over-under track for the automobile sets was lithographed to simulate pavement brick. For train sets, the single oval track used the rail and sleeper (tie) treatment to simulate railway tracks. The center rail was a strip of tin-plated steel with fiber insulators held in place by part of

Lumar Lines floor toys. *Top shelf:* Blue locomotive; red gondola on silver frame. *Second shelf:* Two gondolas. Blue on silver frame; blue on red frame. *Third shelf:* Army version of Lumar Lines floor toy. Olive drab locomotive and gondola with wooden shell load. *Bottom shelf:* Floodlight car; cannon car. H. Diehl Collection, M. Feinstein photograph.

the rail which also was spread to provide tabs to hold each piece. A 708 transformer supplied power. The locomotive looked like a small 0-4-0 Mercury lithographed in red, white, and black with shiny tin-plated stamped wheels. The locomotive bore the number "5151" as did the matching NYC tender. The locomotive was 4-7/8 inches long, 1-3/4 inches wide, and 1-1/4 inches high. The tender measured 4-3/4 inches long, 1-1/4 inches wide, and 1-1/4 inches high.

These diminutive locomotives were well constructed. Nine brass gears were used in the motors with sparklers, and seven brass gears were incorporated in motors without sparklers. The motors were held in by a tab at the front and two screws in the rear, one on each side of the cab. This was similar to the larger O Gauge versions. Motor construction featured bronze bushings at the armature ends, and cloth and rubber-covered wire. All connections were soldered. As small as it was, one version even had a sequence reverse relay. Marx's technique of utilizing one die for all car body shells and then lithographing each one differently to produce a tender, coach, observation, boxcar, hopper, and caboose was well used for this smaller scale train.

Freight and passenger sets were marketed from 1937 until 1939. The lack of additional freight car types did not interfere with Marx's merchandising of freight sets. Marx merely included two boxcars, two hoppers, and a caboose so as to complete a set. Lithography on both the freight and the passenger cars emulated that of the larger six-inch freight cars; the passenger cars were lithographed in red.

Hiawathas

A companion train set, best characterized as the *Hiawatha*, was about the same small size as the channel trains, but of a lesser quality. These small, red, lithographed locomotives had side wing-shaped designs similar to those on the front of the Hiawatha locomotives with silver-enameled shrouds, and a high-mounted headlight. The passenger car had three side windows. The channel track series R & D model from Girard, dated "2/6/1940", was numbered 896, although no such number appeared on the production locomotive.

The locomotive and passenger coach were the only two pieces of rolling stock in this series. Both were lithographed in red, white, and black, except for the coach windows which

Rider-type floor trains. Comparison of the 3000 Ride 'er locomotives. The train on the left may have been repainted; it was never offered in blue. The train on the right is the black "PIONEER EXPRESS". R. Osburn Collection.

had a light blue background to highlight the passengers in the windows. The use of many colors dates the Hiawatha after the Mercury sets when Marx utilized four-color lithography.

The mechanical, small Hiawatha locomotive and matching coach first appeared in 1938 in a set known as the Scenic Mountain Railway. This set came with an oval, undulating track curving up and down, and had a rack stamped into the uphill grades. This rack enabled the locomotive to climb the hills with the aid of a cog wheel.

Other varieties of the Hiawatha locomotive, produced from 1939 to 1941, included two floor toy versions. One had two wooden and two rubber wheels. The other used the Tricky Taxi motor unit consisting of two drive wheels and a third wheel at right angles. This wheel arrangement produced sharp right turns when the sliding front end had nothing to slide on (such as at the edge of a table top).

The Hiawatha coach was lithographed similarly to the smaller Mercury coach, but the Hiawatha's dies were obviously different. Its coach body was higher than the Mercury's and it had five dome-like ventilators embossed in the roof. The Mercury's coupler system was an upturned hook and loop, a part of the car underframe; the Hiawatha-type used a slot in the body end and a dog bone-shaped link, similar to the old link and pin of early railroads.

Others

There were other windup locomotives in the channel track series. One was the 376, similar to the Mercury described above, but stamped to resemble a Pennsylvania torpedo-type, streamlined steam locomotive. Lithographed in gray with multicolor trim, it pulled a train of lithographed freight cars, all of a rectangular design with squared edges. This train ran

on a large tin-plated, lithographed, one-piece layout board embossed with channel track.[1]

Another subminiature train was an articulated Union Pacific M10000 lithographed in yellow and tan or cream and tan. It consisted of a power car, coach, and tail car. It was available with or without a windup motor and came with a one-piece lithographed, tin-plated layout board with embossed channel track.

BATTERY – OPERATED SETS

Commodore Vanderbilt

There was a strong market for battery-operated sets in the mid-1930s since electricity had not yet reached many rural areas. The first battery-operated sets were developed in 1940, when Commodore Vanderbilt motor units were converted to battery usage by replacing field coils with permanent magnets and by deleting the sequence reverse relay. A lithographed metal battery box held six size D flashlight cells for the power. A lithographed metal control box served as a direct contact connector to the track so that the polarity could not be inadvertently reversed by young engineers. Marx later used a similar treatment in 1974 by permanently affixing wires to the track connector and the plastic battery case.

[1] The 376 came lithographed with Walt Disney characters. See *Train Collectors Quarterly*, Winter 1977, Volume 24, No. 1, pp. 22-23.

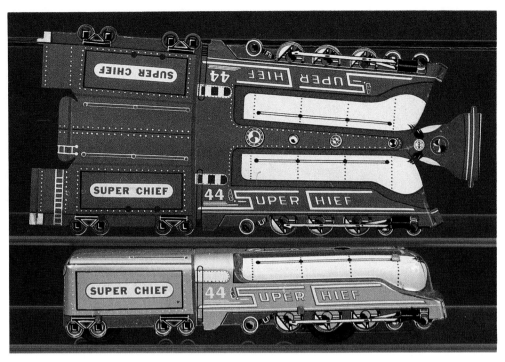

Lithographed plate used by Marx in the manufacture of the Super Chief, shown on the bottom shelf. H. Diehl Collection, M. Feinstein photograph.

Mercury (Articulated)

In the late 1940s, Marx offered a red articulated Mercury passenger train with a tender and two cars. It had a permanent magnetic motor which picked up current from a third rail powered by a six-cell battery box. In 1947, the J. L. Schilling Company offered a plastic O27 train powered by a battery box connected to three-rail track. The Shilling locomotive was short and red, the tender blue, and the two passenger cars yellow. It had semi-automatic, one-way couplers. Marx countered by bringing out a slightly larger, battery train set. It featured a new all- plastic red 198 locomotive, with a blue plastic tender and two or three yellow plastic coaches. The 198 used a one-way coupler very similar to the Schilling model. Other varieties of the 198 locomotive featured either a mechanical or AC electric motor, and the tender was produced in black or blue with red or blue coaches fitted with tab and slot couplers.

590 Set

A postwar O27 battery-operated train set, available in 1956, utilized the sheet steel, 590 series, black locomotive with a one-piece body and a plastic boiler front. This model was also used in mechanical and low-cost electric sets. A small permanent magnetic motor contained in a tin-plated case was also mounted on conventional motor side frames over the front set of drivers. It transmitted power by a crown gear to the axle shaft. Two size D batteries were placed through the rear of the cab into the boiler and were held in place by a wire spring. There was a hand- reversing switch on top of the boiler.

Small Sets (Articulated)

In 1957, a new, smaller battery-powered set appeared with an odd-looking, short, chunky 99 steam locomotive. This articulated floor toy set, manufactured in Hong Kong and distributed through the Glendale plant, had three rather short lithographed passenger cars, two coaches, and a lithographed end car. Inscribed on their sides was "LUXURY LINES" and "MARX". These cars had two wheels each and were coupled at the roof top.

Another version, the Guide-A-Train, had a Civil War-style red locomotive with two cars lithographed like the William Crooks passenger cars. A third version was the Hong Kong battery set which had a number 5 locomotive and lithographed passenger cars reading "Marville Local".

Marxtronic Set

In 1959, Louis Marx & Company introduced another unusual set, the plastic Marxtronic automatic switcher. It came with a battery-powered industrial switcher and two gondolas which could be automatically spotted and loaded on spur tracks. The switches were activated by the passing train.

Plastic Civil War Set

A 1959 vinyl plastic battery set was led by a large, Civil War era 49 locomotive with a funnel smokestack. The vinyl cars had four wheels and were about O27 size. This set was similar to one made by Ideal.

Gd Exc

490 Set

The 490 steam locomotive, used for years in electric and mechanical sets, appeared in battery sets in 1974. Set 2905, "THE RELIABLE", was one of the last sets manufactured. It pulled two Marx plastic, four-wheel freight cars.

A twin set 2915, "THE METEOR", also came out at this time. It had a diesel switcher and three plastic freight cars.

HO Size Hong Kong Set

In 1974 Marx offered a set produced in Hong Kong, similar in size to HO Gauge. It came with a 6914 steam locomotive, 0-6-0, and short, four-wheel freight cars which ran on plastic channel track. The black plastic locomotive dazzles with its red plastic sides and simulated crosshead action. It was powered by two size C self-contained batteries. The wheels were quasi-flanged to operate on a modified channel track. This may not have originally been a Marx locomotive. The picture in the Marx dealer's catalogue bore little resemblance to the actual train. A very similar locomotive made in Japan was imported with a set made of plastic and metal by the Center Import Company of Baltimore, Maryland. In fact, the Marx locomotive on the cover of the box for the Hong Kong 6914 set was a cross between the Marx and Center Import locomotive! The photographs on the Marx box also showed the Center Import track.

Others

Marx offered several other battery sets in 1974 and again in 1975, the last year of production. Three-rail electric sets were adapted to battery operation by providing a DC motor and attaching a battery box to the track. Battery sets available in the 1976 line were actually from previous production runs.

Train toys have been placed in alphabetical order in the following categories to enable the reader to readily locate an item.

Battery-Operated Trains

Channel Track Trains

Floor Trains

Floor Trains (Articulated)

Floor Trains (Rider-Type)

Floor Trains (Small)

Trolley and Handcars

NOTE: The following items are listed in numerical, then alphabetical order within each class.

Battery-Operated Trains

NOTE: Since most of the regular track-type battery-operated domestic locomotives were sold in sets which included American-made cars furnished in other mechanical and AC electrical sets, these cars are not

Gd Exc

relisted. The listing identifies domestic sets by locomotive only, while foreign-made sets do include car descriptions.

5 SET: O27 black plastic Civil War-type engine with funnel stack and gold trim; battery in engine; with two plastic four-wheel Marline "LOCAL" coaches.   8   15

5 SET: 1960, steam-type locomotive made in Hong Kong; small DC motor and interior battery; three lithographed cars connected at roof (same as 99), cars lithographed "MARVILLE LOCAL".
                                                                                                              8   15

49 SET: 1959, 9" black plastic 2-4-0 engine with funnel stack; Marline tender, yellow gondola, red bay window caboose; cars have four wheels; gray plastic 1-3/4" gauge track; dummy knuckle couplers.
                                                                                                             20   30

99 SET: 1957, steam-type locomotive made in Hong Kong; small DC motor and interior batteries; three short colorfully lithographed cars connected at rooftops (like old Flyer Zephyrs); each car with two wheels giving talgo action; lithographed "LUXURY LINES" and "MARX".   10   20

112 LOCOMOTIVE: 1974-75, 112-type diesel locomotive with small DC motor for use on regular three-rail track; exterior battery supply housed in plastic container with track connector.   10   15

198 SET: 1948, short red plastic locomotive with blue plastic tender and yellow plastic passenger cars; one-way semi-automatic couplers.
                                                                                                            150   200

490 LOCOMOTIVE: 1974-75, steam-type locomotive with small DC motor for use on regular three-rail track; exterior battery supply housed in plastic container with track connector.   5   8

2503 SET: 1974-75, black plastic locomotive, no number; small Japanese-made DC motor with interior metal side frames; control lever on top of boiler; Union Pacific 6" tender, 91257 Seaboard gondola, and 3824 Union Pacific caboose, all with plastic wheels; two-rail track with black ties.   8   10

2880 SET: Plastic red, black, or blue locomotive; "MUSICAL TUNE TOOTER"; plastic track with chimes for ties.   15   25

Sparkling Mountain Climber set with 408154 locomotive and 721 "Mountaineer" passenger car. L. Jensen Collection, G. Stern photograph.

Gd Exc

6203 SET: Plastic locomotive, 0-6-0; black metal tender; blue metal gondola; red metal caboose; cars with plastic frames; hook couplers; battery-powered with two C cells. **NRS**

6914 SET: 1974, steam locomotive, approximately HO size, made in Hong Kong; interior battery; set came with short, four-wheel freight cars designed to run in a channel track. Locomotive black plastic with red plastic side rods and crosshead guides. **5 10**

SET: 1948, red Mercury-type locomotive with DC motor for use on regular three-rail track; exterior, track-connected six-battery supply; with set of red articulated 657-type passenger cars. **100 150**

LOCOMOTIVE: 1940, Commodore Vanderbilt with DC motor for use on regular three-rail track; batteries in special metal lithographed box with control and track connector. Note: This was advertised by Sears as also operating from a 38 lb. 6-volt automobile battery, which was a dangerous option. **15 25**

LOCOMOTIVE: 1956, 590-type; black sheet steel body with plastic boiler front and interior batteries; small DC motor. **7 10**

GUIDE-A-TRAIN: 1958, plastic Civil War-type locomotive similar to William Crooks set made in Hong Kong; interior battery; short lithographed cars, "#2 D.R. & G." baggage and "#1 D.R. & G." coach. **30 50**

MARXTRONIC SET: 1959, black plastic industrial diesel switcher with two plastic gondolas (one yellow and one red); locomotive powered by interior battery. (Two versions made: one unscrews at the bottom to remove battery; the other has hood that slides off to remove battery.) **50 75**

Channel Track Trains

376 STEAM LOCOMOTIVE: 1940-47, 0-4-0 torpedo-type; 3-7/8" long, non-flanged floor wheels; upturned hook coupler.
(A) 1940, black wheels; blue-lithographed metal with red and gray stripes; engineer Donald Duck and other Disney motif for Mickey Mouse express; windup motor with start/stop lever. **35 50**

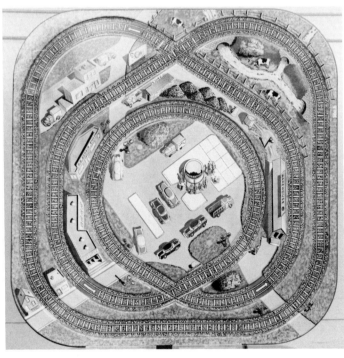

An example of the channel track platform. L. Jensen Collection, G. Stern photograph.

Gd Exc

(B) 1947, gray-lithographed metal with red stripe. **25 35**

557 CABOOSE: 1938-39, simulated cupola lithographed on top roof; design of lithography similar to New York Central 556 O Gauge caboose; non-flanged stamped-tin wheels; 4-3/4" long; upturned hook-coupler in front and loop coupler in rear; red-, black-, and white-lithographed metal. **35 40**

1914 GONDOLA: 1940, yellow interior; black and white frame with non-flanged stamped shiny tin wheels; 3" long; loop coupler in front and downturned hook coupler in rear.
(A) Blue-lithographed, Pluto and other Disney figures on sides. **20 30**
(B) Red-lithographed, Pluto and other Disney figures on sides. **20 30**
(C) 1947, "VIRGINIAN"; lithographed brown with white lettering. **12 15**

3462 TENDER: 1940, 1947, for 376 locomotive; 2" long, loop coupler in front and downturned hook coupler in rear.
(A) 1940, lithographed red with two Mickey Mouse figures on side, "DONALD DUCK RR"; non-flanged stamped shiny tin wheels. **25 35**
(B) 1947, lithographed gray with red stripe and "MARLINES"; non-flanged stamped-tin wheels. **12 15**

5151 MERCURY: 1938-39, 0-4-0 locomotive, 4-7/8" long; "5151" red-, black-, and white-lithographed metal.
(A) Flanged wheels; electric motor with automatic reverse and sparkler feature; stationary coupler loop. (Confirmation requested.) **NRS**
(B) Non-flanged stamped-tin wheels; electric motor with automatic reverse and sparkler feature; movable coupler loop; for use in channel track with third rail (insulated center strip). **50 55**
(C) Non-flanged stamped-tin wheels; electric motor with manual reverse; movable coupler loop; for use in channel track with third rail (insulated center strip). **50 55**

5151 "N.Y.C." TENDER: 1938-39, for 5151 Mercury locomotive; upturned hook coupler in front and loop coupler in rear; 4-3/4" long; red-, white-, and black-lithographed metal.
(A) Non-flanged stamped-tin wheels. **25 30**
(B) Flanged die-cast wheels. **NRS**

5153 "UTOPIA" PASSENGER COACH: 1938-39, for 5151 Mercury group, non-flanged stamped-tin wheels; 4-3/4" long; upturned hook coupler in front and loop coupler in rear; red- white- and black-lithographed metal. **30 40**

5159 "N.Y.C. OBSERVATION": 1938-39, for 5151 Mercury group, non-flanged stamped-tin wheels; 4-3/4" long; upturned hook coupler in front and loop coupler in rear, "N.Y.C. LINES"; rear drumhead; red-, white-, and black-lithographed metal; figure lithographed on rear platform. **30 40**

9049 BOXCAR: 1940, 1947, lithographed yellow with red roof; 3" long; loop coupler in front and downturned hook coupler in rear.
(A) 1940, Mickey Mouse figures on sides and roof; black and white frame with non-flanged shiny stamped-tin wheels; lithographed "MICKEY MOUSE EXPRESS". **25 35**
(B) 1947, "BUILT 1947" and "GREAT NORTHERN"; non-flanged stamped-tin wheels. **12 15**

9712 ERIE HOPPER: 1938-39, "COMFORT COAL CAR" lithographed with various rivet and structural detail; simulated open top also lithographed, design of lithography similar to 554 General Coal Co. O Gauge hopper; non-flanged stamped-tin wheels; 4-3/4" long; upturned hook coupler in front and loop coupler in rear; tan with black and white lithographed detail; red interior. **35 40**

408154 SET: Lithographed red and silver Hiawatha with passenger coach 721 "The Mountaineer"; clockwork with sparking mechanism; key insert on left. **20 30**

Gd Exc

BOXCAR: 1938-39, man lithographed in open door of car; design of lithography similar to 555 C & S O Gauge boxcar; non- flanged stamped-tin wheels, 4-3/4" long; upturned hook coupler in front and loop coupler in rear; white and blue with black- and red-lithographed detail.   35   40

CABOOSE: 1940-47, lithographed red sides with yellow roof; end platform and steps each end; loop front coupler.
(A) 1940, red cupola; Pinocchio and Jiminy Cricket in windows; non-flanged shiny stamped-tin wheels; 2-1/4" long.   25   35
(B) 1947, yellow windows, "MARLINES", "BUILT 6- 41"; non-flanged stamped-tin wheels; 2-1/2" long.   12   15

HIAWATHA: 1938-41, 0-4-0 locomotive; red-, black-, and white-lithographed metal; headlight formed from concave disk projecting above engine front.
(A) 1938, floor toy with Tricky Taxi-type windup motor.   20   30
(B) 1938-39, for use with "Scenic Mountain Railway" set on cog gear track; windup motor with sparkling smokestack feature.   20   30
(C) 1939-40, short frame; windup motor with floor wheels.   20   30
(D) 1941, long frame; motor fitted with die-cast wheels for channel track use.   20   30

PASSENGER COACH: 1938-41, for use with Hiawatha locomotives above; two doors and six windows each side with two people lithographed in each window and train man in doors; two windows each end; red- white- black- and light blue-lithographed metal; stamped-aluminum wheels; dog bone twist-lock coupling link.
                                                             20   30

SCENIC EXPRESS SET: On tin layout, includes 540 black plastic locomotive with attached metal-lithographed simulated "ERIE" tender, 22000 "N & W" hopper, 122390 "A.T. & S.F." boxcar, and 971620 "UNION PACIFIC" caboose.   40   60

SHUTTLIN' CHOO CHOO SET: On tin layout, includes 749 metal-lithographed locomotive and "Automatic LINES" red-lithographed boxcar. "SHUTTLE CHOO CHOO" is written on box. No couplers, locomotive pushes boxcar.   35   50

SPARKLING MOUNTAIN CLIMBER SET: Includes 408154 metal red- lithographed locomotive with sparking mechanism and 721 "Mountaineer" red-lithographed passenger car; channel track sections including sloping cogged section for engine to ride up.
                                                             50   75

UNION STATION SET: On tin layout, includes 540 black plastic locomotive with attached metal lithographed 1243 "ERIE" mail car and 1243 "SILVER DAWN" passenger car.   NRS

Floor Trains

2552 MARLINES: Late 1950s to mid-1960s, 2-8-2 large "FIX ALL" plastic scale locomotive, 14" long, 4-1/4" high, 3-1/4" wide, 1- 1/2" gauge; snap-together construction; all-black except gold drive wheels.
                                                             25   50

M10003: 1936, O27 diesel streamliner passenger train; one-piece construction consisting of locomotive, diner, and coach tail car; orange- and yellow-lithographed metal with windup spring motor as used in Marx tanks.   65   95

LOCOMOTIVE: 1939-41, 1947-49, 0-4-2 with tender attached; Commodore Vanderbilt tender and locomotive with one-piece sheet steel construction; blue- or red-enameled; wooden floor toy wheels.
(A) 1941, "LUMAR LINES" stamped on tender.   10   20
(B) 1947, "ALL AMERICAN" decal scroll on tender.
                                                             10   20
(C) 1940-41, olive drab enameled; with ringing bell.   15   35
(D) Pink-enameled; black lettering.   15   35

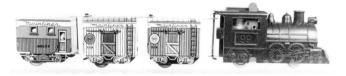

Battery-powered articulated floor train, the "Mainliner". L. Jensen Collection, G. Stern photograph.

Gd Exc

LUMAR LINES CABOOSE: 1940-41, sheet steel construction, with red enamel; wooden floor toy wheels, "PENNSYLVANIA" logo printed on sides.
(A) Black frame.   10   20
(B) Silver frame.   10   20
(C) Yellow frame.   10   20

LUMAR LINES CANNON CAR: 1940-41, sheet steel frame; lithographed cannon with lithographed detail on cannon breech block; olive drab enameled frame; wooden floor toy wheels.   15   35

LUMAR LINES FLOODLIGHT CAR: 1940-41, sheet steel frame; lithographed searchlight with yellow-lithographed detail on light; olive drab enameled frame; wooden floor toy wheels.   15   35

LUMAR LINES GONDOLA: 1939-41, 1947-49, sheet steel construction; high-sided with open truss-rod frame; wooden floor toy wheels; long rectangular slide couplers with down-turned hook; .
(A) 1939-41, white-enameled, printed "PENNSYLVANIA" logo, silver frame; wooden floor toy wheels; long rectangular slide slot couplers with down-turned hook.   12   20
(B) Same as (A), but green-enameled; numbered "2785".   10   15
(C) Same as (A), but blue-enameled; numbered "2785".   10   15
(D) 1947-49, same as (A), but with "FRIENDSHIP" decal on scroll.
                                                             12   20
(E) 1939-41, blue-enamel, printed "PENNSYLVANIA" logo, black frame.   12   20
(F) 1947-49, same as (E), but with "FRIENDSHIP" decal on scroll.
                                                             12   20
(G) 1940-41, supplied with load of wooden shells in cardboard insert; olive drab enameled.   15   40
(H) Pink-enameled.   15   40
(I) White car with silver base; printed "NEW YORK CENTRAL"; "4522".   15   40

LUMAR LINES PASSENGER COACH: 1940-41, sheet steel construction with red enamel and with black or silver frame; wooden floor toy wheels; "PENNSYLVANIA" logo printed on sides.   10   20

Original box from Ride 'er Locomotive, the "PIONEER EXPRESS". B. Allan Collection, G. Stern photograph.

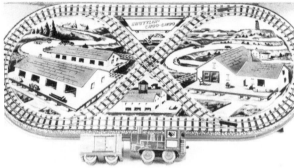

Shuttlin' Choo Choo Train set which included the track layout, the 749 engine and the red "Automatic LINE" boxcar. Note the name on the lithographed box is "Shuttle Choo Choo". B. Allan Collection, G. Stern photograph.

	Gd	Exc

STANDARD GAUGE GONDOLA: Mid-1930s, four-piece sheet steel construction; light green enamel; four flanged tin-plated wheels; Joy Line couplers. — 10 15

STANDARD GAUGE PASSENGER COACH: Mid-1930s, four-piece sheet steel construction with red enamel; four flanged tin-plated wheels; Joy Line couplers. — 15 30

STANDARD GAUGE SET: 13" red steam locomotive with black drivers; 10" red tender; 13-1/2" red coach with black roof; 13-3/4" red gondola, heavy pressed steel; with railing details; Joy Line construction. — NRS

STANDARD GAUGE STEAM LOCOMOTIVE: Mid-1930s, 0-4-0, sheet steel construction, red-enameled; flanged tin-plated wheels.
(A) Battery-operated light. — 25 30
(B) Dummy copper headlight fitting. — 15 25

STANDARD GAUGE TENDER: Mid-1930s, for above locomotive, sheet steel construction, black-enameled; four flanged tinplate wheels; Joy Line couplers. — 10 18

STEAM LOCOMOTIVE AND TENDER: 9" locomotive and 6" tender. — NRS

Floor Trains (Articulated)

WINDUP SET: Plastic locomotive and three lithographed metal coaches.
(A) "JETSON". — 25 40
(B) "FLINTSTONE". — 25 35
(C) "DODGE CITY EXPRESS". — 15 25
(D) "COCOA PUFFS". — 25 40
(E) "MICKEY MOUSE". — NRS
(F) "CASEY JR. DISNEYLAND EXPRESS", black or green locomotive. — 15 25
(G) "CHOO-CHOO TRAIN". — 15 25

	Gd	Exc

(H) "SUPERHERO EXPRESS". — NRS
(I) "DISNEYLAND". — 20 35
(J) "CRAZY EXPRESS". — 20 30

BATTERY-POWERED SET: Black plastic 99 locomotive with lithographed metal coaches.
(A) "D-1 EXPRESS", with two coaches. — NRS
(B) "CRAZY EXPRESS", with four coaches. — 20 30
(C) "MAINLINER", with three coaches. — 20 30

Floor Trains (Rider-Type)

99 LOCOMOTIVE: 1976, black plastic one-piece riding engine and tender (Maggiore). — NRS

333 LOCOMOTIVE: 1974, plastic one-piece riding engine and tender with whistle.
(A) Red. — 2 4
(B) Black. — 2 4

3000 RIDE 'ER: 1939-41, one-piece riding torpedo-type steam locomotive and tender, 27-1/2" long, steel construction with large steel wheels; one-piece steering handle at front; cab roof acts as child's seat.
(A) Red-enameled body. — 50 100
(B) Gray-enameled body; "LIGHTNING EXPRESS" on lithographed sideboards. — NRS
(C) Red-enameled body with Commodore Vanderbilt front; "PIONEER EXPRESS"; no embossed number, name on sides of attached tender. — NRS
(D) Same as (C), black-enameled body. — NRS

LM-22000 GONDOLA: Gray; 19-1/2" long; "MARLINES". — 40 90

"BESSEMER & LAKE ERIE" GONDOLA: 1941, large, 19-1/2" long, steel construction with wooden wheels; long rectangular slide slot couplers; red enamel with black rubber-stamped lettering. (For use with 3000 RIDE 'ER locomotive.) — 90 125

"WHEELING & LAKE ERIE" GONDOLA: 1941, large, 19-1/2" long, steel construction with wooden wheels; long rectangular slide slot couplers; black rubber-stamped lettering. (For use with 3000 RIDE 'ER locomotive.)
(A) Red-enameled body. — 90 125
(B) Blue-enameled body. — 90 125

Floor Trains (Small)

44 SUPER CHIEF: Streamlined lithographed gray and white single-unit locomotive and tender with single axles; windup motor in tender with key on lower right side. — 10 15

93 LUMAR LINES: Streamlined single-unit locomotive and tender; lithographed in black with blue, white, and yellow details; sparkler feature and friction motor; two large rubber wheels and two wooden wheels of the same size on tender. — 5 10

242 LOCOMOTIVE: Black plastic 4-4-2 engine with "SPARKLING FRICTION RR" on attached tender; 10" long; to be pushed for flywheel action. — 5 10

2004-98 SET: One-piece plastic locomotive, tender, boxcar, and caboose. Windup black locomotive and tender; silver-painted boxcar; red-painted caboose. The train runs on a circle of conventional two-rail mechanical track about HO size. — NRS

5400 LOCOMOTIVE: Yellow plastic locomotive and red tender. Tender pulls out to make engine run across floor. — NRS

HO SIZE SET: Small yellow, red, pink, or blue HO size locomotive with coal bunker; three blue-, red-, or yellow-painted stamped-steel gondolas.
(A) Locomotive. — 15 20

	Gd	Exc
(B) Gondola.	10	15

"M10000" LOCOMOTIVE: Mid-1930s, diesel streamlined for three-unit articulated train, "UNION PACIFIC"; power car approximately 3" long; four wheels; both windup and non-powered versions; lithographed.

	Gd	Exc
(A) Tan and yellow.	20	30
(B) Tan and cream.	20	30

M10000 "COACH": Mid-1930s, articulated two-wheel for Union Pacific M10000 above; lithographed tan and yellow.

	Gd	Exc
(A) Tan and yellow.	15	20
(B) Tan and cream.	15	20

M10000 "COACH/BUFFET": Mid-1930s, articulated two-wheel for Union Pacific M10000 above; lithographed tan and yellow.

	Gd	Exc
(A) Tan and yellow.	15	20
(B) Tan and cream.	15	20

"SILVER STREAK" LOCOMOTIVE: Mid-1930s, M10000-type streamlined diesel in silver with black lettering; about 6" long; wooden wheels; "MADE IN USA".

	15	20

"SILVER STREAK" COACH: Mid-1930s, silver; wooden wheels; about 6" long; for use with Silver Streak locomotive.

	15	20

"SILVER STREAK" OBSERVATION: Mid-1930s, silver; wooden wheels; about 6" long; for use with Silver Streak locomotive.

	15	20

Trolley and Handcars

200 TROLLEY: Mid-1920s to mid-1930s, streetcar; for mechanical track or floor toy operation; lithographed in multiple colors, white, red, and spring green, to achieve detail, "12TH ST.", "200 / RAPID TRANSIT / CO" on sides; spring motor with bell.

	Gd	Exc
(A) Non-illuminated.	250	350
(B) Battery-operated headlight.	275	375
(C) Headlight; switch in center of roof; tinplate cowcatcher.	300	400

2002 HANDCAR: 1954-74; electric motor; flanged wheels for three-rail use; two railroad men; plastic frame; metal construction.

	Gd	Exc
(A) 1954-56, one blue man and one gray man; red plastic frame and metal construction.	25	50

	Gd	Exc
(B) 1956-74, one blue man and one gray man; brown plastic frame and metal construction.	20	40
(C) Two yellow men; red plastic frame.	40	65

BARNEY RUBBLE & FRED FLINTSTONE HANDCAR: 1964, windup motor with flangeless floor toy wheels; plastic frame and metal construction.

	35	50

EASTER BUNNY HANDCAR: Early 1930s, printed cardboard bunny and basket; pink frame; flanged O Gauge wheels.

	250	350

GIRARD HANDCAR: Circa 1933-35, two workman figures; light frame and lithographed metal; flangeless floor toy wheels; windup motor.

(A) Shiny nickel frame.	175	250
(B) Brown frame.	175	250

MICKEY MOUSE & DONALD DUCK HANDCAR: 1962-64, plastic frame and metal construction; for platform railway.

(A) 1962, electric motor with flanged wheels for three-rail use.

	20	35

(B) 1964, windup motor with flangeless wheels; yellow plastic.

	20	35

(C) Catalogue number 2008MO, yellow plastic; "TOOLS" embossed on side; plastic wheels; windup motor.

	20	35

MOON MULLINS & KAYO HANDCAR: Windup; metal.

(A) Mid-1920s to mid-1930s, lightweight black frame; Kayo on dynamite box; cheap coil spring motor; flanged O Gauge wheels.

	90	150

(B) Mid-1930s, heavy yellow underframe; Kayo on dynamite box; better windup motor; flanged O Gauge wheels. | 90 | 150 |

(C) Mid-1930s, heavy yellow underframe; Kayo on raised platform; better windup motor; flangeless floor toy wheels. | 70 | 125 |

(D) Yellow handle and base; Kayo on red box; on/off switch; Joy Line windup motor. | 70 | 125 |

POPEYE & OLIVE OYL HANDCAR: Circa 1935-38, heavy underframe; lithographed metal windup motor; rubber figures. Note: The hollow rubber figures usually collapsed and fell off leaving only Olive's shoes. It is extremely difficult to find this handcar with the figures intact.

(A) Larger tin wheels for O Gauge.	200	300
(B) Flangeless tin floor toy wheels.	225	325

Chapter VII

HO Trains and Accessories

by Keith Wills

A portion of this text has been taken from the April 1989 edition of Railroad Model Craftsman with the consent of Carstens Publications.

In the middle of the late 1950s, O Gauge tinplate began to experience a decline. HO maufacturers, sensing a vacuum, started to get into the boxed train set business, offering sectional track, transformer, locomotive and consist, and in some cases, action cars and accessories as play value. They were clearly aimed at children. Varney, Mantua, Athearn, Revell, Herkimer, Atlas, Penn Line and John English, to name some, offered what had previously been the purview of O Gauge tinplate manufacturers. Scale modelers were aghast at this prospect, noting some of the sets had deeper flanges than NMRA norms. Ideal Models, Revell, Ulrich and others made operating accessories. such as crossing guards and coal ramps, in the best Lionel tradition.

Having gained respectability, it seemed HO was going the route of Lionel and American Flyer, particularly since set manufacturers adopted the horn-hook X2f coupler, devised by an NMRA committee, as standard. Would the NMRA then have to establish new standards for HO tinplate? Purists shuddered at the thought after *Model Railroader* seriously raised such a question editorially as perhaps the best solution to the problem.

Other aspects of HO scale modeling were equally upsetting. The small spaghetti-bowl layouts of the era with the tightest of radii led in turn to the "shorty" passenger car. They were slashed to a mere scale 60 feet at a time when the prototype's norm was 72 to 80 feet. Manufacturers deemed these compromises necessary if an HO modeler wanted passenger trains on these tiny layouts and, besides, they sold well.

Another company made liveries the prototype never had. Penn Line made GG-1s in B & O and New Haven-McGinnis red, white and black schemes. This did prompt complaining letters in the hobby press, but they didn't deter the company one bit. If that wasn't bad enough, consider that within a few months of each other, two companies known for toy trains, Marx and Lionel, entered the HO market.

After months of speculation in the press, Marx introduced its new HO line in time for Christmas 1957. Sears showed three sets, one with a smoking die-cast NYC Hudson and the other two pulled by an F-7 Santa Fe unit. At first glance they appeared quite reasonable enough (the illustrations were small) and catalogue copy said they had NMRA horn-hook couplers, nylon trucks and were compatible with other HO equipment. Made in Hong Kong, upon closer inspection they lacked that hard edge of reality. The F-units were ill proportioned, particularly in the cab area. Droopy windshields gave them a sad, beagle-eyed look. The freight cars were equally off, for the boxcar roofs looked a bit too peaked and other details seemed not quite on the mark.

The Hudson had a heavy metal casting for the boiler and cab but was missing a lot of surface detail compared to A. C. Gilbert's more refined version. Oversize drive rods and simplified valve gear were other shortcomings.

Catalogue illustrations show the tender rode on Blomberg diesel electric trucks, rather than the correct six-wheeled Commonwealth types of the prototype. To give the tender proper visual bulk under it, Marx resorted to using dummy trucks from the F-units, which caused the tender to ride too high over the rails.

By 1958, a Geep, which suffered from an equal lack of attention to detail, was added. It had an oversimplified frame and railings and rode on the shallow and coarse Blombergs. An industrial diesel switcher was added in 1959, along with a steam 0-4-0T shunter in 1960. The shell casting of the latter was reasonable, but the drivers lacked connecting rods and had one main rod from the rear set, in the best Marx Commodore Vanderbilt tradition, which slid into a slot in the steam chest.

Action freight cars were miniature versions of the O Gauge line.

Sears sold better Marx HO outfits with flocked plastic landscaped bases and, for several years, it offered a combined railroad/slotcar road race set, reflecting the conflict going on between the two hobby interests.

But Marx was making toy trains, not scale models, geared to children and not their parents. To illustrate this point more clearly, note that Marx applied to the NMRA to change the wheel standards to allow for a .045" deep flange, rather than the approved .035" flange. Marx saw the deeper one as better suited for children, who could be expected to run their trains at top speed, hoping the trains would stay on the rails better.

The NMRA refused the request, but the fact that Marx raised it created fears among scale modelers that HO would at last become a toy train gauge. To its credit, the association did test deeper flanges and concluded that the depth of the flange was not important for tracking, but its shape was — even if it was .025" or less. In a sense, Marx's request can be said to have started research towards the RP25 contour scale wheels we have today.

Marx last catalogued HO sets in 1967, when Sears showed them in contrast with another HO line it started to carry. Tyco was to replace Marx and was more scale-like in appearance, although in some eyes it was equally tinplate, if of a higher degree.

The Marx line was not extensive and changes were made by altering liveries. One Geep was the ugliest ever produced, so mishandled was its Monon paint scheme. At best, the Marx line might have been considered an introduction to HO but geared for children. In its truest sense, it was pure tinplate, and today it has become a collector's oddity.

Marx HO trains can be roughly divided into two major groupings. The first were *scale-like trains* which reasonably approximated NMRA standards. The second were more *toy-like* with less adherence to scale criteria. Some cars appeared in both groups, while others remained unique to one group.

The toy-like group was characterized by larger wheel flanges and large dummy knuckle couplers. Examples of each group follows:

Scale-Like

HO Work Train Set 74642/1.

Western Pacific F-7 diesel A unit.
Western Pacific F-7 diesel B unit.
SFRD 3281 yellow boxcar.
Western Maryland 54201 red gondola.
Rocket Fuel X-415 white tanker.
Western Pacific 645 bay window caboose.

HO Train Set 79537

ASTF 4-6-4, 6096 Hudson locomotive.
ASTF 3281 green boxcar.
Rocket Fuel X-415 red / yellow tank car.
ATSF yellow caboose.

Toy-Like

Battery Train Set 6875

0-4-0 steam locomotive.
NYC tender.
Western Maryland gondola.
NYC caboose.

999 0-4-0 locomotive.

20295 NYC cupola caboose.

20295 no name caboose.

A listing of Marx HO locomotives, cars and accessories follows.

HO Locomotives

	Gd	Exc

10 SWITCHER: 1958, industrial diesel switcher, catalogue number 6910/1.

	Gd	Exc
(A) Blue.	8	12
(B) Green with yellow and silver trim.	10	18

20 STEAM SWITCHER: 1960, 1962, 1965, 1971, 1974, 0-4-0T wheel arrangement; with eight-wheel tender, catalogue number 6910.

	Gd	Exc
(A) "A.T. & S. F.", "SANTA FE" on tender.	8	12
(B) 1960, "NYC RR".	8	12
(C) 1962, 1965, "NEW YORK CENTRAL SYSTEM".	8	12
(D) 1962, "NEW HAVEN".	8	12
(E) 1971, no road name or number.	8	12

21 GP-7 DIESEL: 1958, 1960; "MONON"; with headlight; red and gray body; black lettering; catalogue number 6932; NMRA-type couplers.   15   30

25 F-7 DIESEL: 1971, F-7 diesel, "SANTA FE", "6956"; silver, red, yellow.

	Gd	Exc
(A) Powered A unit.	10	20
(B) Dummy A unit.	8	15
(C) Dummy B unit.	8	15

38 F-7 DIESEL: 1962, "NEW HAVEN"; orange, black, and white; catalogue number 6955.

	Gd	Exc
(A) Powered A unit with headlight.	10	25

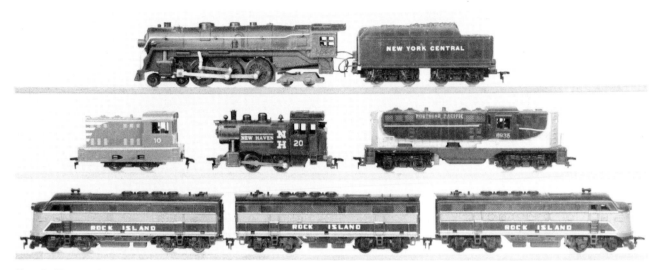

Top shelf: 6069 black locomotive with "NEW YORK CENTRAL" tender. *Middle shelf:* 10 blue switcher; 20 "NEW HAVEN" black switcher with orange lettering; 6935 GP-7 "NORTHERN PACIFIC" diesel, black with gold ends. *Bottom shelf:* 99 "ROCK ISLAND" ABA set. R. Burgio Collection, B. Greenberg photograph.

	Gd	Exc
(B) Dummy A unit.	8	20
(C) Dummy B unit.	8	20

99 F-7 DIESEL: 1959-60, F-7 diesel, "ROCK ISLAND", powered A unit and non-powered B unit; black with red striping; white lettering; number "99" on A unit, no number on B unit; catalogue number 6953, 6953B, or 6953D; NMRA-type couplers.

| (A) 1959, powered A and dummy B units. | 15 | 25 |
| (B) 1960, dummy A unit. | 10 | 15 |

358 F-7 DIESEL: 1958, "WESTERN PACIFIC", powered A unit with light and non-lighted B unit; green, yellow, and red; catalogue number 6942; NMRA-type couplers. — 25 — 35

358 SWITCHER: 1958, green "WESTERN PACIFIC". — 10 — 15

370 F-7 DIESEL: 1962, "NEW HAVEN"; dummy A unit; orange, black, and white; catalogue number 6955.

(A) Powered A unit.	10	15
(B) Dummy B unit.	7	10
(C) Dummy A unit.	7	10

934 GP-7 DIESEL: 1958, "A.T. & S.F."; yellow and gray; red lettering; catalogue number 6934; NMRA-type couplers. — 12 — 20

999 STEAM LOCOMOTIVE: "NYC"; 0-4-0; black; made in Hong Kong. — NRS — NRS

1621 SWITCHER: 1963, "NEW HAVEN"; NMRA-type couplers.

| (A) Black, white, and orange body. | 8 | 12 |
| (B) Black body, orange lettering. | 8 | 12 |

1962 SWITCHER: 1962, "ROCK ISLAND". — 8 — 12

4000 F-7 DIESEL: 1958, "NEW YORK CENTRAL", powered A unit with light and non-lighted B unit, catalogue number 6941.

(A) Orange body; black lettering.	50	75
(B) Black body; white lettering.	20	30
(C) 1958, dummy A unit.	7	10

4938 GP-7 DIESEL: 1962, black and gold, "NORTHERN PACIFIC". — 15 — 25

5772 GP-7 DIESEL: 1962, "NEW YORK CENTRAL", without headlight and handrails, one truck drive; black and white. — 15 — 25

6096 HUDSON: 1957, 1962, 1971, 4-6-4 steam locomotive; die-cast body; plastic wheels; puffing smoke; with 6151 eight-wheel plastic tender; with or without white stripe on engine and tender.

| (A) 1971, no road name. | 20 | 35 |

	Gd	Exc
(B) 1962, "NEW YORK CENTRAL"; with removable boiler front; lighted; two-piece drawbar.	20	35
(C) "NEW YORK CENTRAL"; one-piece drawbar; non- removable boiler front with dummy headlight; not lighted.	20	35
(D) 1957, 1973 "SANTA FE".	25	40

6935 GP-7 DIESEL: 1960, 1962.

(A) 1960, "NEW YORK CENTRAL", with headlight.	15	25
(B) 1962, "NEW YORK CENTRAL", without headlight and hand- rails, one truck drive.	15	25
(C) 1962, "NORTHERN PACIFIC".	15	25

F-7 DIESEL: "UNION PACIFIC"; orange body, black lettering; NMRA-type couplers.

| (A) Powered A unit. | 15 | 25 |
| (B) Powered B unit. | 15 | 25 |

ROLLING STOCK
Boxcars

3281 SANTA FE: 1960, "BLT 2-60".

| (A) 1960, orange body; black lettering. | 3 | 5 |
| (B) 1973, bright green; white lettering. | 4 | 8 |

6147 EXPRESS: 1971. — 2 — 4

6165 REFRIGERATOR: 1971. — 2 — 4

6195 AUTOMATIC: 1971. — 3 — 5

7210 RAILWAY EXPRESS AGENCY: 1959, green body; sliding doors; yellow and white lettering. — 10 — 20

11874 GREAT NORTHERN: 1958, green body; sliding doors; white lettering; catalogue number 6155-1. — 4 — 6

40397 NEW HAVEN: 1958, 1971, black and white body; sliding doors; white lettering; red and white "NH" logo on sides, catalogue number 6155-3. — 4 — 6

77000 BOSTON & MAINE: 1958, blue body; black sliding doors; black and white lettering; catalogue number 6155-4. — 4 — 6

104436 UNION PACIFIC: 1957, sliding doors; catalogue number 6155.

| (A) Dark red body; white lettering. | 4 | 6 |
| (B) Tuscan brown body. | 3 | 5 |

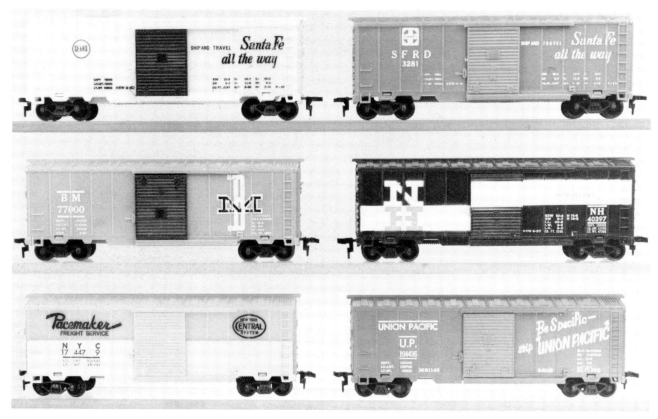

Six HO boxcars. *Top shelf:* Sears orange boxcar with black door; 3281 green "S F R D". *Middle shelf:* 77000 blue "B M"; 40397 black "NEW HAVEN". *Bottom shelf:* 174479 red and gray "N Y C"; 104436 tuscan brown "UNION PACIFIC". R. Burgio Collection, B. Greenberg photograph.

	Gd	Exc

144479 NEW YORK CENTRAL: Red and gray body; black lettering.   4   6

174479 NEW YORK CENTRAL: Red and gray body; "Pacemaker FREIGHT SERVICE".   5   8

174853 NEW YORK CENTRAL: 1958, sliding doors; tuscan body; yellow lettering; catalogue number 6155-2.   5   10

NORTHERN PACIFIC: Blue body; black sliding doors; "FAST FREIGHT"; dummy knuckle couplers.   5   8

SANTA FE: 1960, orange body; sliding black doors; "SEARS" in circle on left (sold in Allstate "Blister" package and also sold in sets).   3   5

Cabooses

C630 NEW HAVEN: Red body; bay window (year not known).   4   6

645 WESTERN PACIFIC: 1959, green body; bay window; yellow lettering.   5   8

646 WESTERN PACIFIC: Green body; cupola; roof antenna; yellow lettering.   6   10

1959 ROCK ISLAND: Bay window; tuscan brown.   4   6

1961 ROCK ISLAND: 1962, ; black cupola; radio antenna.
(A) Red and black body.   5   10
(B) Yellow and gray body.   5   10

2226 SANTA FE: 1958, 1962, 1973, bay window, catalogue number 6196-1.
(A) 1958, "RADIO EQUIPPED" logo.   3   5
(B) 1962, red body; white lettering.   3   5

	Gd	Exc

(C) 1973, smokestack, yellow with black lettering.   3   5

C3008 A.T. & S.F.: Red.   10   20

3903 UNION PACIFIC: 1962, tuscan brown body; bay window; white lettering.   3   5

6196 NEW YORK CENTRAL: 1957, bay window; "RADIO EQUIPPED" logo.   3   5

20295 NEW YORK CENTRAL: 1963, red body; silver cupola; black roof; radio antenna.   6   10

20298 NEW YORK CENTRAL: 1962, bay window.
(A) Tuscan body; white lettering.   5   8
(B) Green body; yellow lettering.   5   8

A.T. & S.F.: 1962, with cupola.   2   4

NEW HAVEN: 1962, cupola; radio antenna; ladders and smokestack; red, white and black body; white lettering.   3   5

NEW HAVEN: Black, orange and white body; black cupola; radio antenna.   5   8

NEW YORK CENTRAL: Tuscan brown body.   3   5

NO NAME: Red body; cupola.   3   5

VALLEY EXPRESS: Red body; black cupola; black chimney; made in Hong Kong.   3   5

Cranes

NEW YORK CENTRAL: 1960, black body; white lettering; operating crane car; crane cab traverses in circle; Brownhoist boom raised and lowered manually.   8   12

Top shelf: Black NYC crane. *Middle shelf:* Two bay window cabooses. C-630 tuscan brown "NH"; 20298 tuscan brown "NYC". *Bottom shelf:* Two cupola cabooses. 20295 red NYC with silver cupola, black roof, and knuckle couplers; "NH" black, orange, and white. R. Burgio Collection, B. Greenberg photograph.

Flatcars

Gd Exc

128 WESTINGHOUSE: 1959, depressed-center; two gray searchlights; white lettering; NMRA-type couplers.
(A) Gray generator unit; black body.   8   15
(B) Blue body; black generator unit.   8   15

161 SEARCHLIGHT: 1958, 1959 and 1971; NMRA-type couplers.
(A) 1958 and 1971, Erie depressed-center.   8   15
(B) 1959, "G.E.X."; depressed-center; black body; white lettering; gray searchlight.   8   15

X-1960 ATOMIC ROCKET LAUNCHER: With controls.
                                                        40   60

6028 ERIE: 1957, 1960, tuscan body; white lettering.
(A) Black body; simulated wood cradle for boat load.   15   30
(B) 1957, with two automobiles.   10   20
(C) 1960, double-decker automobile carrier with four automobiles, maroon base, gray automobile rack.   10   20
(D) Log load.   10   20
(E) Tractor and trailer load.   10   20

6118 WESTINGHOUSE: 1959, 1971, depressed-center flatcar with generator.   5   10

6128 ERIE: 1958, 1971, side rails.   3   5

6129 AUTOMOBILE: 1971, two automobiles.   6   12

6130 FLATCAR: 1958, 1959 and 1971.

Gd Exc

(A) 1958 and 1971, maroon body; white lettering; "IHCX"; two gray bulldozers.   10   20
(B) Same as (A), but two metal yellow and red bulldozers. 10 20
(C) 1959, tuscan body; white lettering; six wood planks lumber load.
                                                         3   6

6138 WELL-TYPE: 1971.   2   3

6145 PIGGYBACK: 1971.   10   20

6160 IHCX: 1958, two bulldozers, "4139".   10   20

6166 ERIE: 1958, 1971, depressed-center; two cable reels. 8 15

6181 SEARCHLIGHT: 1971, twin searchlights.   8   15

6183 ERIE: 1958, depressed-center; two cable reels. 10   20

6185 AUTOMOBILE: 1971, four automobiles.   15   30

6194 WFLX: 1958, tuscan body; white lettering; automatic unloading flatcar with five logs and bin.   35   50

7210 ERIE: 1957, depressed-center die-cast flatcar, NMRA-type couplers.
(A) Black body; white lettering.   5   7
(B) Maroon body; white lettering "BLT 9-57".   5   7
(C) Same as (B), with two brown plastic reels.   5   7
(D) Yellow body; two gray plastic reels.   5   7

10049 LEHIGH VALLEY: 1958, 1962, 1971, side railings; flat lumber; NMRA-type couplers.
(A) Black body; orange lettering.   3   5

Top shelf: 54201 red "WESTERN MARYLAND" gondola; 70018 red "WESTERN MARYLAND" hopper. *Middle shelf:* 36000 blue "CHESAPEAKE & OHIO" gondola; 28233 brown "VIRGINIAN" hopper. *Bottom shelf:* 160149 gray "SOUTHERN PACIFIC" gondola; 109 blue "LEHIGH PORTLAND CEMENT" hopper. R. Burgio Collection, B. Greenberg photograph.

	Gd	Exc
(B) Green body; white lettering.	3	5

NEW YORK CENTRAL: 1958, black NYC flatcar with side rails and hoist derrick. — 10 20

Gondolas

36000 C & O: 1957, 1958, 1971, black body; white lettering; catalogue number 6152. — 2 4
(A) Dark blue body. — 2 4
(B) 1957, light blue body; white lettering. — 2 4
(C) 1958, red body; white lettering. — 2 4
(D) 1971, red body; white lettering. — 2 4

54201 WESTERN MARYLAND: 1958, "FAST FREIGHT"; coal load.
(A) Gray body; black lettering. — 2 4
(B) Red and white body; black interior. — 2 4

160149 SOUTHERN PACIFIC: 1958.
(A) Gray body; black lettering. — 2 4
(B) Dark brown body. — 2 4

WESTERN MARYLAND: Gray; "FAST FREIGHT".
(A) Western Maryland circle herald in second panel from left. — 5 8
(B) Western Maryland circle herald in third panel from left. — 5 8

Hoppers

	Gd	Exc

6154 HOPPER: 1971, (road name not known). — 2 3

25000 LEHIGH VALLEY: 1957, coal load; black body; orange lettering; catalogue number 6154. — 4 5

28233 VIRGINIA: 1958, coal load; brown body; white lettering; catalogue number 6154-1. — 3 5

70018 WESTERN MARYLAND: 1958, catalogue number 6154.
(A) With coal load, black with white lettering. — 3 5
(B) Same as (A), but red body. — 3 5
(C) Open, red body; white lettering. — 3 5

47 HUCX: "HURON PORTLAND CEMENT"; red covered hopper, white lettering. — 5 7

109 LPCX: "LEHIGH PORTLAND CEMENT".
(A) 1960, gray body; black lettering. — 3 4
(B) 1961, blue body; white lettering. — 4 6

Passenger Cars

30246 "SANTA FE": 1958, combination baggage/passenger car; interior lights. — 25 35

71875 "SANTA FE": 1958, passenger coach; interior lights. — 25 35

80971 "SANTA FE": 1958, observation car; interior lights. — 25 35

Six HO flatcars. *Top shelf*: Two 7210 "ERIE" drop centers. Yellow with two brown cables; black with boat load. *Middle shelf*: 6194 tuscan brown "W.F.L.X." with log load; 6028 maroon "ERIE" with automobile load consisting of two plastic late model Cadillacs. *Bottom shelf*: 6130 maroon "I.H.C.X." with bulldozer load; 161 black "G.E.X." with searchlight. R. Burgio Collection, B. Greenberg photograph.

Tank Cars

	Gd	Exc
X-415 U.S.A.F.: 1962, 1971, fuel tank car, U.S.A.F. star insignia, "HYDROCARBON ROCKET FUEL".	3	5
(A) White tank, black base; red lettering.	3	5
(B) White tank, blue base; red lettering.	4	8
(C) Beige tank, black base; red lettering.	7	12
(D) Red tank, yellow base; white lettering.	7	12
2645 CITIES SERVICE: Green, long single tank.	6	12
3827 SINCLAIR: 1958, green tank; catalogue number 6153-1.	7	12
6143 CITIES SERVICE: 1958, 1971, maroon base; two green tanks.	15	25
(6153) ALLSTATE: 1957, 1958, 1971; "ALLSTATE MOTOR OIL".		
(A) 1958, dark blue body; white lettering.	3	5
(B) 1959, light blue body; white lettering.	3	5
78450 HOOKER: Silver and black.	7	15

Work Cabooses

	Gd	Exc
320 MONON: 1959, gray hoist derrick; white lettering.		
(A) Tuscan body.	5	8
(B) Red body.	5	8
645 NEW HAVEN: Tuscan body; white lettering; tan tank.	5	8
6186-2 WESTERN PACIFIC: 1958.	2	5
1958 A.T. & S.F.: 1958, tuscan brown, short gray tank.	2	5
(6190) SANTA FE: 1958, short tank.	2	5
61962 NORTHERN PACIFIC: 1962, tuscan body; short gray tank at end.	4	6
90798 ROCK ISLAND: 1960, tuscan body; toolboxes at end; white lettering.	5	8

	Gd	Exc
499898 NEW YORK CENTRAL: 1971, with toolboxes.		
(A) 1958, red body; catalogue number 6186-1.	3	5
(B) 1971, tuscan body; white lettering; catalogue number 6180.	3	5
(C) Tuscan body; white lettering; gray hoist derrick.	2	5

ACCESSORIES

	Gd	Exc
6000: 1958, uncoupler; track lock-on double terminal.	.50	1
6001S, 6002C: 1957-65, track with hollow steel rail; plastic or fiber ties.	.05	.10
6003: Set of track adapters; each section 3-7/8" long; black plastic ties.	1	2
6007: 1959, crossing; electrical; 90 degrees.	.25	.50
6010: 1958, switchers; pair; electrical, manual.	1	2
6015: 1959, illuminated dead-end bumper.	6	10
6020: 1958, flashing billboard.	3	5
6020AS: Allstate "Powerpack", 18 DC.	2	4
6021: 1958, warning accessory.	3	5
6024: 1957, uncoupling/re-railer.	.50	1
6026: 1971, flashing billboard (set of two in bubble pack); plastic frame with following inserts: "HALO SHAMPOO", "CITIES SERVICE", and "COLGATE TOOTHPASTE"; 3-1/4" wide, 2" high.	5	10
6030: 1958, uncoupler, motor raceway grade crossing.	.10	.25
6030: Transformer, 1.5 amps, 4-18 DC, 18 F.V.		
(A) 1959, "HO Powerpack", AC.	2	5
(B) "HO-Power Pack", DC.	2	5
6040: 1958, switches, pair, electrical, remote.	3	5
6061: 1968, 1971, telephone poles. (Price for each.)	.10	.25

Top shelf: 6143 maroon "CITIES SERVICE" with two green tanks; 320 tuscan "MONON" work caboose. *Middle shelf:* X-415 "HYDROCARBON ROCKET FUEL" tank car, red tank on yellow base; 1958 tuscan brown "A.T. & S.F." work caboose. *Bottom shelf:* (6153) "ALLSTATE MOTOR OIL" tank car, blue tank on black base; 645 tuscan brown "NEW HAVEN" work caboose. R. Burgio Collection, B. Greenberg photograph.

	Gd	Exc
6067: 1958, 1971, set of eight figures.	8	10
6068: 1971, set of 10 railroad figures, JP-1829. Consists of engineer with oil can, brakeman with flag, conductor, red cap, news boy, woman, man with cane, man with coat, man with golf clubs, dog.	10	15
6069: 1958, set of 10 animals.	3	5
6070: 1968, 1971, set of 12 telephone poles.	3	5
6071: Boxed set of 12 telephone poles; brown plastic; 3-1/2" high.	3	5
6072: 1968, 1971, set of two streetlights.	2	4
6074: 1968, 1971, highway light.	2	4
6078: 1958, set of 12 telephone poles.	3	5
6400: Marx store display unit for HO accessories.		NRS
6403: 1959, dwarf signal; bubble-pack mounted, black, three red lights, 3- 4" high.	10	20
6410: 1968, 1971, suburban station with 10 figures.	10	20
6412: 1971, trestle set, 32 pieces.	2	4
6412: 1959, figure eight trestle set, 32 pieces; black plastic trestles (30), gray piers (2); IS-329.	2	4
6415: 1968, 1971, girder bridge, black plastic; "ERIE" herald; 8" long, 1" high, 2-3/4" wide.	1	2

	Gd	Exc
6416: 1958, 1971, floodlight tower; black structure and fence; gray base and floodlight; 6-3/4" high.	5	8
6420(A): 1957, through truss bridge.	2	4
6420(B): 1971, trestle bridge; gray plastic; 8-7/8" long, 3- 1/4" high, 3" wide.	2	4
6421: 1958, twin crossing flasher, black plastic base; vertical mast with crossarms and lights attached, white crossbucks with black "RAILROAD CROSSING"; white sign with black "STOP ON RED SIGNAL"; 2-3/16" high.	3	5
6425: 1968, crossing watchman (also 7425); gray plastic house; blue movable man; black base; 1-3/4" high; two screw connectors; includes section of track; IS-306.	5	8
6434: 1959, overhead twin-signal bridge for two tracks; black plastic with two sets of red and green lights; with three screw connectors; 4-3/16" high.	10	20
6438: 1958, automatic crossing gate.	3	5
6439A: 1958, automatic semaphore (also 7439); black plastic base; support; black arm with yellow stripe; chrome ladder; three screw connectors; 4-1/2" high; includes section of track; IS-306.	3	5
6450: 1968, switchman's tower (also 7450); gray walls and base; black roof; blue movable man; 4-1/4" high.	10	20
6454: 1958, two-light block signal.	3	5

An assortment of HO accessories. *Top shelf:* (6465) gray water tower with red working light on top; (6071) telegraph pole; (6490) black sanding tower; (7450) gray switchman's tower with red window outlines; (6420) gray trestle bridge; (6416) black floodlight tower with gray light and base. *Middle shelf:* (6456) gray automatic barrel loader with yellow forklift and man; (6434) black overhead twin-signal bridge with two red and green lights; (6460) Wheaton station, metal lithographed. *Bottom shelf:* (6439A) semaphore; (7438) black crossing gate; (6415) black "ERIE" girder bridge; (6421A) black crossing flasher with two red lights; (6425) gray crossing watchman with blue man and red details. R. Burgio Collection, B. Greenberg photograph.

	Gd	Exc

6456: 1968, 1971, automatic barrel loader; gray plastic base; gray chute; gray house with black roof; blue man on yellow forklift; control panel included; two screw connectors; 3-1/2" high. **15 25**

6460: 1959, 1971, "Wheaton" lithographed station with remote-control whistle and maroon plastic roof; 8-1/2" wide, 3-1/2" deep, and 4-1/4" high. **20 35**

6465: 1958, 1971, gray water tank on black structure, gray base, red warning light on top; chrome metal ladder; 7-5-8" high. **5 8**

6490: 1968, 1971, sanding tower; movable twin pipes (string over pulley), twin lights on base of tank; black plastic body; 6-3/4" high. **15 25**

7001S, 7002C: 1968, track with hollow steel rail; plastic or fiber ties. **.07 .12**

7007: Crossover; five pieces including 90-degree crossover and four short straight sections; roadbed included. **4 6**

7024: Uncoupling re-railer; black plastic roadbed; 2 tab terminals; 7-1/2" long. **1 2**

7040: Remote-control switch set; left and right hand switches; cream plastic; four-button control panel. **6 10**

	Gd	Exc

7438: Crossing gate; black plastic base and support with crossbucks with white "RAILROAD CROSSING", sign with white "2 TRACKS"; black gate with white stripes; two screw connectors; 3-3/4"; includes section of track; IS-306. **NRS**

7454: Two-light block signal with track section. **NRS**

8020: 1971, curved track. **.10 .20**

8021: 1971, curved track. **.05 .07**

8022: 1971, curved track. **.05 .07**

8024: 1971, straight track. **.05 .10**

8034: 1971, uncoupling straight track. **.05 .15**

JG-5102: Highway light, made in Japan; black plastic base; two screw connectors; chrome metal pole with single light mounted on top; shade provided; 3-3/4" high. **5 9**

JP1829: Figure set, made in Japan. **NRS**

SET: Trackside accessories set. Consists of one semaphore, one water spout, seven signs, five figures, and one "Colgate" billboard. **5 7**

Chapter VIII

Paper Items

The lack of annual catalogues has created a major obstacle in the study and cataloging of Marx trains. The Girard Model Works set the precedent by not producing a catalogue, and Marx followed suit. Marx retailers, however, needed a sales catalogue. The larger retailers, such as Wards, Sears, and Woolworths, as well as wholesale toy distributors such as Allied Toy Distributors, printed their own catalogues or designated a section within their catalogue for Marx trains. These catalogues have become our principal reference sources, although they have limitations. They show only those items offered for sale by that retailer for a particular year. We cannot derive whether it was a new production item or what additional items comprised the entire line.

Sears sold its Marx train stock regularly, and each year's catalogues closely followed actual production. On the other hand, Wards often sold Marx stock that was a year old, probably receiving a discounted price. Woolworth and the other dime stores usually stocked current production items.

Several interesting photographs of Woolworth store displays in Newark, New Jersey, and Brooklyn, New York from the late 1930s or from 1946 to 1950 were seen at the Erie offices in 1978. The photography showed elaborate displays, indicating Marx's involvement with the dime store chains in promoting their trains. It acknowledged that dime store catalogues reflected the most accurate production listings and, in the prewar years, covered the entire train line. After World War II new items deluged the market place and the catalogues only sampled the line. In 1940-1941 a display in an Indianapolis Woolworth's was devoted entirely to Marx trains, including an operating display and an extensive range of accessories. In the early 1950s, Danner Brothers dime stores in Indianapolis also offered an extensive Marx train line.

A source of information of the mid to late 1950s Marx trains was *Model Trains Magazine*. It had a special December issue, called the *Buyers Guide*, which consistently listed some

Marx trains. Other model train publications had similar features. One short-lived publication, *Electric Trains*, carried an article "Trains of the Month" which highlighted two trains, usually not Marx. There is considerable information about Marx in the *TTOS Bulletin* (the publication of the Toy Train Operator Society) and *TCA Quarterly* (the publication of the Train Collectors Association).

Only four postwar *Accessory Catalogues* were issued by Marx prior to the Quaker Oats acquisition. They described accessories and a few train sets. The first was published in 1952, followed by a revised edition in 1953; then a new catalogue was issued for 1954-1955 and finally another new one appeared for 1957-1958. Toward the end of production in 1974-1975, changes took place in the 1974 and 1975 catalogues.

Catalogues issued under the Quaker Oats name are listed in chronological order below. Some of the dates shown for these catalogues were assigned after comparing these catalogues to other items with known dates. Dates of Sears or Wards catalogues were readily apparent from both library and individually-owned copies. A brief description of the train contents is given where such a listing is practical. All catalogue sources are listed under the appropriate year.

Many paper items are whole catalogues with only a few pages devoted to Marx trains. Order forms and instruction sheets are usually one sheet in content. Station boxes and cardboard loads are usually found or offered with the train set. Therefore, no attempt has been made to price these items.

Catalogues

1928 Sears (Fall): Joy Line three-piece freight set with lithographed windup locomotive.

Reproduction of the Marx Timely Table from the 1930s.

1929 Sears (Fall): Honeymoon Express toy and Joy Line freight set on same page (the Honeymoon Express was made in Erie).

1931 Sears (Fall): Joy Line freight set with cast-iron locomotive.

1931 Wards: Joy Line freight and passenger sets.

1932 Sears:

(1) Joy Line sheet steel electric locomotive combination freight and passenger set, with optional passenger cars.

(2) Joy Line mechanical freight set.

(3) Joy Line mechanical passenger set.

1933 Sears: Joy Line sheet steel electric locomotive, combination freight and passenger set, with optional passenger cars.

1933-34 Wards:

(1) Joy Line mechanical freight or passenger set.

(2) Joy Line electric passenger set. Also track and switches for both mechanical and electric Joy Line sets.

1934 Sears:

(1) Joy Line sheet steel electric locomotive passenger set with lighted observation; freight cars optional.

(2) Joy Line sheet steel electric locomotive combination freight and passenger set with optional passenger cars.

(3) Joy Line mechanical passenger set.

(4) Joy Line mechanical freight set.

(5) Floor toy, lithographed, aluminum M10003 streamliner with rubber wheels, 11-1/2" long.

(6) Honeymoon Express with steam-type locomotive.

(7) Standard Gauge Marx floor train (includes gondola and passenger car).

1934 Sears Christmas Catalog

1935 Sears: Commodore Vanderbilt electric sets with six-inch freight and passenger cars, M10000 electric and mechanical sets.

1935 Sears Christmas Catalog

1936 Sears:

(1) Marx M10000 mechanical streamliner, introduced as "New". (Earlier 1935 catalogue shows the M10000. As noted above, the "New" is misleading.)

(2) Commodore Vanderbilt five-unit mechanical set.

(3) Moon Mullins handcar.

1936 Sears Christmas Catalog

1936 Wards: M10000 electric and mechanical sets.

1937 Sears:

(1) Commodore Vanderbilt electric locomotive ten-unit combination freight and passenger set, with optional freight cars.

(2) Commodore Vanderbilt mechanical freight set; seven units and reversing motor.

(3) Commodore Vanderbilt mechanical five-unit passenger set.

1937 Sears Christmas Catalog

1937 Wards: (Page 535) M10005, also Commodore Vanderbilt electric freight set.

1937 Woolworth: Timely Table of railroad accessories with drawing of a locomotive numbered "1396" on front cover.

1938 W. T. Grant and Co.: Timely Table of railroad accessories with drawing of a locomotive numbered "397" on front cover. Note: The cover of this catalogue was identical to the 1937 Woolworth, but the number on the locomotive had been changed to "397".

1938 Woolworth: Timely Table of railroad accessories.

1938: Timely Table without store name on front.

1938 Sears:

(1) M10005 mechanical streamliner five-unit set.

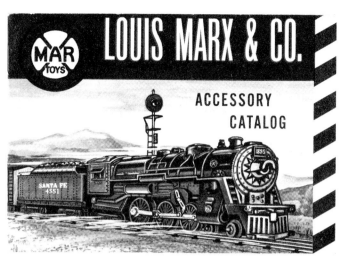

Marx 1954 Accessory Catalog

(2) Commodore Vanderbilt electric six-unit illuminated passenger set with individual light switches to "turn lights off at will" in passenger cars.

(3) Commodore Vanderbilt mechanical five-unit freight set.

1938 Wards: Mechanical and electric sets.

1938 Phillip Morris and Co.: Two pages of Marx trains in Christmas "Toy Land" catalogue.

1938-39 Marx: Color folder, radio control tower one side and train sets on the other side.

1939 Wards: Mechanical and electric sets.

1939 Christmas Catalog: Canadian Pacific locomotive, miniature Mercury set.

1939 Sears:

(1) Mercury mechanical locomotive four-unit set with reversing motor.

(2) Commodore Vanderbilt electric seven-unit combination passenger and freight set.

1939 Woolworth: Timely Table of electric railroad accessories with a locomotive numbered "999" on front, C-408A. Note: Although an artist's version of the 999 locomotive is shown on the cover, it was a year or more before actual production of the 999 locomotive.

1940 Sears:

(1) Commodore Vanderbilt mechanical six-unit freight set.

(2) Commodore Vanderbilt electric seven-unit combination passenger and freight set.

1940 Wards: Mechanical and electric sets.

1941 Marlines: Timely Table, Marlines wing and wheel diagonally across front with two locomotives subdued in background.

1941 Sears:

(1) Commodore Vanderbilt mechanical five-unit freight set with spark generator.

(2) Commodore Vanderbilt electric six-unit passenger and freight combination set.

(3) First reference to Happi-Time toys (bicycles).

1941 Wards: Mechanical and electric sets.

1941 Marlines: Form C-190, eight-page track plan book.

1941 Marx: Timely Table of Marlines railroad accessories.

1941-42 Marline: Repair parts, 999 on cover, four pages.

1942 Wards: First 3/16 scale cars shown with 397 locomotive.

1942 Sears: One mechanical set.

1943 Wards: Marx trains manufactured in 1941 and after, bought by Wards and offered for sale as close-outs of discontinued items in their 1943 catalogue.

1946 Sears: 999 with 3/16 scale cars and a mechanical Commodore Vanderbilt set. Canadian set with six-inch cars including slotted 59 cattle car.

1946 Wards: 999 with 3/16 scale cars, a Canadian Pacific locomotive with six-inch cars, and a Commodore Vanderbilt mechanical set.

1947 Western Auto: Electric and mechanical sets.

1947 Sears: 999 with 3/16 scale cars, a Canadian Pacific locomotive with six-inch cars, and two mechanical sets.

1947 Wards: 999 with 3/16 scale cars and other sets.

1948 Sears: M10005 streamlined passenger set and others.

1948 Western Auto

1948 Wards: Large variety of Marx items.

1949 Allied Toy Distributors: NYC 3/16 scale passenger cars — "New".

1949 Sears: Canadian Pacific set with six-inch cars, M10005 mechanical.

1949 Wards: M10005 mechanical, Commodore Vanderbilt mechanical set, 999 with 3/16 scale freight set.

1950 Sears: 333 locomotive new.

1950 Wards: Mickey Mouse Meteor set and others.

1950 Allied Toy Distributors: 39 West 23rd Street, New York City. Santa Fe 21 and 333 locomotives listed as "new" (Allied made two versions).

1951 Spiegel

1951 Sears

1951 Western Auto

1951 Wards: Mickey Mouse Meteor and others.

1951 Allied Toy Distributors: 18 West 23rd Street, New York City.

1952 Allied Toy Distributors: 18 West 23rd Street, New York City.

1952 Sears: Santa Fe AA combination set.

1952 Western Auto

1952 Wards

Marx 1952 Accessory Catalog.

Battery, Mechanical and Electric Trains, Track and Accessories

1970s Quaker Oats Catalog.

1952 Marx: Accessory catalogue "1932" and "1952".

1953 Sears: NYC diesel (plastic).

1953 Allied Toy Distributors: Price list, 18 West 23rd Street, New York City. (Dated January 1, 1953.)

1953 Wards: Santa Fe diesel (plastic).

1953 Western Auto

1953 Marx: Accessory catalogue "1932" and "now", differs from 1952 edition.

1953 Spiegel

1954 Sears: Santa Fe AA freight set; 1829 combination set.

1954 Western Auto

1954 Wards

1954 Allied Toy Distributors: Price list, 18 West 23rd Street, New York City.

1954 Marx: Accessory catalogue, 1895 locomotive and 4551 Santa Fe tender shown on front cover. Note: The catalogue pictures a 333 locomotive with a Santa Fe tender, but the text describes an 1895 plastic locomotive.

1954 Allied Toy Distributors: Catalogue, 22 West 23rd Street, New York City.

1954 Spiegel: Christmas.

1954-55 Allied Toy Distributors: Catalogue, 22 West 23rd Street, New York City.

1955 Sears: Santa Fe ABA freight set.

1955 Wards

1955 Spiegel: Christmas.

1955-56 Allied Toy Distributors: Catalogue, 22 West 23rd Street, New York City.

1956 Sears: Union Pacific double switcher freight set, Budd RDC.

1956 Wards

1956 Spiegel

1957 Sears: Western Pacific AB green freight set; 666 Army.

1957 (Estimate) Allied Toy Distributors: Large, four-page folder/price list with pictures; 22 West 23rd Street, New York City.

1957 Wards: First year of Marx HO.

1957 Marx: Accessory catalogue, 4311 locomotive on cover.

1958 Sears: Western Pacific ABA gray and yellow passenger and Allstate ABA freight sets.

1958 Wards

1958 Western Auto

1958 Allied Toy Distributors: HO catalogue of Marx trains.

1958 Spiegel

1959 Sears: Allstate switcher, electric William Crooks vinyl freight set.

1959 Wards

1959 Western Auto: Christmas pamphlet with several Marx trains (Marxtronic switcher set).

1959 Spiegel

1959 Model Trains: HO and O Gauge sets.

1960 Sears: William Crooks electric set.

1960 Wards

1960 Spiegel

1961 Sears

1961 Wards

1961 Spiegel

1962 Sears: Rock Island double switcher freight set.

1962 Wards: Windup William Crooks, New Haven AA.

1963 Sears: Two HO Marx sets with scenic base and five O27 sets, also Girard whistling station, single Union Pacific, and New Haven freight sets.

1963 Wards:

1964 Penneys: Toy catalogue.

1964 Sears: One HO train set, one combination HO train and road race set, three Marx O27 sets, one Marx five-unit mechanical train set, and gravel roadbed for track sections.

1964 Western Auto: Christmas.

1964 Wards: Two freight sets; New Haven AA.

1965 Sears: One HO train set, two Marx O27 train sets, one with 57 pieces.

1965 Wards

1965 Marx: Toy catalogue with O27 and HO sets.

1966 Sears: Two Marx O27 train sets.

1966 Wards

1967 Sears: One HO train set with 65-piece plastic town, two O27 train sets.

1967 Wards

1968 Sears: Three O27 train sets, one mechanical four-unit train set with two six-inch, four-wheel cars.

1968 Wards

1969 Sears: Same three sets as shown 1968, also same mechanical set advertised save 10% (the metal cars with metal edges did not meet federal guidelines for safety).

1969 Wards

1970 Sears: Two O27 sets — a repeat of lowest price. 490 sets first offered in 1967-68.

1970 Marx Toys: "Our Fiftieth Year", includes network television campaign schedule (Marx catalogue for the trade).

1970 Wards

1971 Marx Toy Catalog: O27 and HO train sets.

1971 Sears: No Marx trains appear in the Sears 1971 catalogue, (but three new Lionel sets were shown).

1971 Wards: Wards catalogue only shows two Marx trains, the 490 and the 1666 or Big Rail set.

1971 Western Auto

1972 Sears: Four-unit mechanical with three six-inch, four- wheel cars (probably the last offered sale of these forty year old, six-inch cars which did not comply with federal safety standards), and one Marx O27, five-unit freight set, 34-piece cardboard village.

   (1) 490 mechanical set with six-inch metal, lithographed four-wheel cars.

   (2) 702 electric diesel set with plastic four-wheel cars.

1972 Marx Toy Catalog

1972 Wards:

   (1) 1666 Big Rail set.

   (2) Sound of Power set.

1972 Penneys:

   (1) Small electric set.

   (2) Small mechanical set with six-inch, metal, lithographed four-wheel cars.

1972 Western Auto

1973 Sears:

   (1) 490 mechanical set with plastic cars.

   (2) William Crooks electric set with plastic lumber car and caboose.

1973 Marx Toy Catalog

1973 Western Auto

1973 Wards:

   (1) Sound of Power.

   (2) 1666 Big Rail set.

1974 Sears: No listings.

1974 Wards:

   (1) Sound of Power.

   (2) Chug-Chug set.

   (3) Battery-powered set.

1974 Marx Toys: Toy catalogue showing complete line for 1974: one mechanical, four battery, and nine electric freight sets.

1974 Marx Toys: Small, four-page train folder shows track layouts, four train sets, handcar, and accessories.

1975 Marx Toys: Toy catalogue shows one mechanical, three battery, and two electric sets.

1975 Marx Toys: Train catalogue (locomotive 333 on front) shows one mechanical, one import battery, two 6-volt battery, and six electric sets, as well as track, switches, accessories, and display layouts.

1976 Marx Toys: Toy catalogue shows one mechanical, three battery, and two electric sets. Note: Although Marx Toys distributed catalogues in 1976, there was no train production that year. All production ended in November 1975. Items listed in 1976 were from the Girard inventory.

1976 Marx Toys: Train catalogue, 1975 reissue with two sets deleted.

1976 Marx Toys (Spring): No trains listed.

1977 Marx Toys: No trains listed.

Order Forms

Another source of information on Marx train production is the standard order form used by the Girard Model Works Plant. Forms could be obtained by writing to the plant at Girard or, later, the Marx Toy Company in Stamford, Connecticut.

1966

F-29 Mechanical trains and parts.
F-46 Electric trains with automatic couplers, parts, and accessories.
F-56 Electric trains with knuckle couplers, parts, and accessories.

1967

F-46-R-867 Electric trains with automatic couplers.
F-56 Electric trains with knuckle couplers.

1968

F-56-R-468 Electric trains with knuckle couplers.
F-29-R-68 Mechanical trains and battery electric trains.
F-49-R-468 HO railroad parts and accessories.
F-49-R-68 HO parts and accessories.

1969

F-46-R-569 O27 Gauge electric trains with automatic couplers.

1971

F-77 HO parts and accessories.
F-56-R-71 O27 Gauge electric trains with automatic couplers.
F-46-R-371 O27 Gauge electric trains with knuckle couplers.
IS-645 HO Gauge electric engines, cars, and accessories.

1973

F-80 Accessory order form (from Sears Heritage set, William Crooks).

1974

F-30R-74 O27 cars with knuckle couplers (Lehigh Valley set).
F-58R-74 O27 cars with knuckle couplers (Missouri Pacific set).
F-46-R-74 O27 Gauge electric trains with automatic couplers (Wards set).
F-56-R-74 O27 Gauge electric trains with automatic couplers.
F-75-R-74 Typical railroad accessories with sheet of 20 pictures.
F-30-R-74 MCMLXXIV Order Form.
F-56-R-270 MCMLXX Order Form.
F-77 MCMLXXI Order Form.

1975

Mimeograph on Marx letterhead, mechanical.
Mimeograph on Marx letterhead, O27 Gauge.
Printed order form, effective date 2/10/75, covers mechanical and battery sets, 6-volt battery and AC electric sets. Note: The price and order form sheets sent out for 1976 were basically the same as those used in 1975, except for some deleted items and price increases. They even had a 1975 year designation.

Instruction Sheets

Some of the instruction sheets which Marx placed in its sets provided operating and maintenance instructions, while others came resplendent with advertisements for other accessories. Chippy Martin, who prepared these instruction sheets, liked to brag that he had authored hundreds of thousands of Marx publications! His count was probably correct considering that, in some years, when Sears, Wards, and others ordered large quantities, Marx production reached almost 300,000 sets annually.

Close study and cross-referencing of these instruction sheets reveal interesting correlations between the sheets and advertisements for certain sets in a particular year's retail catalogue. For example, the four-page instruction sheet IS-15 has instructions on the first page and three pages of accessories and track layout diagrams. Initially, the instruction sheet had four paragraphs explaining how to connect and operate the transformer. It would seem that IS-15 was issued in 1937. A comparison of IS-15 and IS-38 indicates that IS-38 is simply IS-15 with several revisions. IS-38 has a paragraph explaining how to connect a new five-button control panel which operated both the remote uncoupling track sections and the automatic switches, was missing several track layouts, but added a larger diagram explaining how to connect the five-button control panel transformer and switches was substituted. The revision in itself is not particularly significant until one refers to page 62 of the 1938 Montgomery Ward Catalog and notes that train set 448 was sold with the exact track layout shown in IS-38. The set had two switches, two remote-control uncoupler track sections, and track layout. The 1939 Montgomery Ward Catalog also showed the same train set, 448, on page 56. Thus, it becomes apparent that certain accessories shown in IS-15 were on the market by 1937, perhaps earlier, although no date is shown on either IS-15 or IS-38. Since it is difficult to date Marx trains, any information, even if incomplete, is important to note. Over five hundred instruction sheets are reproduced in our accompanying volume: *Greenberg's Guide to Marx Instruction Sheets*.

Note: *The following are a small sampling of the hundreds of instructions sheets which may help sort out Marx production. Note that most instruction sheets are numbered. B. C. Greenberg's Collection unless otherwise noted.*

IS - 15: Remote-controlled Electric Train Set with Steam Type Locomotive. Ashworth and Whitacre Collections.

IS - 27: Train master block signal.

IS - 114: Real Fun with Real Railroad Whistle Signals. Anderson, Fox, and Gailey Collections.

IS - 140: Important-Refer to instructions covering connection of wires and disregard reference to red, black, and green cables.

IS - 242: Large Radius (O34 Gauge) Remote-control Switches.

IS - 373: 6400 / IED Store Display Unit for HO Accessories. Cimino Collection.

IS - 675: Battery Operated Train Set. Gailey Collection.

1900: Glendale Railroad Station.

2873: Wild West Train Set. Anderson Collection.

75 - R - 74: Typical Railroad Accessories.

Station Boxes

Marx cleverly designed their cardboard set boxes by decorating them with exterior scenes and people to portray a station scene image. There were at least four types of station

boxes used in the 1940-1941 period. The first was a small version measuring 12 x 12 x 6-1/2 inches, whose exterior was printed in red and green as were the later station boxes. This unnumbered station box apparently came with the lithographed 897 locomotive sets of 1940 vintage which were packed in two layers due to the box's size. The duplicate box ends had windows, and the front side had five second-story, four-pane windows and a "Marlines" sign located over two garage doors. A nearby truck marked "For Fun Express" bore a Marx trademark. This side also displayed a door and people. On the rear were four second-story windows, a "Marlines" sign, and a Marx trademark, all mounted over a loading platform displaying boxes and freight. The roof's cross-marked design had a large, centered "M" within a circle.

The second type of station box was larger, measuring about 13 x 17 x 3-1/2 inches, and was issued in 1939 with the 391 Canadian Pacific (Jubilee) locomotive or 897 locomotive. On one side were three large doors numbered "1", "2", and "3" and a window and door marked "Office". The ends bore a Marx trademark and a framed sign. The other side had a raised platform for a loading dock behind which were two large doors, a platform scale, a window, and a man entering an office door. The loading dock was printed with planking and was tucked into the main box at each end. The box lids served as flaps and raised up to fit gabled end flaps which formed a solid-colored peaked roof with an "Airport" arrow running north diagonally across the top of the roof. This station box, printed in green and red, portrayed the details of a station exterior where people busily moved about. It was an attractive accessory requiring minimal assembly: another bargain bonanza from Marx!

Two other types of station boxes were used with the "Lumar Lines" floor toy trains. These stations were 13 x 17 x 4 inches and bore the logo "Ship by Railroad ... North ... East ... South ... West ... & Local" above three freight doors. The 1940 version had plain longitudinal planking printed on the platform, and the ends had impressive columns with a portico roof extending over double doors and matching windows with a brick wall background. The 1941 version had transverse platform planking in simulated wood grain, and the ends were less ornate with two large freight doors showing freight activity within. There was also a station box for a two-train windup outfit from about 1937. Marx army train sets were packed in brown corrugated cardboard boxes which were printed in red and green to depict an army supply depot. The box had a special lid which opened to create a roof for the depot. There was also a red and black version.

Cardboard Loads

Unlike Lionel, Marx frequently used cardboard for car loads in both pre- and postwar train sets. The earlier cardboard sets featured colorful, sample-sized boxes supplied by the manufacturer — green and yellow "Calciwafers", yellow "Bon Ami", blue "F & F" cough lozenges, and orange "Forhan's" toothpaste box were loads for the 552 or 552G gondolas. Other loads of the prewar period were coal for the 554 hopper, which arrived in shiny black ovaloid pills, in packages of about 15 to a cellophane bag and three bags to a hopper; four aluminum-colored wooden milk cans with a stabilizing cardboard insert for the 548 Guernsey Milk gondola; and an odd assortment of unassembled cardboard boxes thrown at random into the set for the young engineer to imaginatively assemble and transport.

Marx again utilized cardboard loads in 3/16th scale cars; this time scale water pipe, sewer pipe, or storm drain pipe moved in flatcars or gondolas. In seven-inch cars simulated concrete blocks, printed packing crates, spools, yellow plastic milk cans and other plastic containers gave purpose and realism to the passing trains. Wooden planks and dowels were supplied with the lumber cars. But the greatest play appeal came from the sample- sized common household products with which the child and his parents readily identified.

Train Boxes

Few collectors find Marx original boxes possibly because these trains did not receive the care afforded to the more expensive Lionel sets. The earliest Marx set boxes were for Joy Line trains. Apparently Marx relied on the "Joy Line" name to help sell trains and prominently placed it on sets produced for Louis Marx & Company before his acquisition of the Girard Model Works. The boxes were constructed of standard brown corrugated cardboard and displayed the New York office address, 200 Fifth Avenue.

After the demise of Joy Line, marketing proceeded under the Louis Marx & Company banner; boxes for the electric trains and some windup sets were again corrugated cardboard. Generally prewar sets were sold in brown corrugated cardboard boxes with blue printing on the top. The words "Streamlined Train" were used to describe the contents and an elaborate three-track illustration glowingly depicted an M10000 streamliner and a Commodore Vanderbilt racing down the tracks side-by-side with a caboose and a portion of a freight passing on the third track. About 13 x 13 inches square, the boxes held early Commodore Vanderbilt sets and late 1934 M10000s. The former sets were still fitted with Joy Line couplers and the M10000 units still utilized Joy Line-type motors. By 1935, M10000 sales volume zoomed, reflecting the train's popularity and the set warranted its own box: an illustrated lid sticker acclaimed this to be the "Official Union Pacific Streamlined Train". Rather than use the traditional color scheme, Marx chose red and silver to replace the tan, red, and cream M10000 sets.

The Mercury sets of 1937 received less fanfare and were marketed in the plain, brown corrugated boxes with blue printing on the lids which inexplicably now read "Stream Line Electric Train" in lieu of "Streamlined Train". It is informative to compare the sticker lid label used in 1936 for M10005 sets with the previous label prepared for the M10000 sets and the early Commodore Vanderbilts. Comparing illustrations used in the 1934 and 1935 labels, it is clear that the label for the 1936 M10005 portrayed the same layout with the M10005 substituted for the M10000. Even in his paper illustrations, Marx reused eye-catching and imaginative graphics.

From about 1946 into the early 1950s, Marx used brown corrugated cardboard with red lettering on the boxtop and black printing on the bottom. A typical box size of this period was 12 x 14 x 3-1/3 inches with the boxtop logo reading "Diesel Type Electric Train" followed by "Made in the U.S.A. by Marx"

and the New York office address. Another box, 13-1/4 x 17 x 3-1/2 inches, announced that inside was a "Stream Line Steam Type Electric Train" with "remote-control." As the 1950s progressed, train sales climbed and Marx sought more attractive packaging. The familiar, unadorned brown cardboard box was succeeded by a coated cardboard, printed in a rich simulated wood-grain with a matching brown ink for the lid printing. Black ink was retained for plain cardboard such as for the Girard (repair) address on the bottom. The lid logo remained the same, reading "Diesel Type Electric Train" followed by the trademark and "Made in U.S.A. by Louis Marx & Co., Inc.", but the box size significantly increased to accommodate the longer units, now 15 x 20-3/4 x 4 inches for freight sets and 15 x 22-3/4 x 4 inches for passenger sets. From the late 1930s to the 1970s, Marx used a lightweight cardboard box to hold low-cost windup sets. The term *cardboard* describes a single layer of fiber board, rather than paste board which is corrugated, multiple layers of fiber board pasted together. These yellow cardboard boxes were 14-3/4 x 9-3/4 x 2-1/2 inches and the tops were printed in red and black to produced a three-color lid; the bottoms were plain and unmarked.

The Sears "Happi-Time" boxes of the 1952 era had a thick white coating over the cardboard and bright blue printing and illustrations on the lid; the bottom was unmarked. The top end said "Happi-Time Toys are sold only by Sears, Roebuck and Co." and there was no mention of Marx as the manufacturer.

In general, the very early accessories came in a neutral-colored, thin cardboard box with exterior blue printing. Later accessory boxes had red exterior printing. The postwar Marx accessories, especially the later plastic accessories of the early 1950s, appeared in larger yellow cardboard cartons with black printing. Boxed accessory sets, such as road signs, were packaged in a red, yellow, and black box, whether metal or plastic items. Both the manual and the remote-control switches were packed in a neutral-colored, thin cardboard box. The box for the manual switches was always printed in green ink, and the box for remote-control switches was printed in red ink. Color coding prevented confusion between the more expensive remote-control switches and the inexpensive manual ones, especially since the box sizes were identical.

In 1948, the box for the 3-1/6-inch scale cars was custom-designed. Made of the usual thin, neutral-colored cardboard, it was printed in red and black to produce attractive three-color illustrations of all the cars in the series. This extra expenditure was justified most likely because Marx intended to sell many of the scale cars as separate items. A large illustration on the carton exterior of the accessory within proved a successful sales technique in the dime store market, where sales of accessories were additions to train sets and buyers bought more or less by impulse. In contrast, Lionel seldom placed pictures on their orange and blue cartons; instead, they published annual catalogues. Marx eliminated the need to include accessory instruction sheets by printing installation instructions on the box sides. Many sales were probably gained because the consumer could, in a few minutes, learn how to easily install a new accessory. And for Marx, that was what it was all about – sales volume through mass distribution.

Chapter IX

Sets

by Robert C. Whitacre

Marx sets are fascinating and challenging to study. Like Lionel and American Flyer, Marx numbered nearly all sets except for some early production. But unlike Lionel and American Flyer, Marx issued only a few catalogues describing their production. This has forced collectors to comb through set boxes recording the contents and gleaning every possible other source. Sources include a few catalogues and "Timely Tables" issued by Marx, some catalogues from Allied Toy Distributors of New York, and the retail sales catalogues of such stores as Sears, Wards, Spiegel, and Western Auto. An extremely important source of information has been Marx collectors who have shared data from their collections with the author. Input from additional Marx collectors is welcome.

Marx train sets evolved from Joy Line sets produced by the Girard Model Works after Louis Marx gained control around 1934. The first of the distinctively Marx sets appeared on toy store shelves around 1934 to 1935. The M-10000 appeared in 1934. The Sears 1935 Catalog offered it in both windup and electric versions. Brand new in 1935 was the Commodore Vanderbilt engine, hyped in the Sears advertisement as the "New Marx Electric Commodore Vanderbilt train." New six-inch metal came with the engine cars. These outfits came with both freight and passenger cars, track, and transformer for only $4.69. From that beginning, in the middle of the Depression, Marx produced literally hundreds of different sets over the next forty years.

Marx developed a systematic set numbering system over the years. While there are some major exceptions, most of the sets fall into fairly well-defined groupings as shown in the accompanying chart.

The Typical Marx Set

What is a typical Marx set? While the cars of a typical set changed colors and numbers, and even changed from metal to plastic over the years, its profile remained very much the same. It was typically a steam freight set with a moderate price tag. In the 1930s and 1940s it included a Commodore Vanderbilt engine and a 551 tender followed by two or three cars such as a gondola, tank car, boxcar, or hopper plus a caboose.

Gradually the Commodore Vanderbilt was replaced by other low-priced engines, such as the metal 591. Later the 400 and 490 plastic engines were widely used. The familiar six-inch cars gradually were replaced with seven-inch cars, and later with economy versions of plastic cars. Of course these sets always came with an oval of track and a small transformer if the set was electric or a key if it was mechanical.

Deluxe Sets

For the lucky boy or girl whose parents could afford a more expensive set, Marx offered a variety of *deluxe* sets. Deluxe is the author's term and refers to higher-priced sets which generally contained more detailed rolling stock and accessories.

One favorite of collectors is the series of switch trains offered in the Montgomery Wards Catalog. The pre-World War II versions were hailed as "Ward's Famous Switch Train" on the top of the set's large box. The special feature of the set was the opportunity for the young engineer to uncouple and switch off cars, and then recouple them by remote control.

Set Numbers	Description
000-999	Windup or mechanical sets
1000-1999	Reversible windup sets
2000-2999	Miniature sets and battery-operated sets
3000-3099	Wards catalogue sets
3800-3999	Earlier sets with four-wheel, six-inch cars
4000-4999	Some earlier deluxe sets, but mostly later sets with 400 and 490 plastic steam engines
5000-5999	Prewar deluxe sets with switches, military sets; postwar sets with metal 591 engines
6000-6999	Japanese and Hong Kong sets
7000-7199	Articulated passenger sets
7200-7999	Small plastic diesel sets
8000-8989	Small and medium metal diesel sets
8990-8999	Sets with 898 engines
9000-9099	Deluxe articulated passenger sets
9500-9999	Sears catalogue sets
10000-10999	Deluxe articulated passenger sets and sets with 994 Meteor engines
11000-11999	Prewar sets with eight-wheel, six-inch cars
14900-14999	Sets with 490 plastic engines
15000-15999	Prewar sets with eight-wheel, six-inch cars with automatic couplers
15600-15699	Sets with 490 plastic engines
16000-17999	HO sets
21300-21999	Wards catalogue sets
24000-24999	Miscellaneous sets
25000-25250	Sets with 999 die-cast engines and scale or plastic cars
25251-26333	Sets with 999 engines and sets with 490 plastic engines
26750-29999	Sets with smaller diesel engines
30000-32999	Sets with 666 and 1666 plastic engines
33000-33999	Sets with 1998 diesel switcher engines
35000-35300	Sets with 333 engines
35566-36566	Sets with 1829 Hudson engines
39360-39365	Twin train sets
40000-44999	Sets with large E-7 plastic diesel engines
45200-45299	Sets with large metal 21 diesel engines
45800-46975	Sets with large E-7 plastic diesel engines
50000-52999	Sets with 666 and 1666 plastic engines
54700-54799	Wells Fargo and other sets headed by William Crooks engines
55800-55999	Sets with 333 engines
56800-56899	Sets with 1829 Hudson plastic engines
60000-79999	HO sets

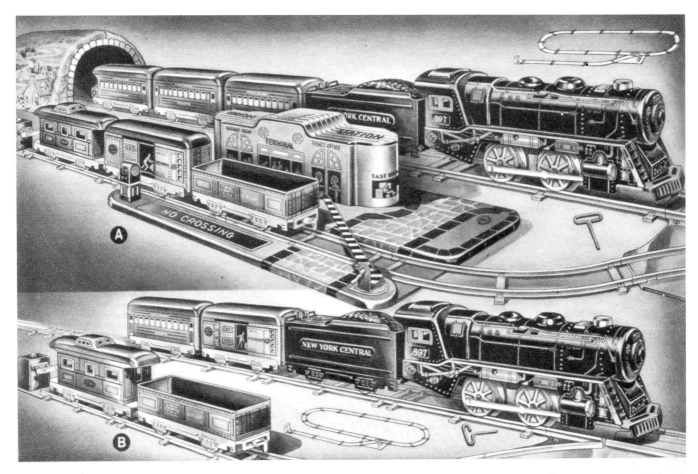

Powerful Wind-Up Trains .. Run Forward or Backward!

(A)   Two Trains in One .. Passenger-Freight; 55 In. Long $2⁸⁹   (B) Passenger-Freight Train . . . 42 In. Long $2²⁹

Looks real. If you want to load passengers at brightly colored metal station, just couple up Steam Type Locomotive and Tender with 2 Passenger Coaches, Observation Car and Baggage Car for a passenger train! If your train is to carry freight, throw siding switch, back passenger Coaches into siding. Then, using Baggage Car as Box Car, return train to main line, close switch and pick up Gondola and Caboose for freight train.

Or use all 8 units and have a combination freight-passenger train almost 5 feet long. Engine has brake and

bell, governor to keep train from jumping track, and will run backward as well as forward. Its strong clock spring cannot be overwound. Engine with Tender is 15 inches long. Entire train 55 inches long. All Metal. 16 sections metal "O"-gauge track—7 straight, 9 curved, right hand mechanical switch and dead end for spur. Metal station and Tunnel brightly colored. Oval track is 137 inches around without spur. Needs 34 by 54 inch "freight yard."
48 T 149—Ship. wt. 8 lbs. 8 oz.............$2.89

Combination Freight-Passenger Train with a Locomotive that runs forward or backward. Bell rings as it speeds around 137 inches of oval track or backs into spur to switch cars. Powerful spring-wind motor can't be overwound. Speed governor keeps train from jumping track. Mechanical Steam-Type Engine with brake and bell; new coal and water-type Tender. Combined length 15 in. Gondola, Box Car and Caboose make freight train; use box car for "baggage," attach Passenger Car and you have a passenger train. Metal, finished in bright colors. Ent. train 42 in. long. 16 sections metal O-gauge track. 7 straight, 9 curved with hand-operated switch for spur, and dead end. Needs space 34 by 54 in.
48 T 147—Combination Passenger-Freight Train. Ship. wt. 5 lbs. 12 oz.$2.29

Advertisement of a Marx set from the 1941 Montgomery Ward Catalog.

This was done with eight-wheel, six-inch cars equipped with one-way couplers. Included in the set were two remote switches, two remote uncouplers, a gantry crane, and enough track to make it all happen. These sets sold for $10.95 in 1939, and included five cars besides the engine and tender.

Many collectors do not realize that Montgomery Ward continued to sell the switch trains after World War II. In the 1952 catalogue, for instance, the train consisted of a 333 engine and scale cars. In 1953 the scale cars were given high trucks and coupled to the new plastic Santa Fe 1095 diesels. The set included seven buildings and over 170 pieces for a hefty $37.95.

One of the most desirable deluxe postwar sets was featured in the Sears 1958 Catalog. Set 9638 came with 8-1/2 feet of train. Pulled by three orange Allstate diesels (one powered and two dummies), the consist had a remarkable assortment

of rarer cars. Included were the Missouri Pacific cattle car in green, the orange Erie flatcar with green tractors, the Seaboard double-door boxcar, the maroon and white Allstate twin-tank milk car, the Southern Pacific depressed flatcar with a large generator, and the orange Allstate bay window caboose. This set sold for $29.89 in 1958. It commands considerably more than that today!

Military Sets

Popular in prewar years and for a while in the 1950s were the military and space exploration sets. Collectors show a great interest in these sets today, too. The most common military engine in the prewar years was the olive 500 Canadian Pacific. Rarer were the electric and windup versions of the lithographed 897 engine. The rarest engine, however, was the olive drab enameled Commodore Vanderbilt. The military sets were outfitted with a variety of appropriate rolling stock including guns, tanks, searchlights, airplanes, ordnance gondolas, vehicle flats, radio cars, and official cars. Frequently the set came in a colorful box that doubled as a military depot. Some sets included flat tin stand-up soldiers, a flag and tents. One set reportedly came with a helmet for the youngster to wear.

Postwar military sets were often made of plastic and were commonly pulled by an olive drab 400 or a die-cast 666. Many of these sets did not survive because they were quite fragile. It is difficult, for instance, to find a rocket launcher car intact. Commonly included in the postwar sets were a platoon of plastic soldiers, tents, flagpole, and military vehicles. Strangely, Marx never produced a plastic, olive drab four-wheel tender. In sets that required a plastic four-wheel tender, the tender was always black.

One of the rarest postwar military sets was issued through Western Auto stores. It came, surprisingly, with a civilian engine, tender, and caboose in Santa Fe markings. The set had the familiar olive flatcar with two plastic military vehicles and the rocket launcher car. But the gem in the set was the plastic deluxe military boxcar. Many collectors have never seen one of these boxcars. The Marx factory may have made only one run, and it is possible that the boxcar came only in this one set.

Other Deluxe Sets

The prewar freight set with the red Canadian Pacific engine is another of the rarer deluxe sets. Besides being headed by a rare engine, the set contained the elusive double flatcars with a single pair of center stakes on each car and a load of rails. These special rails had no crimping from being mounted on crossties. This set also contained the rare wheel car, a cable car, a 550 crane car, and a couple of other more common pieces of rolling stock.

Almost any set headed by a red steam engine seems to attract the attention of collectors. These include sets headed by red Commodore Vanderbilts, Mercurys, and 994 Meteors, as well as the red Canadian Pacific.

Collectors also like sets headed by the blue Mercury. Sometimes called the *Blue Comet*, these passenger sets were headed by a whistling, windup blue Mercury with a matching tender and three blue six-inch passenger cars. Apparently there were several different issues of this set, not only did they come with either plastic knuckle or tab and slot couplers, there were also two different blue tenders. The blue 551 tender came with rivet detail or with a gray band. An interesting question is whether the blue Mercury was issued in a freight set without the blue tender. There seem to be a few extra blue Mercurys floating around without blue tenders. There is also a black 551 tender with blue rivet detail and lettering. Were these the components of those freight sets?

Collectible Late Sets

Rarity and desirability in the collecting of Marx sets are not always related to age. The 1974 production, perhaps Marx's last hurrah, included several choice sets. High on the

list of every collector of plastic Marx is the 41850 Mohawk freight set. This set contained the green Penn Central road diesel pulling the Exxon tank car, the yellow Missouri Pacific cattle car, and the orange Erie gondola.

Also issued in 1974 was the 52750 Champion freight set. In addition to the tender and caboose with the Rio Grande road name, this set contained the red Virginian hopper and the blue and yellow Southern auto loader.

And then there was the 25760 Allegheny set. It had a lowly 490 plastic engine, a common Santa Fe tender, and caboose. There also was a good, but not unusual, New York Central deluxe boxcar. But the big sleeper in this set was the Gulf twin-tank car in blue and orange.

Unusual Sets

Marx had a penchant for producing unusual train sets. The Wards Catalog showed set 3088 with a large cardboard mountain over which the train ran. There were several twin train sets featuring a stop-and-go signal to prevent collisions. A number of sets came with both passenger and freight cars. In later years two or three sets combined train and road race sets. Avoiding collisions was really a challenge! Of course, some enterprising children timed the grade crossing for maximum damage.

The Longest Marx Train Set?

One of the longest O Gauge train sets offered by any manufacturer was the Marx set featured in Montgomery Wards 1939 Christmas Catalog. The caption read: "10 and 1/2 Foot 17 Car Electric Freight Train." Selling for $7.95, this special set pulled by a Canadian Pacific 494 type engine (undoubtedly with weights for traction) and included over twenty feet of track, six gondolas, six refrigerator cars, two hoppers, two tank cars, and one caboose. The set also boasted a Glendale depot and a switch tower. One wonders if anyone ever managed to get all that rolling stock moving at once behind that little engine.

Allstate Sets

Most major train manufacturers catered to their larger retail outlets. Lionel occasionally produced a car with a retail name on it such as "Toys R Us." But Marx went so far as to allow their train sets even to carry the names of the retailers on the box as well as the rolling stock. For Sears there were the earlier *Happi-Time* sets and the later *Allstate* sets. They contained such rolling stock as Allstate diesels, tank cars, gondolas, tenders, and cabooses. The Sears logo was also prominently displayed on the sides of a semi-trailer van which was the load on a flatcar. There were even transformers labeled "Allstate".

To enhance this wedding of manufacturer and retailer Marx used Sears catalogue numbers as their box set numbers. Practically the whole range of numbers from 9500 to 9999 belongs to Sears sets. Marx similarly accommodated Wards catalogue, but much less extensively

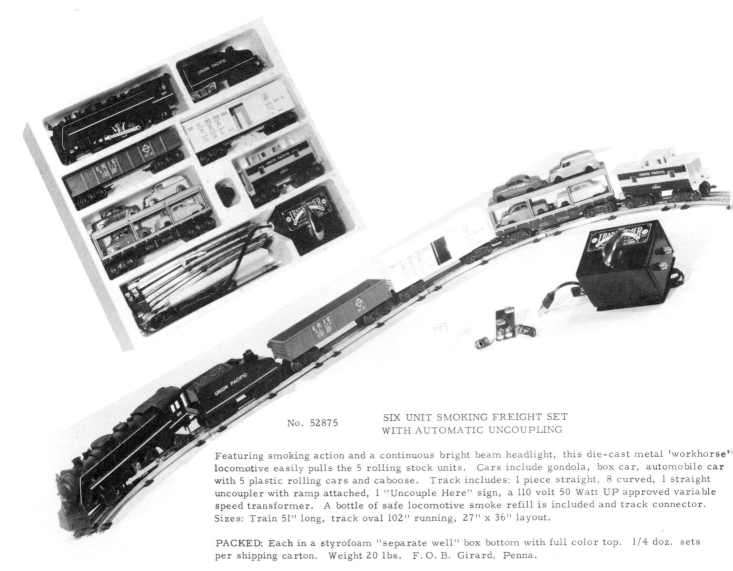

No. 52875   SIX UNIT SMOKING FREIGHT SET
                 WITH AUTOMATIC UNCOUPLING

Featuring smoking action and a continuous bright beam headlight, this die-cast metal 'workhorse' locomotive easily pulls the 5 rolling stock units. Cars include gondola, box car, automobile car with 5 plastic rolling cars and caboose. Track includes: 1 piece straight, 8 curved, 1 straight uncoupler with ramp attached, 1 "Uncouple Here" sign, a 110 volt 50 Watt UP approved variable speed transformer. A bottle of safe locomotive smoke refill is included and track connector. Sizes: Train 51" long, track oval 102" running, 27" x 36" layout.

PACKED: Each in a styrofoam "separate well" box bottom with full color top. 1/4 doz. sets per shipping carton. Weight 20 lbs. F.O.B. Girard, Penna.

LOUIS MARX & CO., INC., 200 FIFTH AVE., NEW YORK, NEW YORK, 10010

Promotional photograph used by Louis Marx & Co., Inc. showing set number 52875.

Many Questions Remain

While a great deal of information on Marx sets has come to light in the last decade, there are many questions that will continue to tantalize the imagination of Marx collectors for years to come. To name a few: How many sets did Marx produce? Why wasn't there a green tender for the green Commodore Vanderbilt? Why didn't Marx make a complete prewar eight-wheel military set? (Or did they?) There are, in addition, dozens of questions concerning which cars and which engines came in which sets.

Gradually many of these questions are being resolved; but perhaps some questions will remain mysteries. And, maybe that is part of the fascination of collecting Marx train sets.

Chapter X

Track, Transformers, and Miscellaneous Items

Although engines and rolling stock may be the main objects in a train collection, without track, transformers, and accessories railroad operations would abruptly come to a standstill.

TRACK

Track design changed infrequently. In fact, the catalogue numbers for straight and curved track, 601 and 602, respectively, remained essentially the same from 1935 through 1975. The earliest track, produced for Joy Line windup trains and later adapted for their electric sets, resembled early American Flyer O Gauge track more than it did the lower profile O27 track usually associated with Marx. Early Marx crossties were tin-plated and rail height was equal to that of O Gauge track. Each track section had three ties which secured the rails, but the curved track ties were "stepped-up" across the tops to provide super elevation. The first 1934 M10000 sets, as well as the mechanical Animal Express (popularly known as the Bunny Train), came with super-elevated track.

Early regular O27 track had tin-plated ties (which were not super-elevated). This type was used from about 1935 to 1939 and was then replaced by the same type of track, but with black-oxidized ties. This black tie O27 variety became the most common Marx track which Marx designated in his advertisements as O Gauge. Marx probably chose the O Gauge designation because O Gauge was perceived a premium quality track compared to O27. The switch and crossing base for this type were tin-plated, but later appeared with a black base. Just before and after World War II, this type of track became all black because tin-plated sheet metal was unavailable. Oxidized black sheets had to be used for both windup and electric track. Tin-plated Marx O27 track did become available later in the postwar period.

The O34 Gauge curved track was first produced in 1939 so that parallel double-tracked layouts could be built. The system worked well with short locomotives and cars; but, when the 333 locomotive, the long diesels, and long 3/16-inch scale passenger cars were introduced, the system no longer provided adequate clearance. For example, a 333 locomotive on an inner loop of O27 track would overhang to the extent that it would strike a long passenger car on an outer loop of O34 track. Marx literature suggested double-track layouts as late as 1958 and the O34 curved track was available for many years. The large metal 21 diesels were originally sold with O34 regular length (8-1/2") curves. Later Marx made 10" straight track sections to go with the O34 curves.

The Montgomery Ward 1953 Catalog showed regular five-tie straight track sections which came in train sets with wide radius curved track before development of the 1801 long straight sections. Sears Happi-Time sets of 1952 also came with the regular straight five-tie section for use with O34 curves. The final type of O27 track, having all plastic ties and rails, was used with windup, as well as battery-operated sets.

Still another type of special track dates from 1937 when Marx manufactured a miniature, electrically-powered train of about HO Gauge proportions. A mechanical version followed in 1940. The cars were lithographed similarly to the larger six-inch cars, but they ran on sheet metal channel-shaped track, which was lithographed to simulate ties, rails, and roadbed ballast. Apparently these miniature sets were only available from 1937 to perhaps 1940.

About 1955, Marx began to develop HO trains, and in 1957 marketed HO straight and curved track. In 1958 switches appeared and, in 1959, 90-degree crossings followed. In 1958, Wards sold Marx HO sets with Atlas track, while Sears sold Marx HO sets with Marx track.

The O27 plastic roadbed with tie indentations for inserting the track came with some sets. Plastic roadbed for O27 track used in Allstate sets for Sears appeared in 1961-1962. In the 1940s and 1950s Marx two-rail and three-rail track used a solid track pin, but in the late 1960s Marx developed a notched pin similar to Lionel's. The distinguishing difference is that Lionel's pins had pointed ends while Marx's were rounded.

Plastic track for battery-operated sets made in Hong Kong had different cross-sections, as did the Marxtronic O Gauge black plastic track. Prewar mechanical tin-plated ties were plain; postwar black ties had a dimple in the tie where the third rail would have been placed.

———————

In the following listings the word "gauge" is used as most train collectors utilize it, i.e. O27 Gauge track means track with curves of about a 27" diameter. The actual Gauge or distance between rails is the same as O. "S" in the item number indicates straight track, "C" indicates curved track. An identifying characteristic of Marx track is that the edges are crimped downwards.

	Gd	Exc
Number Unknown: 1928-36, Joy Line O Gauge windup track with three tin-plated ties; super-elevated; 10" straight section; a circle of four pieces with a diameter of 19-9/16".	.50	1
Number Unknown: 1930-34, Joy Line O Gauge electric track, three tin-plated ties, super-elevated.		NRS
Number Unknown: 1937-40, approximately HO size electric and windup track; lithographed sheet steel with inverted channel.	1.50	3
Number Unknown: 1960, O27, electric straight track with three black-oxidized ties; plastic roadbed constructed with integral unloading platform for use with operating milk car.	.40	.60
Number Unknown: 1961-62, O27, electric straight track with three black-oxidized ties; with plastic roadbed notched out for track connector.	.30	.40

	Gd	Exc
0501S, 0502C: 1963-75, O27, windup multi-tie, one-piece black plastic rail; also for later battery sets only. (Quaker Oats produced this track in a grayish version from 1973-75.)	.10	.15
501S, 502C: 1935-41, O27, windup track with three tin-plated ties and two rails; 10-1/4" straight section; a circle of eight sections with diameter of 26-3/4".	.10	.20
501S, 502C: 1946-72, O27, windup track with three black-oxidized ties.	.10	.15
501S, 502C: Same as above, but with black rail.	.10	.15
601S, 602C: 1935-38, O27, electric with three tin-plated ties, slightly longer than later track.	.10	.20
601S, 602C: 1940-42,1946, same as above, but rails and ties black-oxidized.	.10	.20
601S, 602C: 1939-75, O27, electric track with three black-oxidized ties.	.10	.20
701S, 702C: 1939-75, O27, electric track with three black-oxidized ties; mounted on plastic roadbed.	.15	.25
811S: 1940-56, O34, electric (8-3/4" long) straight track with five black-oxidized ties.	.25	.40
812C: 1940-56, O34, electric curved track with five black-oxidized ties.	.25	.50
1801: 1955-63, O34, electric (11-1/4" long) straight track with five black-oxidized ties.	.25	.50
1802: 1939-63, O34, five black-oxidized ties, curved only, electrical.	.25	.50
6001S, 6002C: 1957-65, HO, plastic or fiber ties, non-solid steel rail.	.10	.15
7001S, 7002C: 1960, HO, plastic or fiber ties, non-solid rail, attached to gray or black plastic roadbed.	.12	.20
8020: 1971, HO, curved track with terminals.	.20	.30
8021: 1971, HO, curved track.	.07	.10
8022: 1971, HO, curved track.	.07	.10
8024: 1971, HO, straight track with rerailer.	.10	.15
8034: 1971, HO, uncoupling straight track.	.15	.25

SWITCHES AND CROSSINGS

Chippy Martin, a retired Marx executive, has remarked on the frequency with which Marx designs changed. He pointed out the profits to be realized from the sale of switches as compared to that from train sets. In fact, some switches were more expensive than some sets. And, each time Lionel changed switches, Marx followed suit. In general, a Lionel engine could negotiate Marx switches, but Marx locomotives could not easily pass through a Lionel switch. It was not until the 1950s that Marx reduced and recessed its drive wheel gear diameter on the larger diesel locomotives allowing Marx trains to clear the flange-ways of Lionel switches. With this innovation, Marx no longer limited its train buyers to Marx switches.

The potential profit from the sale of crossings was never as great as that from switches, so crossing design changes were usually introduced only as a result of changes in production techniques and market conditions. Toward the end of production, federal guidelines for toys dictated hazard-free construction causing Marx to change the metal edges of the switches and crossings. As a result, they were given plastic bases.

The study of switches and crossings is of some help in dating train sets. The early practice of tin-plating bases later yielded to the use of black-oxidized finishes or dull black enamels. Metal switch motor housings on automatic electric switches were at first painted red and later black. Manual switches had the control mounted on a stand, as contrasted to the Lionel version which was flat on the base. There was a lighted metal automatic variety with a large jewel reflector on the housing. In the early and late 1940s the rails, as well as the bases on switches and crossings, were oxidized black instead of being tin-plated. Some tin-plated bases may have been made in the 1950s, but black was generally used after World War II. There was a 90-degree crossing encased in roadbed material to match track with roadbed that came in sets.

The following listings are numerical within each category.

Switches

	Gd	Exc

Number Unknown: 1933, Joy Line, two-rail windup; tin-plated, 10" x 5-1/2"; red and green bull's eye. — 2, 3

Number Unknown: 1933, Joy Line, three-rail, manually-operated; tin-plated, 10" x 5-1/2"; red and green bull's eye. — NRS

Number Unknown: 1952, two-rail windup, manually-operated; plastic black, monolithic rail and tie. — 1, 1.50

510: 1939, O27, pair, two-rail windup, manually-operated; tin-plated base; red and green indicator. — 1, 1.50

510: 1946, O27, pair, two-rail windup, manually-operated; black-oxidized base; red and green indicator. — 1, 1.50

608 Right / 609 Left: 1937, O27, pair, three-rail, manually-operated; tin-plated base; red and green bull's eye. — 1, 1.50

610: 1939, O27, pair, three-rail, manually-operated; tin-plated base, red and green indicator. — 2, 3

610: 1941, O27, pair, three-rail, manually-operated; black-oxidized base, red and green indicator (also made with black-oxidized rail). — 1, 1.50

640: 1957, O27, pair, three-rail, manually-operated; black plastic. — 5, 7

740: 1973, O27, pair, three-rail, manually-operated; black plastic. — 3, 5

810: 1956, O34, pair, three-rail manually-operated; black plastic. — 3, 5

1588 Left / 1588 Right: 1937, O27, remote control; tin-plated base, with 1585 control panel, no indicator or light. — 2, 3

1590: 1950, O27, pair, three-rail, remote control; black-oxidized metal base with controller. — 3, 5

1610: 1939, O27, pair, three-rail, remote control; tin-plated base with light. Variation: controller panel has additional button for automatic uncoupling and additional terminals. — 1, 1.50

1610: 1940, O27, pair, three-rail, remote control; black-oxidized base with light and controller. — 4, 5

1610: 1951, O27, pair, three-rail, remote control; black-oxidized base with light and controller. — 3, 5

1640: 1957, O27, pair, three-rail, remote control; black plastic base with light and controller. — 3, 3

	Gd	Exc

1740: 1973, O27, pair, three-rail, remote control; black plastic base, no light with controller. — 3, 4

1810: 1955, O34, pair, three-rail, remote control; black plastic base with light and controller. — 6, 9

6010: 1958, HO, pair, electric, manually-operated; tin-plated hollow rail, plastic base. — 1.50, 2

6040: 1958, HO, pair, electric, remote control; tin-plated hollow rail; plastic base; with controller. — 3, 5

Crossings

Number Unknown: 1951, two-rail windup, 90-degree; black plastic; combined rail and tie. — 1.50, 2

507: 1937, O27, mechanical, 90-degree, tin-plated base, 7-1/2" wide. — .50, 2

507: 1946, O27, mechanical, 90-degree, black-oxidized base, 7-1/2" x 7-1/2". — .50, 2

604: 1936, O27, electrical, 90-degree, open tin-plated base, 7-1/2" wide. — .50, 2

607: 1937, O27, electrical, 90-degree, tin-plated base with underplate. — 1, 2

607: 1941, O27, electrical, 90-degree, black-oxidized base. — 1, 2

607: 1954, O27, electrical, 90-degree, black plastic base and ties. — 1, 2

607C: 1957, O27, electrical, 90-degree, black plastic base, 7-3/8" x 7-3/8". — 1, 2

1807: 1955, O34, electrical, 90-degree, black plastic base. — 1, 2

6007: 1959, HO, electrical, 90-degree, plastic base, tin-plated rail. — 1, 2

UNCOUPLERS AND RELATED TRACK ITEMS

307: 1939, track lock (to hold track sections together at joints). — .35, .50

309: 1939, boxful of track separators (to hold O27 and O34 tracks apart when in parallel run). — .60, .75

600: 1946, track connector — double terminal (O27). — .25, .50

1088 AET: 1937, short insulated rail clip for accessories. — .75, 1

1089 AET: 1937, long insulated rail clip for accessories. — .75, 1

1602: 1938, remote uncoupler unit for one-way automatic couplers. — 2, 3

1603: 1938, "accessory controller" for remote uncoupler unit 1602. — .25, .50

1605: 1940, remote uncoupler unit for one-way automatic couplers (control included or combined with switch control panel in certain sets); green light when in use. — 1, 2

1624: 1942, uncoupling ramp track for tilt-type automatic couplers with "Uncouple Here" sign included (for regular O27). — 1, 2

1624: 1962, uncoupling ramp track for O27 with plastic roadbed, snap-on (used with Sears special Happi-Time track) for tilt-type automatic couplers. — 1, 2

1824: 1955, uncoupling ramp track for tilt-type automatic couplers with "Uncouple Here" sign included (for O34). 2139 AC to DC converter for speedway track with two terminals. — .50, 1

5008 AET: 1930, track connector — double terminal. — .25, .50

5009 AET: 1937, track connector — single terminal. — .30, .50

	Gd	Exc
5008 AET: 1930, track connector — double terminal.	.25	.50
5009 AET: 1937, track connector — single terminal.	.30	.50
6000: 1958, track lock-on double terminal (HO).	.25	.35
6024: 1957, uncoupling/re-railer for HO Gauge.	1	2
6030: 1958, motor raceway grade crossing/HO Gauge track section, non-solid rail.	.50	1

TRANSFORMERS

When the Girard Model Works decided to make an electric Joy Line cast-iron steam locomotive about 1930, development of a transformer was as important to them as development of the electric motor itself. Joy Line transformers were first produced about 1930 with a 25-watt rating. Some earlier transformers were made with detachable cords, using two round male prongs in a shield on the transformer case end and a female plug similar to those used on old electric irons of the 1930 period. By about 1956, at the peak of Marx train production, the largest transformer had a 150-watt rating. The higher wattage reflected the growing use of accessories, of engines with smoke units, and of layouts with extensive track systems, all of which required greater transformer capacity.

Most transformers were produced to compete in the toy market, but a few, in the early years, were produced to meet non-standard electrical distribution systems in parts of the United States and elsewhere. Marx also made 220-volt transformers for export to South America and Europe. The Girard Model Works produced all Marx transformers and the fact that early Marx transformers provided five more watts than their competitors was an important sales feature of the 1930s.

Knowledge of transformer types can often aid in dating a train set. In addition, it is sometimes possible to relate known transformer design changes to undated catalogues. It is known, for example, that Marx went from a square case to a rounded-corner version of the 709 and 729 transformers. The last year that a square case was offered by Marx was in the 1939 Montgomery Ward Catalog. If one looked at the small print in undated Woolworth-Marx brochures, attention was directed to the new rounded-corner case, which was described as an improved safety design. This information implied that the Woolworth-Marx catalogue was issued circa 1938 to 1939.

Note: Many transformers came in other colors with other labels than those listed here. The authors are always interested in learning more about transformer variations.

	Gd	Exc
POWER HOUSE: Lithographed enclosed building; "Girard Model Works"; transformer inside.		NRS
JOY LINE: Circa 1930, 25 watts, secondary voltage 7-13; square case with red vertical rheostat arm on side.		NRS
JOY LINE: 1932, 25 watts, secondary voltage 7-13; square case with red vertical rheostat arm on side, rectangular shield on end for plug-in two-hole connector similar to iron plug.		NRS

	Gd	Exc
309: 1950, 25 watts, secondary voltage 5-10; rounded-edged case with two posts on rounded side, small Bakelite pointer on top, riveted lithographed nameplate.	1	3
309: 1952, 25 watts, secondary voltage 5-10; early 309 case with logo printed in white on top of case and insulated separator between two terminal posts on flat side of case. Also numbered 319.	2	3
319: 1955, 30 watts, secondary voltage 7-13; 309 case, two posts, plastic pointer-type handle on top, lithographed logo plate riveted on top and circuit breaker button on side.	2	4
329: 25 watts, small square blue-green case with white plastic knob; two posts on side.	2	4
421: 1936, control rheostat, painted black.	3	5
422: 1939, control rheostat, chrome-plated or black.	10	15
709: 1940, 45 watts, secondary voltage 7-13; square case with red vertical rheostat arm; logo stamped on case only.	2	4
709: 1938, 45 watts, secondary voltage 7-13; rounded case with red vertical rheostat arm, two posts; additional logo on gold decal.	2	4
709: 1950, 50 watts, secondary voltage 7-13, rounded-edged black case with red vertical rheostat arm on side, two posts.	2	4
709: 40 watts, secondary voltage 5-11, rounded case, two posts.	2	4
709: 25 watts, secondary voltage 6-11, rounded case, two posts.	2	4
729: 1936, 45 watts, secondary voltage 7-13, 12 fixed voltage; square case with red vertical rheostat arm; logo stamped on case only.	2	4
729: 1938, 45 watts, secondary voltage 7-13, 12 fixed voltage; rounded case with vertical rheostat arm, four posts; additional logo on gold decal.	2	4
729: 1940, 50 watts, secondary voltage 7-13, 13 fixed voltage; rounded-edged black case with red vertical rheostat arm on side, four posts.	2	4
(729CB): 1940, same as 729, except circuit breaker added on top.	2	4
809: 1938, 55 watts, secondary voltage 7-13, 13 fixed voltage; large rounded case with long-handled throttle lever, three posts; circuit-breaker and reversing button.	5	8
909: 1938, 45 watts, secondary voltage 7-13, 13 fixed voltage; otherwise same as 809, approved by Hydro-Electric Power Commission.		NRS
1209: 1947, 45 watts, secondary voltage 7-13; rounded sheet metal case, two posts on flat end, tin-plated handle on top; patent number same for internal parts as prewar patent number; lithographed nameplate on top. Also numbered 1229.	2	4
1209: 1949, 50 watts, secondary voltage 7-13; 1209 case with increased wattage.	2	4
1229: 1950, 50 watts, secondary voltage 7-13, 13 fixed voltage; black-enameled sheet metal case (1209) with tin-plated operating handle on top, four posts on flat end.	2	4
1239: 1950, 50 watts, secondary voltage 7-13; same as 1209, but with circuit breaker.	2	4
1239AS: 1956, 50 watts, secondary voltage 7-13, 13 fixed voltage; 1209 case, lithographed background on label in red or pink (supplied with Allstate sets).	2	4
1249: 1947, 45 watts, secondary voltage 7-13, 13 fixed voltage; 1209 case with four posts on flat end and circuit-breaker reset above posts.	2	4

Gd Exc

1409: 1938, 75 watts, secondary voltage 7-13, 13 fixed voltage; other side same as 809.   6   10

1540: 1952, 70 watts, secondary voltage 7-13, 13 fixed voltage; 1209 case, circuit breaker labeled "reset"; four posts on flat side of case.   4   6

1546: 1953, 65 watts, secondary voltage 5-15, 15 fixed voltage; 1209 case with four terminal posts on flat side of case.   NRS

1549: 1954, 70 watts, secondary voltage 7-15, 15 fixed voltage; 1209 case with four terminal posts on flat side of case.   4   6

1549: 1954, 75 watts, secondary voltage 7-15, 15 fixed voltage; 1209 case with lithographed label background in blue (supplied with Happi-Time set) and circuit breaker; variation: brown base with blue-lithographed label.   4   6

1559: 1955, 75 watts, secondary voltage 7-15, 15 fixed voltage; square sheet metal case with tin-plated sheet metal handle on top of case; lithographed nameplate riveted on top; four posts and circuit breaker on side.   4   6

1669: 1955, 100 watts, secondary voltage 5-15, 15 fixed voltage; rectangular sheet metal case with chrome-plated rounded sheet metal handle on top of case; four posts and circuit breaker on small side of case.   5   10

1859: 1956, 150 watts, secondary voltage 0-15, 15 fixed voltage; black or blue Bakelite sculptured case with die-cast pointed operating lever on sloped front part of case; logo on metalized label; circuit breaker and binding post on rear; deluxe model.   30   50

1859AS: Same as 1859, but with Sears "Allstate" label.   30   50

6020: 1960, 1 amp, 18 volts DC; small metal case with knob-type controller on top of case, two posts on side, for small HO sets, DPDT switch for reversing.   2   4

6020AS: 1 amp DC, 18 fixed voltage DC; black metal case, 3-1/2" x 2" x 2-1/2"; fiber disk speed control and forward, neutral, and reverse controls lithographed on top to resemble control panel; "ALLSTATE power packs" and circuit breaker.   3   5

6030: 1957, 1.5 amps, 4-18 volts DC, 18 fixed volts AC; gray metal case with vertical plastic handles at each end, one for reversing and one for rheostat control; four posts on side; logo printed in white on top of case, "HO POWERPACK" for use with HO trains and race sets.   2   4

6030: 1.5 amps, 4-18 volts DC, 18 fixed voltage DC; gray metal case, fiber disks through top of case for direction and speed; yellow logo on top of case "HO-Power Pack"; four posts on side, deluxe model.   3   5

6049: 1957, 1.5 amps, 0-14 volts DC, 15 fixed voltage AC; deluxe HO power pack with single lever on top, forward one way, reverse the other; four posts.   3   6

MOTORS

Marx produced a large number of variations in the motors which they used over the years to power their trains. An outstanding testimonial to the design endurance and staying power of the Marx motor configurations can be found in the seven basic gear train designs that were used. Every motor configuration, and there were many, used the same armature. The only alteration made to the armature in over 50 years of motor production was to lengthen the pinion gear, and supply difference types of bearing supports. The exceptions, of course, were the battery-operated can motors and the hand-cars. The motor listing which follows is divided into mechani-cal and electrical groups. Within the electrical group, direct current (DC) motors are identified as such; all others are for alternating current (AC) use. A variety of motor related items, such as governors, brake levers, reverse levers, and sparkler features are noted, whereas other items, like the puffing smoke feature which is exterior to the motor unit, are not listed. One interesting feature provided on the postwar blue and also black Mercury mechanical motor was a melodious whistle device actuated by a fan which whistled the code for a grade crossing: two long, one short, then one long whistle. There was a gear with tabs that was struck by a lever that opened and closed the air opening on the whistle housing. Another innovation was the mechanical smoke unit which utilized a rubber bulb filled with baking powder that "puffed" the powder as "smoke" when struck by a lever.

Mechanical Motors

Gd Exc

M-1: 1925-28, early Joy Line, wire coil spring, stamped gears, no brake, frame integral with locomotive body. Not sold separately.   NRS

M-2: 1929-31, second Joy Line, clock-type spring wound by a square shaft key, fitting over a hollow square-bore brass projection.   NRS

M-3: 1931-35, third Joy Line, clock-type spring wound by a threaded hollow socket projection into which a threaded key screws; ringing bell, stamped-steel wheels, on/off lever underneath and some with sparkler feature.   10   15

M-4: 1935-36, both with or without drive rods, Marx non-reversing type, ten-spoke die-cast drivers, bell; wound by a screw-in key produced with two governor types: 1. Early M10000 or 2. CP or M10005.   6   9

M-5: 1936-38, for Canadian Pacific, M10005, or Commodore Vander-bilt; both with or without drive rods, Marx reversing type, ten-spoke die-cast drivers, wound by a screw-in key; vertically protruding reverse lever with three positions: up/reverse, mid-position/stop, and lower position/forward; lever slightly curved or bent-over at top and fitted with a detent spring at motor frame.   15   20

M-6: 1936-41, 1946-50, Marx non-reversing type, stamped-steel, eight-spoke drivers (wheels may be either tin-plated or steel blue-blacked); wound by a square shaft key fitting into a hollow square socket; brake lever engages gear train; some with sparkler feature.   4   6

M-7: 1934, 1946-50, Marx reversing type, stamped-steel, six-spoke drivers (the wheels may either be tin-plated or steel blue-blacked); wound with a square shaft key fitting into a hollow square socket. Reverse same as M-5.   10   15

M-8: 1950-75, Marx non-reversing type. Two versions: early type: stamped-steel, six-spoke blue-blacked steel drivers; later type: die-cast 17-spoke black-oxidized drivers; both units with sparkler attach-ment and centripetal governor; large blue strap steel spring wound by square shaft key fitting into a hollow square socket.   4   6

Electric Motors

The following drawings of the gear arrangements of the locomotive motors were drawn solely for the purpose of identifying the motor by its gear arrangement. We have not attempted to show the exact number of gear teeth. We have labeled the various motor types A through L (we did not use Type I to eliminate possible confusion between the number, 1, and the Roman numeral, I). Motor Types A through E, and L, have cast gears to the edge of the wheel flanges. Motor Types F through K have recessed gears on the wheels.

Type A

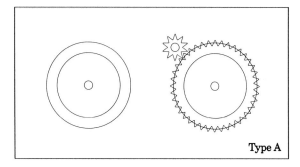

Type A

Gd Exc

E-1: 1930-32, early Joy Line, for cast-iron locomotives, large gear mounted on front wheel directly driven by small gear on armature shaft, (no intermediate gearing); single roller-type pickup, riveted brush holder. **NRS**

Type B

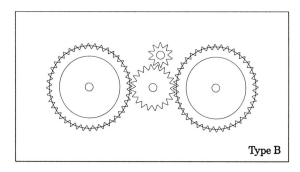

Type B

Gd Exc

E-2: 1932-34, second Joy Line, for stamped-steel locomotives; intermediate gear between small gear on armature and geared wheels; rear wheels made of black rubber, tin-plated stamped-steel front wheels (also found with all four wheels tin-plated); single-roller pickup; some with hand reverse in cab; riveted brush holder. **10 15**

E-3: 1934-36, third Joy Line, for stamped-steel locomotives and earliest M10000 streamliners, intermediate gear between small gear on armature and large gears on wheels; rubber wheels with "Girard" lettered in between spokes (some with tin-plated stamped-steel wheels); one-piece sliding shoe pickup, some with reverse lever in cab; riveted brush holder. Rubber drive wheels were made of natural rubber. The rubber was originally the consistency of pencil eraser rubber, but has hardened over the years. Surviving rubber drivers appear "hard" due to age. **10 15**

Type C

The Type C motor design was "the work horse" of the Marx stable of motors beginning in 1934 and continuing through 1973. Except for a very few locomotive types, this familiar gear arrangement was used in virtually every engine style Marx had including the Commodore Vanderbilt, Mercury (regular), 62 B & O, 6000 Southern Pacific, 999, all of the stamped-steel engines such as 897, 898, 591, 595, and 994, and the Canadian Pacific varieties 494, 495, 391, etc.
This design was also used quite extensively in the inexpensive plastic and diesel engines. Although the composition of the motor plates

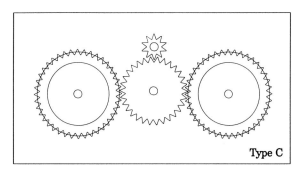

Type C

themselves changed over the years, from steel to a fiber board construction, the basic gear arrangement remained the same. Some of the later engine types employing this motor design were the 490 and 400, along with some variations of the GE 70-ton switcher

Gd Exc

E-4: 1934-37, Marx, early Commodore Vanderbilt-type with single intermediate gear, 10-spoke, die-cast wheels; three-piece sliding shoe pickup; manual reverse lever through boiler section; coil- type springs and brushes in tubular holders; painted side rods. **8 11**

E-5: 1936-38, Marx, second Commodore Vanderbilt-type, 10-spoke, die-cast wheels; three-piece sliding shoe pickup; two-position sequence reversing relay unit with hand-cutoff lever; brushes and gearing same as E-4 model. **4 7**

E-6: 1938-41, Marx, second Commodore Vanderbilt-type, no reversing relay cutoff lever; all else same as E-5. **4 7**

E-7: 1939-41, Marx, second Commodore Vanderbilt-type, except brushes in stamped cylinder holder with coiled spring positioned transversely to apply pressure from spring end against brushes, all else same as the E-5. System retained for subsequent motors. **4 6**

E-8: 1939-41, Marx, third Commodore Vanderbilt-type, no reversing relay cutoff lever; all else same as E-7. **4 6**

E-9: Circa 1946, Marx, transitional, 10-spoke wheels; new one- piece sliding shoe pickup; cutoff lever for reversing relay unit removed, did not reappear. **4 6**

E-10: Circa 1946-57, Marx, common, Baldwin disk drivers; one- piece sliding shoe pickup; otherwise similar to E-7, but no cutoff lever. **4 6**

E-11: 1937-41, Marx, DC, 10-spoke, die-cast wheels, but field created by permanent magnet instead of windings; designed for DC operation, came in sets with metal "BATTERY CONTAINER" and "CONTROLLER" for battery train sets; battery holder for six flashlight dry cells or a 6-volt "Hotshot" battery; reversed by using "forward" or "reverse" buttons on train controller. (Some were made after World War II.) **9 12**

E-12: 1949-55, Marx, DC, second version, construction similar to E-10, except with permanent field magnet in lieu of coil windings; designed for DC operation with batteries as was E-9, but no reversing relay. **4 6**

E-13: Circa 1955-72, Marx, four Baldwin disk-type wheels, non-reversing, single intermediate gear, short one-piece sliding shoe pickups; fiber side frame similar to E-21 (low price loss leader). **2 3**

Type D

The Type D motor was utilized almost exclusively in the 21 Santa Fe tin lithographed diesel. The 21 diesel, designed to compete with Lionel's F units and Unique's tin lithographed Rock Island diesel, was very successful from a merchandizing viewpoint simply because of low cost. This motor design was another example of the skilled Marx engineers who minimized cost by using two of the single intermediate

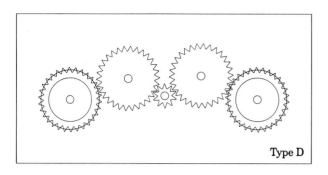

Type D

reduction gears found in the Type C motor, and part of their inventory, to produce a rather resourceful double-reduction motor.

Gd Exc

E-14: 1950-54, Marx, heavy duty, used primarily for tin- lithographed 21 Santa Fe diesel; double intermediate gears with unblackened solid die-cast wheels, 1-1/8" flange diameter, 7/8" running surface diameter; without traction tires; wheels concealed by die-cast truck frame; one-piece collector; reversing relay unit; cast-iron weight; steel motor frame; with large top- side mounting bracket.   **5   8**

Type E

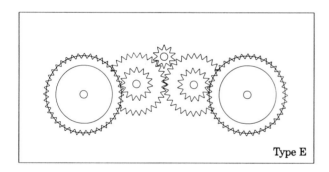

Type E

Gd Exc

E-15: 1950-73, Marx, heavy duty, for Alco S-3 switchers; stepped intermediate gears with same wheels as E-14; wheels concealed by truck frame; one-piece pickup shoe; reversing relay unit; many with cast-iron weight; without rubber traction tires on wheels; steel motor frames with large steel overhead mounting bracket.   **8   16**

Type F

E-16: Circa 1937-40, Marx, special, with extra powered gear for operating accessories; 10-spoke wheels; three-piece pickup; elongated frame with stepped intermediate gearing and small gears on driving

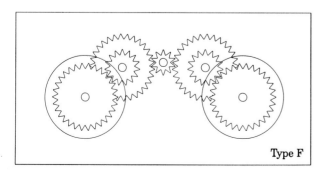

Type F

Gd Exc

wheels; reversing relay unit at rear instead of front; large (about 2" in diameter) gear meshed with forward intermediate gear as a power take-off gear for a device shooting sparks up stack.   **8   12**

Type G

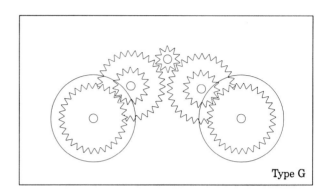

Type G

Gd Exc

E-17: 1952-75, some Marx GE 70-ton switchers; Baldwin disk wheels, with or without side rod bosses on wheels, depending on application; stepped intermediate gears, double reduction; special mounting bracket for front mount when used in GE 70-ton switchers. Also used in the diesels, 666 and 1666, William Crooks, and others.   **4   8**

E-18: Marx, Baldwin disk drivers; double intermediate gear, but with regular length side frames for motor; with E-12-type reversing relay unit and one-piece sliding shoe pickup.

(A) 1956-75, no liquid smoke unit.   **4   6**

(B) 1961-70, with liquid smoke unit.   **5   8**

Type H

E-19: 1950-73, Marx, heavy duty, for Alco S-3 switchers; stepped intermediate gears with same wheels as on E-14; wheels concealed by truck frame; one-piece pickup shoe; reversing relay unit; many with cast-iron weight; with or without rubber traction tires on wheels; steel/aluminum motor frames with large steel overhead mounting bracket. Note: Special mounting brackets for motors used in Alco S-3 switchers. No cast weight used on motors installed in switchers.   **8   16**

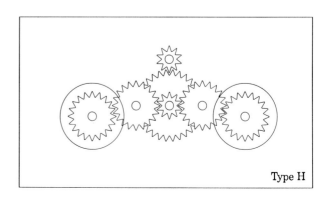

Type H

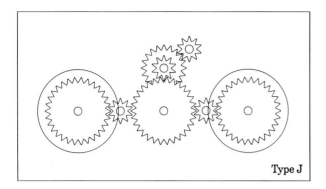

Type J

Type J

Gd Exc

E-20: 1952-59, Marx, three-axle, six-wheel motor; multi-spoked wheels with flangeless center pair of wheels; stepped intermediate gear between pinion gear on armature shaft and left center wheel; one-piece sliding shoe pickup and reversing relay unit; used in 333 and 1829 locomotives.   **15   20**

Type K

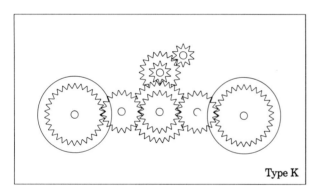

E-20B: 1952-59, similar to E-20, but fitted with liquid smoke unit, used on later 333s and 1829; has different gear arrangement so that gears and wheels of (A) will not interchange with (B).   **18   25**

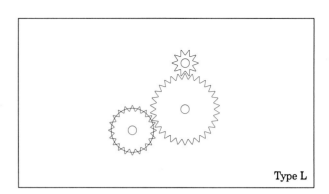

Type L

Type L

Gd Exc

E-21: 1948-52, possibly later, Marx, second version, for postwar M10005 streamliners, small, non-reversible motor with single-axle fiber side frames and small die-cast wheels; front set of stamped-steel wheels, not connected to motor unit, used in low-priced road diesels.   **5   10**

E-22: 1955-63, Marx, small motor for handcars; non-reversing; drive gear train, with several intermediate gears to one wheel only; plain die-cast wheels slightly larger than regular car wheels; individually sprung sliding shoe pickup; small brushes specifically for this motor type.   **5   10**

E-23: 1959-75, Marx, later battery motor; DC permanent magnet field for smaller motors than in E-11 and E-12; mounted in boiler; front axle gear driven only through a crown gear, multi-spoked die-cast type wheels used with mechanical motor (M-8) and batteries – two "D" flashlight cells – held in boiler cavity; produced in Hong Kong for later Marx battery sets; with or without driving rod.   **2   3**

E-24: 1974-76, Marx, six-volt DC can-type motor with small metal gears powered by lantern battery in "power pack"; heavy metal die-cast frame holds small vertical-mounted Japanese "RE-35" motor; all other gears nylon; thin, 17-spoke die-cast drivers, front set non-geared; for three-rail track; 112 Lehigh Valley GE 70-ton switcher, perhaps other types.   **3   5**

Marx Trains Glossary

AC: Alernating current; the type of electrical current used to operate most Marx trains.

A C L: Atlantic Coast Line Railroad.

A T & S F: Atchison, Topeka & Santa Fe Railroad (commonly called "Santa Fe").

Alco S-3 switcher: A type of diesel locomotive used by the real railroads for light-duty tasks, such as switching cars in a train yard. Marx made a model of this unit, which has a distinctive vertical front.

Allstate: A brand name used by Sears for products ranging from automotive batteries to insurance. Beginning in 1965, Marx used this label on some train sets produced for Sears.

Armature: The moving section of an electric motor; it has windings and commutator.

Articulated: An adjective used to describe cars that share a common truck; for example, two articulated cars might have a total of three trucks.

B & L E: Bessemer & Lake Erie Railroad.

B & M: Boston & Maine Railroad.

B & O: Baltimore & Ohio Railroad.

Bakelite: Synthetic resin or plastic used in the early manufacture of toy trains.

Baldwin driver: A term used to describe a wheel with teardrop shapes between spokes.

Bay window caboose: Caboose with no cupola, but with extended side windows.

Boiler front: Disk-shaped cover on front of locomotive boiler.

Boom: Adjustable beam on a crane used to support and lift cargo.

Brush: Part of an electric motor; the carbon cylinder touching commutator.

Brush-holder: Part of an electric motor; holds the brushes next to the commutator.

Budd R D C: Self-propelled Rail Diesel Car; resembles a passenger car.

Bull's-eye marker: Round red lights used on the rear of a car (usually a caboose) to indicate the end of a train or the position of a train for safety.

C & O: Chesapeake & Ohio Railroad.

C & S: Colorado & Southern Railroad.

C B & Q: Chicago, Burlington & Quincy Railroad (commonly called "Burlington").

C R I & P: Chicago, Rock Island & Pacific Railroad (commonly called "Rock Island").

C V: Abbreviation for Commodore Vanderbilt.

Canadian Pacific: A type of streamlined steam locomotive commonly referred to by its markings, which are patterned after the Canadian Pacific Railroad.

C. E. Carter Company: Firm acquired by Louis Marx & Company in 1933.

Channel track: U-shaped track used for trains with flangeless wheels.

Choo-choo mechanism: Brass strip struck by a bar to make a choo-choo sound.

Circuit breaker: Device for cutting off power in case of too much current; i.e., a short circuit.

Clockwork: Refers to windup (spring-wound) motors in locomotives and toys.

Combination set: A set that contains accessories, as well as trains and track.

Commodore Vanderbilt: Type of steam locomotive — named after owner of N Y C.

Commutator: Part of an electric motor; brass disk on armature against which brush makes contact.

Coupler: The part of a car or locomotive that allows it to attach or *couple* to another car or locomotive.

Coupler pockets: Long slots at end of frames for couplers.

Crossarm: As on a street lamp holding the downward globes.

Crossbuck: The X-shaped warning sign commonly found where railroads and vehicular roads cross.

Crosshead: Part of a steam locomotive; stamped-steel piece at end of drive rod that slides on parallel guides.

Cupola: Raised area on the roof of a caboose.

DC: Direct current; the type of electrical current used to operate most of Marx's HO and battery-operated locomotives.

Deck: Part of a searchlight car; refers to platform holding a searchlight.

Deluxe: A series of Marx cars; found in boxes marked "DELUXE".

Depressed-center: Refers to flatcar with sloping section in floor center.

Die-cast: Metal bodies or wheels formed in a die.

Dome: One of the protrusions on top of a steam locomotive boiler.

Door guide or runner: Strip for holding a movable door in place.

Drumhead: The lighted logo at the end of the observation car.

Dunbee-Combex-Marx Ltd: Purchased from Quaker Oats 1976.

Ear flap markers: Part of a steam locomotive; small lighted markers on forward side of locomotive boiler.

Eccentric linkage: Part of a steam locomotive; extra action rod on 333 and 1829 locomotives.

Embossed: Raised or depressed in a flat surface.

EMD FT diesel: The first of the popular "F-series" locomotives made by the Electro-Motive Division of General Motors; reproduced in miniature by Marx.

EMD F-3 diesel: A type of diesel locomotive.

EMD F-7 diesel: A type of diesel locomotive.

Erie Archives: Part of the Marx plant in Erie, Pennsylvania where R & D models and production samples were kept.

Facade truck: Simulated truck with one axle instead of two.

Fairbanks Morse: One of the manufacturers of full-sized locomotives; Marx produced a diesel locomotive based loosely on a Fairbanks Morse design.

Firebox: Part of a steam locomotive; area below cab containing the fire.

Fixed voltage: Refers to parts on transformers for accessories.

Flanged wheel: Wheel with ridge or lip on inner side to keep train on track.

Flangeless wheels: Wheel with flat surface around perimeter; used on trains made for channel track and on floor toys.

Floor train: To be pushed or pulled; no track, flangeless wheels.

Frame: Bottom part of a car, to which wheels or trucks are attached.

GE 70-ton switcher: Small industrial switcher used on real railroads. Marx made a model of this locomotive that is distinquished by its slanted front.

Girard Model Works: Added to Louis Marx & Company in 1934.

Girder bridge: A type of bridge using girder construction.

Grab-iron: A short section of railing on a car or locomotive, provided for railroad personnel to hang on to.

Grille: The air intake on a diesel locomotive.

Hafner: Competing toy train company; Marx bought dies in 1955.

Happi-Time: Marx label used for some Sears sets.

Heat-stamped: A type of decorating process in which heat is used to impress a color (in the shape of letters or logos) into a plastic surface, such as the side of a boxcar.

High-sided gondola: Higher sides than ordinary gondola, esp. 3/16" scale.

HO: The name for a small gauge train; one-half of O Gauge.

I C: Illinois Central Railroad.

I C G: Illinois Central Gulf Railroad (successor to I C).

I-G N: International Great Northern Railroad (Missouri Pacific).

Journal box: Small square-shaped box over axle end on a truck.

Joy Line: Trains produced 1927-1934 by Girard Model Works.

K C S: Kansas City Southern Railroad.

L & N: Louisville & Nashville Railroad.

L N E: Lehigh & New England Railroad.

L V: Lehigh Valley Railroad.

Linemar trains: Marx production in Japan.

Lithography: Method of printing a design onto a flat, metal surface.

Logo: Insignia, herald, or trademark of company or railroad.

Lumar Lines: Refers to Marx floor trains and toys.

M P: Missouri Pacific Railroad.

Marxtronic set: Label used by Marx on an inexpensive, battery-powered set that included a switcher and two gondolas.

Mercury: Shrouded New York Central steam locomotive made as a toy by Marx.

NKP: Nickel Plate Road (name of a railroad).

N Y C: New York Central Railroad.

Notch-front tender: Similar to flat-top, but with notch at front top.

O27: Refers to O Gauge track with 27" diameter.

O34: Refers to O Gauge track with 34" diameter.

Observation car: Usually the last car in a passenger train; equipped with an open platform or special windows at the rear to provide a better view for passengers.

One-way coupler: An early automatic coupler with male and female ends.

Ornamental horn: A detail part found on locomotive models; called "ornamental" to distinguish it from functional (noise-making) horn mechanisms sometime hidden in locomotives or transformers.

Overlapping: The use of two colors painted on each other to make a third color.

P F E: Pacific Fruit Express (trade name used on refrigerator cars).

PRR: Pennsylvania Railroad.

Penney's Special: Marx set made specifically for J. C. Penney.

Pickup: Sliding shoe or roller found on underside of locomotives and some cars; used for electrical contact.

Pilot: Another name for a cowcatcher on a locomotive.

Plastic knuckle coupler: 1953 non-operating coupler used on cheaper sets.

Plastimarx: Marx train production in Mexico.

Punched tab coupler: Dimple in coupler shank attached at frame floor.

Quaker Oats Company: Purchased Marx domestic plants 1972.

R & D: Research and Development; the corporate department or division engaged in the task of designing new models, tools, techniques, etc.

R P O: Rail Post Office; part of a passenger train.

Recessed gear: Gear smaller than outside rim of drive wheel.

Reefer: Abbreviated name for refrigerator car.

Rivet lithography: Dots which resemble rivets.

Rubber-stamped: Method of applying letters or numbers with inked stamp.

S A L: Seaboard Air Line Railroad

S O U: Southern Railroad

S S W: St. Louis Southwestern Railroad

St. P & P RR: St. Paul & Pacific Railroad (Milwaukee).

Scale: Proportionate in size to a life-sized car or locomotive.

Secondary voltage: Refers to posts on transformer for running the train.

Side frame: Side of truck, either plastic overlay or stamped-steel.

Side rod: Part of a steam locomotive; rod from rear drive wheel that moves when wheel turns.

Sideboard: Shelf-like sides on Canadian Pacific locomotives.

Silk-screening: Method of stenciling color through silk mesh to form letters.

Simulated truck: Facade truck with only one axle.

Slope-back tender: Sloped toward rear with simulated light.

Solid door: Non-movable door, sometimes called a plug door.

Stack: The exhaust port on top of a steam locomotive boiler; allows smoke to escape.

Stacker: A person who placed lithographed sheets carefully in a stack as they came off the production line.

Stake pockets: Part of a flatcar; the receptacles for the vertical stakes used to restrain loads.

Stamped-steel: Method of forming metal bodies or wheels by a stamping process.

Standard bodies: Bodies than can be used to produce many different cars.

Standard Gauge: Approx. 2-1/2" or more, referring to floor toys.

Steel strap motor: Refers to motor in windup locomotive.

T & P: Texas & Pacific Railroad.

T C A: Train Collectors Association.

T T O S: Toy Train Operator's Society.

Tab and slot coupler: Coupler shank bent into tab that fastens into a slot.

Tabs: Slip through slots in a frame to secure it to the body.

Tail banner: Logo on tail end of observation car.

Talgo coupler: Part of an articulated car; fits notch on next car or locomotive.

Teardrop: Refers to shape of domes or stacks on CP, CV, Mercury steam locomotives.

Tender: Coal or oil car coupled with steam locomotive.

Tilt automatic coupler: Replaced the one-way coupler in 1941.

Tinned or tin-plated: Covered or plated with tin or tin alloy.

Truss bridge: Bridge supported by a rigid framework of beams.

Twisted tab coupler: Coupler with twisted shank fastened to car frame floor.

U P: Union Pacific Railroad.

Unique Art Company: Rival company with lithographed trains in early 1950s.

Vestibule: Enclosed entrance at end of passenger car.

W P: Western Pacific Railroad.

Wagon-top tender: Flat on top with rounded edges.

Walkway: Pathway on roof of boxcar or reefer for brakeman.

Wedge-type tender: Narrow at rear, wider at front as viewed from top.

Windup: A locomotive with a steel spring driving mechanism wound with a key.

Work car: Usually a modified caboose/flatcar; used on real railroad for maintenance.

Wrecker car: Same as a crane.

Yoke: Metal or plastic holder fastening searchlight to body.

Index

Listings for both Volume I and Volume II are incorporated into this index. "I" before the page number indicates that the item will be found in Volume I; "II" indicates Volume II. Color photographs are designated by "-C" following the item number.